HOMOSEXUALITY:

Its Causes and Cure

Books and Monographs by Albert Ellis

An Introduction to the Principles of Scientific Psychoanalysis (*Journal Press*, 1950)

The Folklore of Sex (*Charles Boni*, 1951; rev. ed., *Grove Press*, 1961)

Sex, Society and the Individual (with A. P. Pillay) (*International Journal of Sexology Press*, 1953)

Sex Life of the American Woman and the Kinsey Report (*Greenberg*, 1954)

The American Sexual Tragedy (*Twayne*, 1954; rev. ed., *Lyle Stuart*, 1962; *Grove Press*, 1963)

New Approaches to Psychotherapy Techniques (*Journal of Clinical Psychology Press*, 1955)

The Psychology of Sex Offenders (with Ralph Brancale) (*Charles C Thomas*, 1956)

How to Live with a Neurotic (*Crown*, 1957)

Sex Without Guilt (*Lyle Stuart*, 1958; *Hillman*, 1959)

What Is Psychotherapy? (*American Academy of Psychotherapists*, 1959)

The Place of Values in the Practice of Psychotherapy (*American Academy of Psychotherapists*, 1959)

The Art and Science of Love (*Lyle Stuart*, 1960)

The Encyclopedia of Sexual Behavior (with Albert Abarbanel) (*Hawthorn*, 1961)

Creative Marriage (with Robert A. Harper) (*Lyle Stuart*, 1961)

A Guide to Rational Living (with Robert A. Harper) (*Prentice-Hall*, 1961)

Reason and Emotion in Psychotherapy (*Lyle Stuart*, 1962)

If This Be Sexual Heresy ... (*Lyle Stuart*, 1963)

Sex and the Single Man (*Lyle Stuart*, 1963)

The Origins and the Development of the Incest Taboo (*Lyle Stuart*, 1963)

The Intelligent Woman's Guide to Man-Hunting (*Lyle Stuart*, 1963)

Nymphomania: A Study of the Over-Sexed Woman (with Edward Sagarin) (*Gilbert Press*, 1964)

The Case for Sexual Liberty (*Seymour Press*, 1964)

Homosexuality: Its Causes and Cure (*Lyle Stuart*, 1965)

Homosexuality: ITS CAUSES AND CURE

by *Albert Ellis, Ph.D.*

with an Introduction and a Terminal Essay:

**HOMOSEXUALITY
AND THE MYSTIQUE OF THE GIGANTIC PENIS**

by DONALD WEBSTER CORY

LYLE
STUART
INC.
NEW
YORK

Table of Contents

Introduction

by Donald Webster Cory

Only a generation ago, a wall of silence surrounded the subject of homosexuality; today, it is one of the most discussed of all subjects, finding its way into novels, movies, theater, political analyses, journalistic popularizations, women's magazines, and occasionally, although rarely, a sober scientific work. Such a book is the present one by Albert Ellis.

It is indeed a rare pleasure, that may be dismissed by some with a scornful sneer about mutual admiration, but that involves two people who have come to similar views from different vantage points, for me to say a word in introduction to the work of a man who, some decade and a half ago, introduced my first book to the public. Since that time, amid the hundreds of articles and dozens of books, I have awaited, often with impatience, the contributions of the original and seminal mind of Albert Ellis on this difficult and often tragic area of human personality and behavior. To those who will approach this book with open mind (and, alas, they are few), they will find herein exciting and original answers.

I

Once the name was Edmund Bergler: today it is Albert Ellis. Public enemy No. 1 of the homosexual, the whipping boy of the homophile press, the *bête noire* of the friend of the deviant, Albert Ellis is scorned, laughed at, ridiculed, hated, feared—and admired. And although he has spoken up in courts, at public forums, in books too numerous to mention, at lecture halls, and in homosexual publications, in favor of the legal and social rights of the sexual nonconformists, he continues to be denounced with a fury that might be expected were he on a puritanical crusade, a McCarthy investigating committee, or a vice squad rampage.

What is there, then, about the work of Albert Ellis, in the area of homosexuality, that has made him the ultra *persona non grata* of so many people whose rights he indubitably upholds and whose interests he vigorously defends? There is a deepgoing schism between Dr. Ellis and the homophile movement, and I speak on it, one might say, from both sides of the fence, as a friend of the author and as one who agrees almost entirely with his position—and at the same time as a recognized and accepted person of leadership, influence, and prestige within this movement.

The agreement that I have arrived at with Dr. Ellis started, I might say, when he wrote the introduction to my book, *The Homosexual in America.* In fact, I would trace it to an even earlier origin, when the late Dr. Kinsey, having read the manuscript of that book, met me in the old Hotel Pennsylvania, spoke enthusiastically about my work, and explained that he could not contribute an introduction to it, because of the special position he was in.

"There is only one person I know who ought to do this for you—and that's Albert Ellis." He gave me Dr. Ellis's address and telephone number, and added: "He is just about the most consistent liberal on sex of anyone in America."

Over a period of years, I have found myself more and more in agreement with Dr. Ellis's basic position, and this agreement seems to have been arrived at independently by the two of us, he largely (although not exclusively) from a clinical practice, and myself from observations and interactions with homosexuals on a level of friendship and within the homophile social protest movement. In the dialogues that have ensued, I readily admit that I have been influenced by his orientation; I have come to believe that, to a lesser degree, he has at times been influenced by mine; but essentially—and I stress this because of the significance of the convergence of two views from such divergent sources—we arrived rather independently at an area of consensus.

For reasons that are quite readily understandable, namely, that groups under pressure from an unaccepting society tend to accept criticism from within that would be rejected from without (as witness the racial joke, which a Jew can tell to Jews about Jews, but would be resented if told by a Christian or in the presence of Christians), the homophile movement has been somewhat less reluctant to aim its big guns at me than at Dr. Ellis, although the concepts that he brings forth are not noticeably different from those I have stated, amid considerable applause.

Now, what are the major points that make Albert Ellis appear in the light of a menace to those he is studying, describing, and defending? I should say that they can be reduced to two:

1. That homosexuals, in this society, if they are exclusive or near-exclusive in their erotic interests in their own sex, are disturbed individuals, and the state of being a confirmed homosexual is hence a disturbance. These people, Dr. Ellis insists, are not sinful, they are not immoral, they are not antisocial; but they are compulsive, neurotic, have poor sex-role identification, have rigid fixations, tend to be goofers, to be self-destructive, to make poor relationships with fellow human beings, and, in fact, they are frequently borderline psychotics. Unfortunately, the last phrase has become an epithet, rather than a scientific description, and for that reason, it is my opinion that it should be excluded from serious literature, except when intended solely for the eyes of the technically trained.

2. Although deeply ingrained in the entire fabric of the personality, homosexuality, as a learned condition, can be unlearned while the converse is equally true; fear of and flight from hetero-

sexuality, which characterizes these deviant persons, can be diminished and entirely removed. This would, in the word of Dr. Ellis, constitute a "cure," which is to say that it would leave the individual free from compulsions which uncontrollably drive him toward the same sex (although it would not leave him free from desire and interest in other men), while at the same time leaving him free and unfettered, without irrational blocks, to enjoy sexuality with the other sex.

Dr. Ellis, of course, is not the first to contend that homosexuality is curable; a change of orientation has been reported by numerous others, including Richard Robertiello, who devoted an entire book to a full-length discussion of the life and analysis of a lesbian; Clifford Allen, a noted contemporary British writer; and Irving Bieber, who recently published a study of attempted change of orientation with upward of 100 male patients; as well as a host of others, mentioned by Dr. Ellis in the text and cited in the bibliography. None of these people, including Albert Ellis, contend that the process is easy, or that it is usually successful. Dr. Bieber, who offers considerable statistics, demonstrates beyond a doubt that most of his and his collaborators' patients did not change (he had far more "failures" than "successes"); that those who changed (the minority) were somewhat more bisexually oriented, rather than exclusively homosexual, at the beginning of therapy; and that some of the "successes" were bisexual at the end of therapy, as well.

Yet, the name of Dr. Bieber is met with considerable derision in homophile circles, as is the work of Dr. Ellis. For it must be admitted that homosexuals are indulging in a campaign, not to discover whether cure is possible, not to find out under what conditions it occurs and how frequently and what the nature of the new personality might be, but to "prove" that change of orientation is utterly impossible. "Show me one person who has changed," they will challenge; and since such a person cannot easily be brought forth to face public exposure, they denounce a host of men of science as liars and charlatans.

Victim as he is of a cruelty at the hands of his fellow-men, and seeking to alleviate his position in society, the homosexual fears that the work of Drs. Ellis, Bieber, and others, will serve to reinforce the anti-homosexual prejudices of the society. Some might suggest, viewing homophiles at a meeting, that they fear heterosexuality itself, that they are in flight from it, and the case history of a reported change is a threat to their own egos, which require as a defense a belief in the unchangeability of their own conditions. This somewhat psychoanalytic interpretation may indeed be valid; but an even stronger reason for homosexuals castigating therapists, such as Drs. Ellis and Bieber, who show how they have cured some confirmed members of the gay world, is their pervasive fear that their fight against public persecution and for social acceptance will be impeded by the belief, among health authorities and in the educated areas of public life, that they could change and enjoy heterosexual outlets, if only they had the will and would make the effort.

The man of science can be deeply interested in the uses to which his findings are put, but he cannot legitimately distort his findings so that they will be useful to one group rather than another. He cannot be committed to a conclusion because it will support goals; he cannot permit his science to become the tool of ideological prejudices. So, even if it were true (as I contend it is not and need not be) that the work of Drs. Ellis, Bieber, Robertiello, and other psychotherapists, would prove inimical to the struggle of the Mattachine Society, the Janus Society, and other groups which fight against the persecution of homosexuals which is still rife in our society—groups with which I am affiliated and in which I have long played an active role—it would in no way invalidate the conclusions of these men of science. Even if the psychotherapists were to find, *as they have not,* that the reorientation of a willing homosexual is a quick and easy process that has almost unanimous chance of success, this should not serve as a signal for the homophile movement to denounce these scientists, but should motivate this movement to re-evaluate some aspects of its struggle for personal freedom and human dignity for homosexuals.

The denunciation of the psychotherapists and of other scientists working in this area stems from a completely irrational and self-defeating viewpoint: that if a person can be changed and does not avail himself of this opportunity, he is no longer worthy of acceptance in the family of humanity. Underlying this view is an entire series of false assumptions:

1. Homosexual behavior must be antisocial, must be worthy of punishment by society, and should be eradicated at all costs.

2. However, if it cannot be eradicated, if it is as inborn as having only one kidney or being color blind, society will come to tolerate it as a necessary evil, a condition that ought not to be, but that cannot be avoided.

3. Hence, since we are fighting against the intolerably cruel attitude of society, we must convince others, and ourselves, that it is ineradicable, and anyone who says the opposite is a menace to human freedom.

Now, supposing we were to reject these assumptions entirely, and start from some others:

1. That homosexuality is no more antisocial than claustrophobia, and should be no more of a reason for ridicule, formal and informal punishment, and discriminatory practices than fear of heights.

2. That like other fears, phobias, compulsions, and emotional difficulties and disorders, homosexuality can sometimes be alleviated, and where this is possible it is desirable for the individual that he be encouraged to do so.

3. In most instances of severe emotional phobias, alleviation is difficult, drawn out, and anxiety provoking (because the phobia

is sometimes a defense against a greater fear or because it is a symptom that is viewed by its victim as being not only inconvenient but shameful). Consequently, treatment may not be possible, or it may be partially or entirely unsuccessful. Nonetheless, any degree of success in dealing with this phobia may be highly desirable.

4. Since the condition of confirmed homosexuality is not intrinsically immoral or antisocial, but is personally difficult for the individual involved; since the difficulties in treating it are immeasurably complicated by the senseless persecution by society; and since the alleviation of the condition is an arduous process, complex and frequently unsuccessful, the struggle for a change in the persecutory legal and social attitudes toward this type of deviant should be continued and enhanced.

5. This struggle may perhaps be complicated and impeded by the cases of cures, as published by Drs. Ellis, Allen, and others; but this is because their work is misunderstood. The misuse of findings of a man of science is not an argument against the findings, but merely a reason for those who understand his work to make greater effort to combat such misuse.

I am more and more convinced that the homophile movement in the United States is fighting a righteous struggle, for justice, freedom, and personal dignity; that it will do great harm to its struggle if it gets into a head-on clash with men of science whose work it finds threatening; and that there is nothing inconsistent between acceptance of the work of psychotherapists who report success, nay cure, and struggle for the right to participate in the joys of life for those who cannot, will not, or do not undergo such change.

II

I should not like to close this introductory work without reference to Dr. Ellis's admonition to the patient whose case he reports in the second verbatim recorded series of interviews in this book, that he should refrain from homosexual relations because, in this society, it is illegal and self-defeating. The reader of this work, taking the taped interview out of context of the *entire series* of therapeutic sessions, may possibly get the impression that Dr. Ellis is urging that we become a highly conforming society. He might seem to be speaking, in this interview, not only in favor of blind conformity to the social norms at all times, no matter what the individual idiosyncracies and preferences might be, but also in favor of upholding every law, under all conditions, no matter how much one opposes it in principle.

Albert Ellis, on the contrary, vehemently opposes a society of mass conformity, and he is himself hardly an ultra-conformist, as those who have read any of his books know, and as one soon discovers when attending a lecture at which he is talking to a middleclass audience in a university hall, and where he does not hesitate to use language which is shocking to some of the people in the audience.

The conformity that Dr. Ellis urges in this book is directed to a patient, in trouble with the law and under therapy, a patient who has indulged in practices which have given him little pleasure and over which he has no control. We should be able to differentiate between the nonconformist who is spontaneous, creative, iconoclastic, and the nonconformist who is unable to control those urges which, in spite of himself, drive him to violation of the norms. We should not find it too difficult to discriminate between the nonconformist who is compelled despite himself to choose a path, and one who desires to choose it; between the man who is guilty and ashamed and remorseful because of his nonconformity, and the man who has rationally dissociated himself from the ordinary, the plebeian, and even, in some instances, the legal.

Let me close by saying that this book is a major contribution to an understanding of homosexual behavior, and one that will be read, studied, pored over, hailed and denounced for many years to come. The homosexual is indeed fortunate, as is the entire society, that the pen of America's foremost sexologist has been used to throw light on the still greatly misunderstood problem of the inner and outer conflicts of the homosexual.

November 3,
1964.

HOMOSEXUALITY:

Its Causes and Cure

Foreword

No definitive book on homosexuality has yet been written nor is likely to be for some time to come. For the world of the homo- sexual has many complicated aspects: it has a long history behind it; it involves many kinds of homophiles: the "fairies" and the "butches," the oldsters and the youngsters, the gay boys and the lesbians, the Madison Avenue executives and the Forty-Second street prostitutes; it has many interesting anthropological facets; it has a fascinating sociology; and its psychological and clinical components themselves could easily fill a weighty tome.

The present volume concentrates largely on the psychology of homosexuality—particularly on its causes and its treatment. As a psychotherapist and a sexologist, I have been engaged in the study and therapy of fixed homosexuals for the last twenty years; and during this time I have seen over a hundred of them for intensive treatment and several hundred more for briefer series of interviews. In the course of this experience, I have devised a somewhat unique approach to inducing confirmed deviates to overcome their strong fixations and compulsions and to be able to have highly enjoyable and successful heterosexual rela- tionships. Although I have written about this rational-emotive therapeutic approach to the treatment of confirmed homosexuals in several articles and chapters in my various books, I have not previously outlined it in detail in any publication.

The present book, taking off from where my other writings on this subject have stopped, much more lengthily discusses why homosexuals are the way they are, how emotionally disturbed

19

they tend to be, and exactly what can be done to help them overcome their fixed homosexuality. It is by no means a complete
handbook on homophilism (and will be followed, in fact, by an
Encyclopedia of Homosexual Behavior on which Donald Webster Cory and I have been working for some time, and which we
hope to have ready for publication in a year or two). But it is
designed to give a fairly comprehensive picture of the causes and
cure of homoeroticism in our society. It not only gives the usual
kind of psychological information on sex deviates, but includes
two verbatim transcripts of recordings of psychotherapy sessions
with homosexual patients. To my knowledge, this sort of material
has not previously appeared in print; and it is hoped that its
inclusion in this book will encourage the publication of verbatim
material of other psychotherapists who have successfully treated
this difficult kind of patient.

Albert Ellis, Ph.D.
New York City

chapter 1

*Constitutional Factors in
Homosexuality:
A Reexamination of the
Evidence*

~~~~~~

Most of the early authorities on human sexuality were quite convinced that homosexuality is largely of constitutional origin. Writers such as Carpenter (1911, 1914), Bloch (1908), H. Ellis (1936), Forel (1907), Hirschfeld (1920), Krafft-Ebing (1886), and Robinson (1914) stoutly held that either some or all homosexuals are born rather than conditioned to be attracted to members of their own sex and that hormonal or genic imbalances lie at the bottom of confirmed homosexualism. Many later writers also echoed these views on the primacy of constitutional factors in homosexuality: for example, Abrams (1918), Bauer (1940), Curran (1938), Glass and McKennon (1937), Neustadt and Myerson (1940), Newman (1936), Lang (1940), Rosanoff (1938), Sanders (1936), Steinach (1940), Sorensen (1938), Witschi (1932, 1942), and Wright (1938, 1941).

Nonetheless, in spite of the early and later contention by many outstanding authorities that homosexuality is fundamentally inborn and that it is therefore almost impossible to change the basic sexual drive of a confirmed or exclusive homosexual, the opposing view of the psychoanalytic schools, that homophilism is largely an early-acquired sexual anomaly, and that despite the stubborn resistance to change of most homosexuals their sex proclivities sometimes can be definitely changed in the direction of hetero-sexual interests and activities, has fairly well conquered the field of psychiatric thinking and is subscribed to by the great majority of psychotherapists. Notable psychoanalytic proponents of the theory that homosexuality is environmentally rather than con-stitutionally caused have included Adler (1917, 1939a), Bieber and his associates (1962), Bergler (1956), Brill (1913), Freud (1924, 1938), Ferenczi (1916, 1926), London (1933, 1937), Money-Kyrle (1932), Schilder (1942), Silverberg (1938), Stekel (1922), and Wittels (1929).

Not only the psychoanalysts, but many other psychiatrists—such as Allen (1949), Barahal (1940), Caprio (1952), Hamilton (1929, 1936), Glueck (1956), Henry (1941, 1955), Kahn (1937), and West (1955)—have also espoused the view that homosexuality is not caused by hormonal, constitutional, or genetic factors but is the result of psychological or environmental influences. And these experienced practitioners have been joined by a host of psychologists, sociologists, and other sex researchers who have similarly denied the significant influence of direct constitutional factors in the causation of homosexuality—including Allen and Broster (1938), Cory (1961, 1963), Davis (1929), Dean (1936), Devereux (1937), Fielding (1932), Hammer (1957), Kelly (Ter-man and Miles, 1936), Kinsey and his associates (1941, 1948, 1953), Pollens (1938), Pomeroy (1958), Swyer (1957), and Westwood (1953). The present writer (Ellis, 1945, 1958, 1959a, 1959b, 1961, 1961b, 1962a, 1962b, 1963a) has also been one of those who has stoutly held, and presented experimental and clinical evidence in favor of the hypothesis, that confirmed homosexuality is not an inborn trait and that it can very definitely be cured with active-directive, rational-emotive psychotherapy.

Curiously enough, however, in spite of the great preponderance of modern authorities who oppose the view that there are direct constitutional factors in the etiology of homosexuality, this view strongly persists. Homosexuals themselves for the most part believe it; and so do probably the majority of heterosexual laymen. Moreover, the somewhat influential homosexual press—which in the United States mainly consists of three publications, *One, The Mattachine Review* and *The Ladder,* and which in other countries publishes various other journals—regularly and often vociferously promulgates the doctrines that (*a*) homosexuals are born the way they are; that (*b*) they are usually just as psychologically normal or non-disturbed as heterosexuals; and that (*c*) there is no point in trying to treat them so that they can make good heterosexual adjustments.

In view of the persistence of the idea that homosexuality is a congenital or inherited human trait, and in view of the large volume of recent publications that have both defended and opposed this view (including papers on the latest findings in genetics and in chromosomal determination of the sexuality of animal and human cells), it was deemed advisable to reexamine the hypothesis of inborn homosexuality and to see how it still stands up in the light of modern evidence. The present chapter will therefore review the evidence on the direct inheritance of homosexual traits.

The genetic hypothesis. The most convincing evidence that homosexuality may be constitutionally caused has been presented by several genetic investigators. Krafft-Ebing (1886) was apparently the first authority to offer fairly strong data in this regard. Quoting from Casper, Ulrichs, Griesinger, and Westphal, and collecting all known cases of homosexuality published up to 1877 where something was known on the family backgrounds of the homosexuals, Krafft-Ebing concluded: "I have designated this peculiar sexual feeling as a functional sign of degeneration, and as a partial manifestation of a neuro- (psycho-) pathic state, in most cases hereditary,—a supposition which has found renewed confirmation in a consideration of additional cases."

Following Krafft-Ebing, various other investigators studied the incidence of homosexuality and allied disorders in families and came to somewhat similar conclusions, although most of these investigators have not agreed with his viewing homosexuality as a degenerative disease. Thus, Sanders (1936) reported that of seven uniovular pairs of twins with one member being homosexual, in six cases the other twin was also homosexual. Goldschmidt (1938), on the basis of experiments conducted with gypsy moths, contended that homosexuals are probably true genetic intersexual individuals. Hirschfeld (1940) reported that about 35 per cent of homosexual males have brothers or other close family members who are also homosexual. Lang (1940) and Jensch (1941a and b) both noted that the sex ratio among siblings of male homosexuals is significantly above that of ordinary male-female expectation.

None of these studies has been very conclusive; and all of them have been roundly, and rather justifiably, criticized by geneticists and other investigators with opposing views (Darke, 1948; Koller, 1942; Rubin, 1960). The most extensive and best controlled genetic study of homosexuality has been that of Kallmann (1952a, 1952b). Kallmann found that although more than half of the dizygotic co-twins he studied showed no evidence of overt homosexuality, concordance as to the overt practice and quantitative rating of homosexual behavior after adolescence was observed in all 40 of the monozygotic pairs of twins that were investigated. If Kallmann's data were to prove true of all one-celled twins, and were to indicate that when one member of such a pair is homosexual the other also invariably is, while this is only partly true of two-celled twins where one member of the pair is homosexual, then strong evidence in favor of the genetic transmission of homosexuality would exist.

Kallmann's conclusions have been attacked by various critics— such as Scott (1961)—on the grounds that even if identical twins do show much higher rates of mirrored homosexuality than do fraternal twins, this may not be the result of genetic influences but may arise from the fact that identical twins, because of their very identity, have a more closely similar environment than non-identical twins. The main objections to Kallmann's findings, however, have actually been presented, although in somewhat muted and unclarified form, by Kallmann himself in his original papers reporting his study. These objections are as follows:

1. Kallmann notes that although he found rampant homosexuality among both the identical and fraternal twins that he studied, "of the 85 fathers only one is known at present to have had a history of overt homosexual behavior, in addition to several convictions for pedophilic acts." Obviously, however, if homosexuality is a directly inherited human trait, it could only be reasonably expected that the fathers of homosexual twins would also, in a very high percentage of cases, have distinct homosexual histories. Since this was not found, and since there is no other evidence showing that homosexuals have fathers, uncles, or other male relatives who, in a significantly high percentage of cases, also prove to be homosexual, it seems highly unlikely that true hereditary factors are directly involved in homosexuality. Congenital factors, possibly; but hardly hereditary ones.

[In reading the manuscript of this book, Donald Webster Cory thought that I had dealt with this particular point too briefly, considering its great importance in any consideration of the possible hereditary origin of homosexuality. He therefore appended the following more detailed note:

"The proponents of the theory of inborn homosexuality are never quite sure whether homophilism is congenital and hereditary or congenital without being hereditary—that is, present at birth but caused by prenatal influences rather than genic factors. The theory that homosexualism is truly hereditary immediately runs into several difficulties, for the evidence shows that (a) many more males than females in our society are confirmed homosexuals; (b) that fixed homosexuality significantly increases in various regions at certain times (as it apparently has increased in the United States following World War II); (c) that it also significantly increases whenever males are isolated for reasonably long periods (as happens when they are imprisoned); and (*d*) that all manners and degrees of homosexuality exist, ranging from rigid exclusiveness to highly labile ambisexuality (Kinsey, Pomeroy, and Martin, 1948).

"Perhaps the main reason why the hypothesis of hereditary homosexuality appears to be untenable is the fact that although a high percentage of heterosexuals marry and have children, a low percentage of homosexuals have either legitimate or illegitimate offspring. The great majority of parents of homosexuals are themselves distinctly heterosexual, even though a few have had one or both parents who are homophilic. If, as seems to be the case, the chances of having children are significantly lower for individuals who are presumably carrying a hereditary homosexual gene, by the usual process of evolution this gene would tend to disappear in any population over any considerable period of time. This is not because homosexuality is necessarily a disease or a great handicap (since many pathological conditions are hereditary and still survive in our population); but because it is simply the type of condition that makes it much more likely that the carrier or 'affected' person will not have offspring.

"In and of itself, this is not sufficient evidence to exclude the possibility of inborn homosexuality: because there are, on the one hand, non-hereditary congenital predispositions; and, on the other hand, there are recessive hereditary traits. But no one has seriously suggested that homosexuality is a recessive trait in a father (or mother) who then passes it down to a son in such a fashion that it then causes dominant and manifest homosexual behavior.

"For lack of evidence to the contrary, the logic of the laws of heredity, so far as these are known to us today, would tend to exclude homosexuality as a truly inheritable characteristic, because the dynamics of the condition itself would then lead to its own diminution and eventual disappearance."]

2. The great majority of the identical twins used in Kallmann's

study were not only homosexual but schizophrenic or borderline schizophrenic as well. Thus, Kallmann tells us that "six of the index cases classified as monozygotic and concordant as to overt homosexuality have also been concordant with respect to schizophrenic episodes either before or after the manifestation of their homosexual tendencies ... Of the remaining subjects in the group of monozygotic twins concordant as to homosexuality, at least 22 index cases are classifiable as definitely schizoid, severely unstable with obsessive-compulsive features, or excessively alcoholic. Evidence of transvestism has been observed in seven cases of the total sample. Altogether, only 10 twin subjects of the monozygotic series and 18 subjects of the entire sample [of 85 pairs of twins] have been diagnosed as sufficiently adjusted, both emotionally and socially."

In other words, Kallmann's study was not really an investigation of homosexuality in monozygotic and dizygotic twins, but of homosexuality in *basically psychotic* twins. And it hardly comes as a surprise, to anyone who is familiar with the behavior of psychotics, that when one of them is overtly homosexual the other one is also most likely to display distinct homosexual behavior.

3. Recognizing the limitations of his own study, Kallmann did *not* conclude that it indicated that homosexuality is a directly inherited trait. On the contrary, his conclusions were that "apparently, only two males who are similar in both the genotypical and the developmental aspects of sexual maturation and personality integration are also apt to be alike in those specific vulnerabilities favoring a trend toward fixation or regression to immature levels of sexuality. The most plausible explanation of this finding is that the axis, around which the organization of personality and sex function takes place, is so easily dislocated that the attainment of a maturational balance may be disarranged at different developmental stages and by a variety of disturbing mechanisms, the range of which may extend from an unbalanced effect of oppos-

ing sex genes to the equivalent of compulsive rigidity in a schizoid personality structure."

In other words, Kallmann seems to be saying here that males normally develop from immature to mature—and presumably heterosexual—levels of sexuality; but that if they are seriously enough disturbed, they may easily become fixated on or regress to immature—or homosexual—levels. Homosexuality itself, therefore, is not directly inherited; but both a labile sexual predisposition and a tendency toward psychosis are probably inherited; and a combination of these two traits may easily lead to homosexuality.

If Kallmann's data are typical, therefore, they at most seem to show that psychosis runs in human families and that if one psychotic male displays overt homosexual behavior—as a great many psychotic males, of course, do—then there is a very good chance that his one-celled twin brother, if he has one, will also be largely or exclusively homosexual.

There is, however, some contradictory data that throws further doubt on the hypothesis that homosexuality is directly inherited. First of all, several cases have recently been reported in the literature where one member of a set of identical twins was homosexual and the other twin was distinctly heterosexual. Thus, Rainer, Mesnikoff, Kolb, and Carr (1960) intensively studied two sets of identical twins, one male and the other female, in whom the development of the overt psychosexual role was divergent in the sense that one of each pair was heterosexual while the other was homosexual. They found that "neurological and various biochemical examinations failed to reveal differences between these identical twin pairs divergent for homosexuality and heterosexuality." In commenting on this paper, Kallmann (1960) again notes, as Hutchinson (1959) also suggested, that the most probable mode of operation of gene-specific components with a pleiotropic effect may be "on the rates of development of neuropsychological mechanisms involved in identification processes and other aspects of object relationships in infancy." In other words, defective genes may cause tendencies toward serious emotional disturbance, which may in turn lead to homosexuality.

Other recent investigations of direct genetic factors in the causation of homosexualism have produced uniformly negative results. Barr and Hobbs (1954) examined five cases of marked male transvestism and showed that the subjects all had regular male XY chromosome patterns. Polani, Hunter, and Lennox (1955) demonstrated that in cases of Turner's syndrome, where individuals with female secondary sexual characteristics are shown to be genetically male, homosexuality rarely occurs. Early studies by Neugebauer (1908), followed by more recent studies by A. Ellis (1945), Money (1961), Jones and Scott (1958), and many other investigators, have shown conclusively that both true and pseudohermaphrodites ordinarily have sex urges not in accordance with their genetically based sexual constitutions but in accordance with the manner in which they, often quite accidentally, happen to be raised. Pare (1956) took mouth scrapings from 50 male homosexuals, chromosomally sexed these mouth scrapings and compared them with the results obtained from similar studies in 25 male and 25 female controls. He found that the chromosomal sex in the 50 homosexuals was male in all cases and did not differ, in the incidence of chromatin spots, from normal male controls.

All this evidence would seem to clearly indicate that the hypothesis that homosexuality is directly attributable to genetic factors is not only as yet unproved, but seems to be highly questionable. Homosexuals may possibly inherit some tendencies, such as schizoid dispositions, which indirectly prejudice them in favor of deviated sex behavior, but there is no presently available data which indicates that they directly inherit their sexual proclivities.

The hormonal hypothesis. Some authorities, who do not necessarily believe that homosexuality is directly inherited, feel that there are distinct hormonal differences between homosexuals and heterosexuals, and that these hormonal differences cause homosexuality. Vague allegations to this effect have often been made by many sexologists, such as Benjamin (1958, 1961), Brunori (1958), and Rasmussen (1955).

More specific claims that imbalances of sex hormones may be directly responsible for the causation of fixed homosexuality have been put forth by several investigators. Thus, Neustadt and Myerson (1940) assayed the urine of a group of homosexuals and non-homosexuals and found what seemed to be significant differences between the two groups, with the homosexuals showing unbalanced male hormone ratios. Wright (1941) treated 9 homosexual prisoners with antuitrin S and follutein and found that at least three of them reported a decrease in their homosexual urges. Glass and Johnson (1944) used sex hormones with 11 homosexuals and showed some benefit in three of these cases. Massion-Verniory and his associates (1957) found that the average elimination of 17-ketosteroids was lower in 30 sexually deviated males than in the average non-deviated population. Lenz (1958) reported one case in which, after undergoing a testes amputation because of the development of a seminoma, a 48 year old teacher received an oestradiol stab implantation and a series of four injections of estrogens, and that he then became more attracted to the male sex, often experienced homosexual dreams, and showed homosexual tendencies toward his students. Hughes (1914) presented the case of a homosexual male who, after his entire testes were excised, lost his erotic inclination toward males but showed a social inclination toward asexualized ladies.

Such evidence as this, which indicates that homosexuality may have a hormonal causation, is remarkably sparse in the medical and psychological literature, and it has usually resulted from poorly controlled rather than double-blind studies. It is also contradicted by other evidence. Thus, in the studies cited in the last paragraph by Neustadt and Myerson, Wright, and Glass and

Johnson, only very partially good results were obtained when sex hormones were used to treat homosexuals. Neustadt and Myerson, in fact, who strongly espoused a hormonal theory of homosexuality because of their finding significantly less male hormones in the urine of homosexuals, were forced to report that "treatment of a few cases by testosterone injections produced no essential changes in the homosexual feelings or conduct, although the urinary findings were changed." Rosenzweig and Hoskins (1941) gave massive doses of male hormone to a homosexual male and reported no change in the direction of his sexuality. Barahal (1940) gave testosterone to seven overt homosexuals and discovered that it merely resulted in an increase rather than a decrease in their homosexual drives. Brown (1950) tried androgen treatment of 300 homosexuals, with quite unsuccessful results.

After reviewing all the known data on the hormonal treatment of homosexuality, Kinsey, Pomeroy, Martin, and Gebhard (1953) concluded that "in connection with the clinical treatment of homosexuality there are, of course, reports of 'good results,' but no adequate data to show that the behavioral patterns of such subjects have ever been modified by hormonal treatments. We have the histories of an appreciable number of males who had received hormonal treatments, but we have never seen an instance in which a homosexual pattern had been eliminated by such therapy."

Other negative evidence in regard to hormonal influences on homosexuality is provided by the fact that, as Rubin (1960) shows, "castration—which would deprive the individual of the glands which produce sex hormones—has also not caused a change in sexual orientation, though it has had many other effects upon the body and upon sexual desire and ability." Furthermore, as we have shown in the previous section of this chapter, hermaphrodites, who almost certainly are as mixed up as they can possibly be in their hormonal makeup, and females who have been virilized by tumors of the adrenal cortex, are almost always sexually oriented in relation to the sex in which they were raised, rather than in relation to the sex whose hormonal and anatomic characteristics they largely possess.

Finally, as Allen, Broster, and their associates (1938) point out, "one frequently finds that the strongest homosexuals are the most perfect physical specimens and have well-developed masculine bodies with no trace of glandular disease. Surely it would be more reasonable to assume that the hormone in this case, as in others, acts quantitatively. If homosexuality is due to endocrine dysfunction it should be easily correlated in every case with physical variations—which it is not."

In the light of the evidence just cited, it seems clear that not only has it never been established that an imbalance of sex hormones is directly responsible for fixed homosexual behavior, but it seems highly unlikely, in the face of the existing data, that this ever will be established.

The body-build hypothesis. One of the most frequently cited so-called evidences of the constitutional origin of homosexuality is the fact that male homosexuals are frequently effeminate and female homosexuals masculine in their body types. Thus, Weil (1924) compared measurements of 380 homosexuals and 1,000 heterosexual males, found that the former were generally smaller and more effeminate in body-build, and concluded that "more than one-half to two-thirds of all homosexuals show deviation from the 'norm'; anatomical deviation, which means that there is a different physical build and constitution than in heterosexual men." Hirschfeld (1936) insisted that "even before reaching puberty, a child, who later becomes homosexual, shows characterological traits of being differently constituted than other children, who when grown up will have heterosexual feelings: that is, a girlish appearance in the boy and a boyish appearance in the girl." Lichtenstein (1921) reported that "a physical examination of such people (lesbians) will in practically every instance disclose an abnormally prominent clitoris. This is particularly so in colored women."

Havelock Ellis (1936) noted that in ten cases of lesbians who were genitally examined, "in only four were the sexual organs normal; in others they were more or less undeveloped . . . The clitoris is more usually small than large; women with a large clitoris (as Parent-Duchatalet long since remarked) seem rarely to be of the masculine type." He also observed that "the greater part of these various anatomical peculiarities and functional anomalies point, more or less clearly, to the prevalence among inverts of a tendency of infantilism, combined with feminism in men and masculinism in women. This tendency is denied by Hirschfeld, but it is often well indicated among the subjects whose histories I have been able to present, and is indeed suggested by Hirschfeld's own elaborate results."

Rosanoff (1938) held that in feminized homosexuals whom he studied, "the desire to play the passive part seems to be determined by an unusually high erogenous value possessed by the oral and anal regions in these subjects." Dickinson (1941) examined 31 lesbians and found that they had unusually early onset of menstruation; had exceptionally frequent erectility of their nipples; and had glans clitorises which averaged over one-third larger in the median line or antiposterior diameter than the average measurement of non-homosexual women. Barahal (1939) reported that 40 per cent of a group of homosexual males he examined had a feminine-type distribution of their pubic hair, as against 29 per cent of non-homosexuals. Schlegel (1957), after examining body measurements of about 10,000 persons, held that homosexuals have several kinds of special body-types that mirror their sexual inclinations. Nedoma and Freund (1961), investigating a group of 126 almost exclusively homosexual male adults and comparing them with an equally large group of heterosexual men, found the homosexuals to have significantly lower body weight, shorter biacromial distance, and larger width of penis.

Henry (1933, 1934, 1941) and Henry and Gailbraith (1934) produced a series of publications on the constitutional aspects of homosexuality. They indicate that homosexual males have relatively narrow hips, boyish form, long legs, feminine carrying angle of the arm, large muscles, deficient hair on the face and chest, feminine distribution of pubic hair, a high-pitched voice, small penis and testicles, and the presence of a scrotal fold. The homosexual female, they say, is characterized by deficient fat in the shoulders and abdomen, firm muscles, excess hair on the face, breasts and lower extremities, a tendency to masculine distribution of pubic hair, a small uterus and either over- or under-development of the labia and clitoris.

At first blush, these data on significant anatomical differences between confirmed homosexuals and heterosexuals look rather impressive. But when examined more closely, the following lapses in this evidence become clearer:

1. Few of the reported studies were systematic or well-controlled. Weil's often-quoted findings about the femininity of body-build of homosexuals were sharply challenged by Wortis (1937), who showed that his control group of heterosexual males was an atypical group, and that many of his conclusions about anatomical femininity were based on wrong data and inferences. Lichtenstein's and Dickinson's claims that lesbians have large clitorises are directly contradicted by Havelock Ellis's contention that they usually have small clitorises; and all three of these investigators are contradicted by Henry, who insists that lesbians have both over- and under-developed labias and clitorises. Weil's data showing that male homosexuals have larger hips than non-homosexuals are directly contradicted by Henry's data, which indicate that they have relatively narrow hips.

2. Most of the observed group differences tend to be rather

small, and leave much leeway for considerable overlapping of groups and for individual variations. Most of the homosexuals and lesbians who were measured seem to be well within the normal range for their sex groups; and the group differences that are found often seem to stem largely from the inclusion of a relatively few oddly constructed individuals in the homosexual groups.

3. The main consistent findings seem to be not that homosexual males have feminine body-builds and lesbians have male body builds, but that both homosexuals and lesbians have immature anatomies. As Hadfield (1933) notes: "It would be truer to say that in both cases there is a *physiological immaturity*. The female homosexual is often said to be masculinoid; in dress and in manner this is often so, but she is not really masculinoid in physiological development. There are such masculinoid hairy women, but they are not usually or typically homosexual. The feminine homosexual has the boy-like figure, not the man's figure. She is, in other words, immature, lacking in adult female characteristics—roundness of body, large hips, etc., typical of the female. Similarly with the homosexual male, he is not so much feminine as juvenile and immature. He is effeminate only in the sense of being undeveloped as a man."

If homosexuals differ from heterosexuals in that a certain number of them are physiologically immature rather than that they have the physical characteristics of the other sex, this may mean that their physiological immaturity makes it difficult for them to adjust to a regular heterosexual way of life and therefore *in*directly rather than directly predisposes them to homosexuality. It has frequently been found, for example, as Bieber (1962) and his associates recently show, that homosexuals tend to shy away from and do poorly in sports activities when they are children. It is therefore possible that because they are physically immature they tend to do poorly in sports; and, recognizing this fact, and not wanting to keep disadvantageously competing with other boys, they withdraw from such competition in many instances, and protectively begin to take on female traits and manners.

It is also possible that physiological immaturity is often a reflection of psychological immaturity as well; and that, as Kallmann's study (quoted above) indicates, homosexuals sometimes inherit a distinct tendency toward both physical and psychological disturbance rather than a tendency toward homophilism *per se*. Their defective psychophysical inheritance may then *in*directly predispose them toward many kinds of aberrant or pathological behavior, including fixed homosexuality. Henry (1933), for example, found that anomalies of the genitalia and evidence of arrested sexual development were conspicuous not only in the homosexual group he studied but in a highly narcissistic group of psychotic patients as well. If, as some data indicate, psychotics as well as fixed homosexuals have unusual, immature types of body-build, homosexuality may well be more closely linked to inborn tendencies toward psychosis than to anatomical differences themselves.

4. There is considerable evidence for the theory that if homosexuals are often anatomically different from heterosexuals, their less masculine appearance indirectly but still environmentally favors their becoming homosexual rather than, on purely physiological grounds, directly causes their homosexuality.

a. As many astute observers—including Barahal (1939), Bloch (1908), Freud (1925), Rosanoff (1938), and Ellis (1936)—have pointed out, we frequently find, among homosexual individuals, those who are exceptionally strong and masculine in their appearance—and those who are unusually weak and effeminate in their body-build. In Freud's words: "Sporadic secondary characteristics of the opposite sex are very often present in normal individuals, and well-marked physical characteristics of the opposite sex may be found in persons whose choice of object has undergone no change in the direction of inversion; in other words, in both sexes *the degree of physical hermaphroditism is to a great extent inde-*

pendent of the psychical hermaphroditism." If physical appearance were *in*directly rather than directly connected with homosexuality, this irregular correlation of effeminate body-build in males with homophilism is exactly what we would expect to find.

b. Some psychoanalysts, such as Menninger (quoted in Barahal, 1939) and Kunkel (1936), have pointed out that changes in body-build may result psychogenically. Girls, for example, who wish to repudiate their femininity for psychological reasons and to make themselves into butch-type lesbians, may consciously or unconsciously manage to flatten their chests, narrow their hips, and masculinize their faces; or, if this seems a little far-fetched, they may certainly by actual practice develop a deep voice, strong muscles, a man's stride, and other physical traits normally possessed by men. Similarly, males who want to be inverts, and to adopt the sex-role of females, may make real efforts to stay away from athletics, to stick to a feminine diet, to keep their skins soft and creamy, and to do other things which may actually make them take on, at least to some degree, a more feminine body structure. Moreover, by deliberately employing, for many years at a time, opposite-sex ways of walking, talking, gesturing, painting their faces, doing up their hair, etc., many homosexuals may adopt a false look of effeminacy (if they are males) or masculinity (if they are females) that readily confuses observers and leads to their identification as having an opposite-sex body-build that they really do not possess (Sherman, 1938).

c. Physiologically normal males who just happen to fall into the low end of the masculine scale as far as appearance is concerned—who, for example, happen to have soft features, or large hips, or large breasts, or feminine gestures—may more frequently tend to be approached by confirmed homosexuals and given inducements to join the homosexual ranks than may be beefy, rough-looking, and brawny males. Thus, among the Sakalavas of Madagascar, Bloch (1933) tells us, a group of delicate-appearing boys, called the *sekrata,* are commonly treated as girls and induced to assume feminine ways and permit pedication by other males. In our own society, parents may treat a boy as a girl because he happens to have a girlish figure and features, a wealth of hair, etc. (Ferenczi, 1916); and in lower class and delinquent neighborhoods feminine-appearing males, because they are more attractive to active homosexuals, may be more frequently and more vigorously the objects of homosexual seduction (Reckless, 1943). As Margaret Mead (1935) notes, in cultures where anatomical differences in maleness and femaleness are considered to be very important, and where a man's neighbors are convinced that if he has an effeminate body he must be psychologically effeminate, this man may be firmly pushed into becoming a transvestite and a homosexual. In cultures, however, where anatomical differences are not considered to be so important, little or no homosexuality may exist.

d. In competitive societies such as our own, where a person's looks are closely related to his degree of sexual, social, and business success, an effeminate-looking male or a masculine-looking female—of whom there are literally millions, in accordance with the normal laws of individual variation—will often tend to be handicapped in social-sex relations. Such a person will actually have a hard time attracting suitable members of the other sex; or else, believing that he or she will have difficulty (when, actually, this may not be true) such a person may easily develop severe feelings of social-sexual inadequacy, and may refrain from active heterosexual participation. The more such an effeminate-looking male or a masculine-looking female shies away from heterosexual participations, the less practice in such affairs he or she will get, and the greater his or her feelings of social inadequacy will usually become. In time, such a person frequently feels quite estranged from the other sex, and is then easily susceptible to homosexual proselytizing. This does not mean, of course, that all young people in our society who feel sexually inadequate and who consequently turn to homosexuality are drawn from the ranks of physically anomalous or ill-endowed boys and girls, but it may well mean that the boy who is not the football hero type and the girl who would never get close to Hollywood are more likely to become homosexual than those who measure more closely up to our ideals of brawn and beauty.

5. Several studies of homosexuals have produced little or no evidence that these sex deviants *do* have unusual body-builds. Thus, Kelly and Terman (1936) measured 33 passive male homosexuals and found that their physical measurements did not differ markedly from those of army and college men, although there was a slight tendency for their means to be somewhat smaller than those of the other male groups. None of the 33 cases for whom a physical examination was possible showed the slightest defect of the genital organs. The only significant difference found between the homosexual and the heterosexual men who were studied was that the former had smaller amounts of body and leg hair and as a rule their beards were considerably less heavy than those of the average men.

Scott (1958) studied 64 prisoners convicted of homosexuality and found that there was no evidence of endocrine disorder or characteristic body build. Only a small minority showed effeminate traits or behavior. Suzanne Prosin (1962), in a study of twenty lesbian couples who had been "married" to each other and were living together for a period of at least a year, reported that "it would appear that little can be said of the lesbians, as a group, that will support the stereotype presented in the literature and accepted by the public . . . There was no relationship between the size of the person and the choice of role, nor correlation in terms of role within any given pair . . . The picture of the lesbian, as an overly masculinized woman, cannot be supported on the basis of the physical appearance of the subject group."

All told, it would appear that the evidence in favor of the hypothesis that homosexuality is directly related to or is caused by the peculiar body-build of homosexual individuals is far from clearcut, is often contradictory, and applies, at most, to a small minority of confirmed deviants. That there is *some* correlation between homosexuality and human anatomy may well be possible; but, if so, there would appear to be more of a connection between confirmed homosexuality and physical immaturity of both males and females than between homophilism and the possession of the anatomic characteristics of the other sex. Moreover, the low degree of positive correlation that may exist between homosexuality and the secondary sex characteristics of both males and females would indicate that there is no direct connection between these two traits, but that anomalous body-build may in *some* (and even at that, probably in relatively few) instances have an *in*direct influence on an individual's becoming a fixed homosexual.

The untreatability hypothesis. A good many writers on homosexuality have insisted that, since it is very difficult or impossible to cure confirmed homosexuals, in the sense of changing their desires from exclusive preoccupation with members of their own sex to exclusive preoccupation with members of the other sex, homosexuality must be an inborn trait. This argument has been strongly stated by Hirschfeld (1936) as follows: "That the homosexual urge is not acquired but inborn is apparent from the phenomenon of its tenacity. Were it caused by external influences, it would be necessary to assume that it would yield to extraneous influences. In such a case, it would be possible not only for the heterosexual individual to become homosexual, but also, for a homosexual to become heterosexual. Both assumptions are at variance with the results of abundant experience. It is certain, on the other hand, that men and women of extraordinary strong character and will-power were unable to change the direction of their sex urge in spite of great effort."

Hirschfeld's view on fixity, and therefore the innateness, of confirmed homosexuality has been endorsed by numerous writers, all of whom more or less claim that it is impossible for a true homosexual to change his spots and to become heterosexually oriented. Exponents of this view include L. Allen (1960), Bauer (1940), Bloch (1908), Bredstchneider (1959), a British Medical Journal editorialist (1958), Carpenter (1911), English and Pearson (1937), Haggard and Fry (1936), Healy (1938), Hemphill, Leitsch, and Stuart (1958), Mercer (1959), Neustetter (1962), Rosanoff (1938), Sauls (1960), Vincent (1961), Wildeblood (1955), and the Wolfenden Report (1957).

A somewhat more optimistic, but still essentially negative, attitude toward the treatment of homosexuality is taken by a good many other authorities, including Sigmund Freud (1925), who noted: "The removal of genital inversion or homosexuality is in my experience never an easy matter. On the contrary, I have found success possible only under specially favorable circumstances, and even then the success essentially consisted in being able to open to those who are restricted homosexually the way to the opposite sex, which had been till then barred, thus restoring to them full bisexual function." In a famous letter to the mother of a homosexual, Freud (1960) also stated that "in a certain number of cases we succeed in developing the blighted germ of heterosexual tendencies, which are present in every homosexual; in the majority of cases it is no more possible."

This view of the enormous difficulty of curing homosexuals has been mirrored by many other writers, including the British Medical Association's committee on the study of homosexuality (1955), Curran (1938), Freund (1959), Hooker (Russell, 1962), and Maslow and Mittelmann (1941). Although such a view appears, upon cursory examination, to be quite convincing, and to indicate that homosexuality may very well be an inborn trait, a closer examination reveals some very interesting flaws and inconsistencies:

1. An unusually large number of writers who have stoutly held that homosexuality is incurable—such as L. Allen, Carpenter, Hirschfeld, Mercer, Vincent, and Wildeblood—turn out, unsurprisingly enough, themselves to be confirmed homosexuals.

This may be publicly stated by me, because these homosexual writers are either now dead or have recently in print confessed to being homosexual. What I cannot presently state because of our libel laws, but which I nonetheless know to be a fact, is that many of the other most vociferous upholders of the view that homosexuality is incurable and consequently inborn are also themselves sex deviants. Their testimony, consequently, is hardly unbiased or reliable. Many of the other authorities who take a very pessimistic view of treating homosexuals—such as English and Pearson, Healy, and Maslow and Mittelmann—have obviously been influenced by early Freudian views, and are adhering closely to Freud's original formulations. Modern psychoanalysts, who increasingly subscribe to less Freudian positions, almost always take a more optimistic view of the treatment of homosexuals.

2. The criterion of cure that is demanded by those who are most pessimistic about the treatment of homosexuals is quite unrealistic. In the treatment of non-homosexual neurotics and psychotics, for example, no one seems to demand that "cure" consist of completely eradicating, in the patient, all possible vestiges of emotional disturbance. If the psychotherapized neurotic becomes, as a result of being treated, *reasonably* free of anxiety and hostility, he is considered to have made notable gains. No one, of course, would expect him to become *totally* well-adjusted. Similarly, "cure" in the cases of homosexuals should not unrealistically be conceived as total eradication of homosexual interests and desires, but the replacing of exclusive homosexuality with *some* degree of spontaneous heterosexual urge and with successful and enjoyable heterosexual participation (A. Ellis, 1959a, 1960, 1962b, 1963a). But those who take a very pessimistic view of the treatment of homosexuality almost always define the "cure" of homosexuals in a most unrealistic manner, and consequently overlook the many therapeutic (and, for that matter, self-induced) cures that actually occur.

3. It is quite obvious, as has been often reported in the literature,

that most homosexuals who come for psychotherapy do not change their obsessive-compulsive, exclusive patterns of homosexuality because they make no serious attempt to do so. Bein (1934), for example, investigated 17 exclusive homosexuals who came to him for psychotherapy and discovered that not one of them really wanted to become more heterosexual, but all came for their general neurotic disturbances. Westwood (1960) reported that very few of the 127 homosexuals he intensively studied in the course of a major research on homosexuality underwent psychotherapy, and of the few who did half gave up for some reason in less than three months. "By far the majority," he notes, "said either that treatment would not help or that it was not necessary . . . These 82 contacts present a very difficult problem. They have adopted a defensive attitude to their homosexual condition and they resent the suggestion that they are suffering from any kind of disease or need any kind of treatment." Westwood also points out that it would be unthinkable for most older homosexuals to change their basic sex patterns because "for most of them it would amount to starting a new life with new friends and in a new place. Even if at first they entered the homosexual coteries with reluctance and purely as a defense against outside pressures, so many of them have perforce had to make this adjustment that to expect them to abandon their whole way of life at this stage of their careers would be demanding the impossible."

Confirmed homosexuality, in other words, is a condition that has distinct disadvantages in our society, but that has direct sexual rewards as well. The homosexual *does* derive sex satisfaction from relations with males; he *can* easily get sex partners; he *is* prejudiced in favor of males; and he often *has* built an entire way of life around his homosexuality. Consequently, in some instances he is no more likely to *want* to change his pattern of living and to become exclusively heterosexual than the successful criminal is to *want* to get a relatively low paying job and to work honestly for the rest of his life. Both practicing homosexuals and the successful criminals may occasionally be *forced* or *induced* to change their methods of living; but obviously, a radical transformation in their ways of behaving will be most difficult to bring about. This, however, hardly proves that either the homosexual or the criminal was *born* a social deviant.

4. The fact that it is difficult or even impossible for an individual to change his mode of behavior, once this mode is strongly fixed, by no means proves that it is an innate or congenital way of behaving. As much recent research on imprinting in ducklings and other animals has shown, once an animal is strongly imprinted, early in its life, with a tendency to become attached to certain individuals or objects, it is almost impossible, later in this animal's life, to un-imprint it again and to induce it to be equally strongly attached to another kind of individual or object. Similarly, as Brown (1961) and Money (1961) have reasoned, once human beings are strongly imprinted with homosexual or transvestite tendencies, it may be almost impossible to get them completely to change these early-learned tendencies.

Even when animals are conditioned later in life, it has been found that it is inordinately difficult, and sometimes impossible, to recondition or decondition them again. Thus, Liddell (Hoch and Zubin, 1950) found that, by forcing sheep to be protractedly vigilant, he could induce them to behave neurotically; but once he got them to be neurotic, it was almost impossible to help them be non-neurotic again.

Similarly, Solomon and Wynne (1954), after conditioning experiments in creating fears in rats and dogs, conclude that a principle of the partial irreversibility of traumatic anxiety reaction exists and that, according to this principle "there will be certain definite limitations on the 'curing' of behavior arising from early, 'primitive' traumatic experiences. This will also hold true for psychosomatic symptoms which may be more direct manifestation of early conditioning. Complete freedom from a *tendency* to manifest such symptoms could not be expected, even with the most advantageous course of therapy."

If these experimenters are correct, then there would seem to be no reason why, even if confirmed homosexuality were not inborn but followed from early conditioning, it would still be easily curable.

5. It is often assumed that fixed homosexuals become sexually deviated early in life and are virtually incurable for the rest of their lives, but this is far from true. First of all, many homosexuals have a completely enjoyable heterosexual history for several years, sometimes a decade or two, before they become confirmed deviants. Still others begin their sex lives as exclusive homosexuals, then become quite heterosexual, and later become exclusively homosexual again. The notion, espoused by the orthodox Freudians, that all males go through a pregenital, then a genital phase, that they then undergo a latency period, and that they finally experience a homosexual phase, on which they may become fixated or from which they may graduate into a heterosexual phase—this idea is entirely hypothetical and has no scientific evidence in its support. Actually, different individuals may go through several kinds of phases before they finally wind up in the homosexual or heterosexual camp.

Secondly, there is much reason to believe that literally thousands of fixed homosexuals, without any formal psychotherapy whatever, manage to become quite heterosexual in their orientation. Usually, such individuals change their sexual orientation when they are relatively young. But I have seen several cases where men and women in their thirties and forties simply forced themselves to forego all homosexual contacts and propelled themselves into heterosexual relations; and within a year or two of so doing, these individuals had become largely or exclusively heterosexual in their desires and activities and were no longer bothered by homosexual urges. I have even seen one case where a male homosexual and a lesbian deliberately married each other for reasons of convenience; but when they began experimenting sexually, largely because they happened to share the same bed, they eventually learned to like heterosexual more than homosexual relations, and divested themselves of their fixed homosexual leanings.

If these spontaneous, non-therapeutically helped changes often take place in confirmed homosexuals, as I am convinced that they do in a surprisingly large number of instances, it seems most unlikely that homosexuality is either incurable or inborn.

6. The view that it very definitely *is* possible to cure confirmed homosexuals by psychotherapy, and to help them to be largely or exclusively interested in heterosexual relations after they have had such therapy, is espoused by many authorities, including Adler (1939a), Berne (1947), Branson (1959), Fain and Marty (1959), Fry and Rostow (1942), Menninger (1939), Pascoe (1961), Stearn (1963), and Thouless (1929). More importantly, case studies and statistical reports on homosexuals who have been successfully treated by various kinds of psychoanalytic and directive methods of psychotherapy have been reported in the scientific literature by a great number of therapists, including C. Allen (1949, 1952), Bien (1934), Bieber and his associates (1962), Buckle (1949), Caprio (1952), Cowles (1954), A. Ellis (1959a, 1959b, 1960, 1962b), Fink (1954, 1960), Foster (1947), Anna Freud (1951), Fried (1960), Hadfield (1958), Harper (1959), Henry (1941, 1955), Karpman (1954), Laidlaw (1952), Lewinsky (1952), London (1937), London and Caprio (1950), Maclay (1960), Mendelsohn and Ross (1959), Monroe and Enelow (1960), Morse (1961), Nedoma (1951), Poe (1952), Robertiello (1959, 1961), Rubenstein (1958), Shentoub (1957), Socarides (1960), Srnec and Freund (1953), Stekel (1922), Tarail (1961), Wasserman (1960), Westwood (1953), and Woodward (1958). Not only has successful individual treatment of fixed homo-

sexuals often been reported, but their effective treatment by group therapy methods has also recently been demonstrated—for example, by Hadden (1958), Smith and Bassin (1959), Thompson (1961), and Yalom (1961). And, in addition to the list of individual therapists noted in the last paragraph who have reported cures of fixed homosexuals, Clifford Allen (1947) has collected reports of successful treatments by Bircher, Frey, Gordon, Laforgue, Lilienstein, Naftaly, Ross, Serog, Strausser, Sumbaer, and Virchon. Altogether, therefore, there would seem to be clinical reports by at least fifty different authors attesting to significant or complete changes in confirmed homosexuals and the achievement of heterosexual desire and pleasurable activity by these fixed homosexuals. The number of successful cases reported by these authors, moreover, runs well into the hundreds.

In view of all this evidence, it now seems quite preposterous to hold that fixed homosexuality cannot be cured or that the impossibility of changing confirmed homosexualism is good proof of its inborn nature. Conversely, the cure of homosexuality does not completely prove that this condition is *not* innate, since it is certainly possible, by corrective therapy, to improve or cure certain physical conditions, such as congenital syphilis or deformed limbs, with which an individual may be born. But the fact that confirmed or exclusive homosexuality is definitely amenable to psychotherapy is at least presumptive evidence that it is not a directly inherited characteristic.

The brain damage hypothesis. A few writers have tried to trace the causation of homosexuality to brain damage. Thus, Thompson (1949) postulates the existence of a hypothetical cerebral center discharge without normal cortical control, and he suggests that sexual anomalies, including homosexuality, may be a kind of release phenomenon, similar to Parkinsonism and athetosis. Hoffer (1957) hypothesizes that Oscar Wilde's homosexuality was caused by his having cerebral syphilis. And other observers, noting that lobotomies and other brain injuries sometimes lead to disordered sexual behavior, have wondered whether homosexuality and cerebral damage are closely correlated.

Although this is an interesting hypothesis, there seems to be no concrete data to support it. It is certainly possible that in some instances brain damage encourages homosexuality—for example, in the cases of some arteriosclerotic males who, although previously normal sexually, attempt to have sex relations with boys after they are cerebrally afflicted. If so, however, it seems most likely that only a very small minority of practicing homosexuals are motivated by brain injuries. And it also seems likely that, in those instances where cerebral damage is correlated with sex deviation, it is only an *in*directly causative factor. That is to say, the cerebral trauma probably leads to general lack of inhibition and of good judgment, which in turn may encourage all kinds of prohibited sex behavior, including homosexuality, attacks on children of the other sex, public masturbation, etc. Any direct connection between cerebral malfunctioning and confirmed homosexuality is as yet unestablished.

The historical and cultural hypothesis. It has often been contended that since homosexuality is found in all parts of the world, in many different kinds of cultures, and in all historical epochs, it must be biologically inborn. Thus, Dingwall (1959) has indicated that "in human societies there exists every variation of heterosexual and homosexual activity. The 'perfect male' and the 'perfect female' are far rarer than has been supposed. As far as we know, examples of homosexual love have been recorded from the earliest times and among a great variety of peoples." Berrios (1961) has pointed out that even in a state so carefully organized as ancient Peru homosexuality was commonly known. And Hirschfeld (1935) has contended that in almost every country of the world the number of homosexual males is three out of every hundred—and that it is exactly the same percentage among silkworm moths!

This argument for the universality, and hence innateness, of confirmed homosexuality breaks down at several points:

1. From all the anthropological evidence that we now have available, it would appear that Hirschfeld was quite mistaken. Although there is probably *some* amount of homosexuality everywhere in the world, the rates vary enormously, with certain peoples displaying virtually no overt homophilism while others (who are often of the same ethnic stock) have considerable homosexuality (Mead, 1935).

2. Homosexuality flourishes, among any given cultural or geographic group, much more under some conditions than under others. Thus, although only about four per cent of American males are fixed homosexuals during their entire lives, a much higher percentage engage in exclusively homosexual acts when they are isolated from females—as they often are in prisons, in boys' schools, on long ocean voyages, etc. The fact that confirmed homosexuality is often directly proportional to the availability of heterosexual partners is excellent evidence against Hirschfeld's and others' hypotheses that it exists everywhere at a pretty steady rate and is therefore inborn.

3. The observation that homosexuality tends to exist in every part of the world at every period of history is easily accounted for by the hypothesis, which most sexologists and psychologists still accept, that human beings are born with an ambisexual tendency, which allows them to be raised to be heterosexuals in most instances, but which is sufficiently labile to permit homosexuality to develop under somewhat unusual circumstances and in many individual cases under fairly usual conditions. No innate predisposition which would directly cause some individuals to become fixed deviates is needed to account for the widespread, if quite variable, homosexuality which exists all over the world.

Summary. Several hypotheses concerning the possible innateness or direct constitutional causation of confirmed homosexuality have been examined in this chapter, including the theories that it is genetically caused, is hormonally based, is directly connected with an individual's body-build, is almost completely untreatable, is the result of brain damage, and is historically and culturally uniform in incidence. When critically reviewed, all these hypotheses are seen to be unsupported by objective, confirmatory evidence of a scientific nature. What has been found, at most, in the course of this survey, is that certain genetic, hormonal, and anatomic factors may well help indirectly to produce homosexuality in some subjects—and particularly, perhaps, in those who are born with tendencies toward severe emotional disturbance, hormonal imbalance, or physiological immaturity.

chapter 2

The Psychological Causes of Homosexuality

~~~~~~~~~~~~~~~~~~~~~~~~~~~~~~~~

There are many environmental or psychological reasons why individuals whom one would normally expect to be heterosexual, or at least to be bisexual, tend to become mainly or exclusively homosexual. In fact, there are *so* many influences that psychologically predispose a male or female to become homosexual that one has a difficult time deciding which of them is truly important; and authors who insist that there is one *paramount* reason are to be suspected of giving a one-sided presentation. For each point that such authors unduly emphasize, they seem to leave out fifty or a hundred *other* significant factors. Some of the main environmental factors in the etiology of fixed homosexuality will be considered below.

Factors of general conditioning and learning. Several authorities —such as Brown (1961), Cory (1963, 1964), Cory and LeRoy (1963), Kelly (Terman and Miles, 1936), Kinsey, Pomeroy, Martin, and Gebhard (1948, 1953), Henry (1934, 1941, 1955), Henry and Gross (1941), Money (1961), Pomeroy (1958), West (1955), and Westwood (1953)—have talked about the conditioning or learning elements in the causation of homosexuality. Some of the points that have been raised in this connection are the following:

1. Just as imprinting takes place in certain animals, such as ducklings, when they are at a rather young and critical age, so that they then become attached to specific objects or other animals and remain so attached for the rest of their lives, it is possible that

some young children become attached to a homosexual role, or to members of their own sex, or to certain kinds of sexual activities, when they are children or adolescents, and that this early acquired "imprinting" strongly biases them for the rest of their days, and makes them continue to be attached to homophilic ideas and participations.

2. Some children are specifically raised to dislike members of the other sex and to respect, like, or love members of their own sex. Thus, parents or teachers may deliberately raise a boy to believe that most females are dangerous or horrible creatures and that males are fine and praiseworthy.

3. Children may have experiences with members of the other sex that are unpleasant and experiences with members of their own sex that are pleasant, thus prejudicing them against heterosexual involvements. Thus, one of my homosexual patients had several sisters and female cousins who treated him nastily when he was a youngster; and one of my lesbian patients had an uncle who bullied her into having repeated sex relations with him when she was between her eighth and twelfth years.

4. Children may be raised almost exclusively with members of the other sex, and may therefore come to acquire their tastes, interests, and desires. A boy raised with several sisters and aunts may learn to get along so well with females that he never feels too comfortable with rough and unruly boys and finds it difficult to take an active interest in their kinds of pursuits—including the pursuit of the female as a sex object.

5. Children may be raised almost exclusively with members of their own sex and may therefore find that they get along most comfortably with this sex and that they are rather uncomfortable when they are in the presence of opposite sex members. They may experience their first intense sex desires when only members of their own sex are around; may matter-of-factly have affairs with these same-sex members; and may consequently find that their sex ideation is bound only to these homoerotic partners.

6. Even when children and adolescents are normally raised with members of both sexes, they may have their first satisfying sex relations with a member of their own sex and may consequently become fixated on homosexual involvements. Young males who are seduced by older males or by their peers will *usually* not become fixed homosexuals for that reason alone, since most of them will later try heterosexual affairs and may even become exclusively heterosexually oriented. But in *some* instances, particularly where the youngster has difficulty competing for heterosexual favors, his early pleasant homosexual experiences will induce him to keep seeking the easier, more available sexual pathway and to remain largely or exclusively homosexual.

7. Children and adolescents who have early heterosexual experiences may find that these are so traumatizing or unsatisfying that they may later retreat to exclusive homosexual relations. Thus, the boy who has a guilt-ridden, loveless, inept experience with a prostitute, or the girl who has initial intercourse in a very painful manner with a man who has no consideration for her as a human being, may withdraw from the field of heterosexuality and may, accidentally or by design, become involved in homosexual relations thereafter.

8. In certain cultures or subcultures individuals may receive definite social approval for engaging in homosexual rather than heterosexual activities and may therefore become homosexually predisposed. Thus, some societies—as ancient Greeks (Eglinton, 1964; Licht, 1932; Wood, 1961) or modern Mohave Indians (Devereux, 1937)—have institutionalized homosexuality, with males receiving approval and prestige for playing homosexual roles. In some groups in our own culture—such as groups of adolescent boys or groups of males in prison—homosexuality is an accepted way of life, and males who do *not* engage in this kind of activity may be considered aberrant or looked down upon as being outsiders.

9. Isolation with members of one's own sex, particularly for a

prolonged period of time, encourages some individuals to become conditioned to homosexuality, even when they have previously had an exclusively heterosexual history. Thus, men who are incarcerated in prisons or in hospitals; or who are isolated with other males in the armed forces; or who are working in regions where females are not generally available—many such men are driven to engage in homosexual behavior, and some of them continue to do so after their period of isolation has ended and when females are freely available.

In the great majority of these cases, where the individual is somehow conditioned or biased, usually at an early age but sometimes later in life, to favor homosexuality, there are profound factors *other than* environmental conditioning involved in his becoming a fixed homophile. For one thing, he must obviously be born with the *tendency to be conditioned*. For if humans were relatively nonconditionable sexually, as many of the lower animals are, and had clearcut sexual intincts which literally drove them into one kind of sex activity (such as heterosexual copulation), they surely would not be as easily influenced by environmental training as they are. The fact remains, however, that they are not born with clearcut instincts, which impel them to be unidirectional in their sex pursuits, but instead seem to be born with sex drives that have an innate *power* but little innate sense of *direction* (Ellis, 1945; Money, 1961). Because they are naturally plurisexual, they are *easily* conditioned toward heterosexuality, homosexuality, or some other monolithic pathway; and in many instances, in fact, they never become quite channelized toward any single path of sexuality, but all their lives participate in a many-faceted kind of sexuality.

Humans, moreover, have a good many physiological predispositions which often make it easy for them to be conditioned in a *specific* sex channel. Thus, a given male may be born with a tendency to be highly sexed, to be physically small and weak, and to be timid and passive in his social relations. If so, he will tend to desire *some* form of sexuality to a high degree, but may feel that (in our competitive society) he is not quite "manly" enough to achieve the heterosexual conquests that he would like to have. Under *these* conditions, any early environmental factors (such as seduction by an older male) that occur in *this* male's life and that predispose *him* to homosexual participation will probably be taken more seriously by him than would be exactly the same factors that might occur in *another* male's life; and, consequently, he might very well turn into a confirmed homosexual, while another male, in similar circumstances, would only engage in occasional or temporary homosexuality.

The point is that environmental conditions *themselves* very rarely, if ever, cause human beings to do anything: since environment can only work on the *living organism,* which itself is physiologically predisposed to accept or reject its influences. External conditioning, moreover, is an exceptionally complex thing: since it is both reinforced *and* contradicted by other external factors. A given male may be deliberately raised by his mother to be girlish; but he may also be reared in a neighborhood where (*a*) his peers are a rough set of boys who will not tolerate any effeminacy, or (*b*) his peers are a highly cultured group of boys who are somewhat effeminate themselves. Depending on whether neighborhood factors *a* or *b* are operating during his childhood, the strong influence of his mother to raise him as a girl may be reinforced or overridden.

To make matters still more complicated, it should be recognized that homosexuality itself is hardly a monolithic, well-defined trait, but instead has at least two major components: sexual desire and sex-role inversion tendencies. Many male homosexuals are mainly or exclusively driven toward other males for their sex satisfactions, and yet they are just as strongly taken with the normal male role of their society and are not effeminate in their voice, manners, gestures, dress, or interests. Aside from the fact that they enjoy going to bed with other males, they would easily be taken for fully "masculine" men by anyone who knew them intimately.

On the other hand, there are a good many homosexuals who are true sex-role inverts, in that they not only desire other males sexually but also think and act like most women in their cultures do. These are the "fairies" or the "pansies," some of whom are so extreme in their "feminine" outlooks that they loathe their male bodies, and try to become transsexualists—that is, individuals who have their sex organs surgically removed or changed, so that they can "truly" become feminized and adopt the regular life of a woman (Benjamin, 1961).

Finally, there are still other males who are heterosexual in their sex orientation, but who love to wear women's clothing and adopt other female ways. These are called cross-dressers, transvestites, or eonists (Allen, 1949; Brown, 1961; H. Ellis, 1936; Kinsey, Pomeroy, Martin, and Gebhard, 1953; Overzier, 1958; Storr, 1957; Thoma, 1957).

When, therefore, a given environmental influence, such as a mother encouraging a boy to be effeminate, turns an individual toward one form of sex deviation (that is, homosexual sex-role inversion or transvestism), another set of environmental factors, such as the movie and TV screens telling him *ad nauseam* that he is supposed to lust after females, may turn him into nondeviational channels. The result may well be, consequently, that if Johnnie, Joey, and Jimmie are all conditioned by their mothers to play a female role in our society, Johnnie may become a sex-role invert who lives in Greenwich Village, displays overt effeminate ways, and who only looks for butch-type homosexuals to go to bed with and to be subservient to; Joey may become an average homosexual who dotes on baseball games and poker, reinforces his masculine self-image by taking up weight-lifting and karate, but who keeps looking for male bed companions; and Jimmie may become a happily married heterosexual transvestite who keeps privately giving in to the urge to dress in his wife's clothing and at times to masquerade in public in female dress.

In sum: conditioning factors may be very important in the causation of fixed homosexuality; but they only operate within the framework of the individual's total social sexual relations, and they are themselves influenced by his innate biological makeup.

Factors related to parental and familial conditioning. Psychoanalytic writers, ever since the latter part of the nineteenth century, have stressed the role that familial and parental factors play in the psychological causation of homosexuality. Thus, from a variety of Freudian and non-Freudian views, familial etiological agents have been stressed by many authorities, including Adler (1917, 1939a, 1939b), Allen (1949), Barahal (1940), Bergler (1956), Bieber *et al.* (1962), Caprio (1952), Cory (1963, 1964), Devereux (1937), Ferenczi (1916, 1926), Fielding (1932), Freud (1924-1950, 1938), Hamilton (1925, 1929, 1936), Hammer (1957), Kahn (1937), London (1933, 1937), London and Caprio (1950), Money-Kyrle (1932), Pollens (1938), Schilder (1942), Sprague (1962), Stekel (1922), and Wittels (1929). Some of the points that have been raised in this connection are:

1. The child who is strongly attached to his same-sex parent may also become sexually attracted to this parent and may become homosexual in an effort to have symbolic relations with this parent or with someone resembling him.

2. The child who is weakly attached to his same-sex parent, or who feels dislike or hostility toward this parent, may find it difficult to identify with his own sex, may retreat into identification with members of the other sex, and may therefore become homoerotic.

3. The child who fears his own-sex parent, or who feels he is much weaker than this parent, may become afraid to compete with this parent for the affection of the other-sex parent (or for the affection of any member of the opposite sex) and may retreat into homosexuality.

4. The young male who is attached to his father and who wants

to keep the love of this father may symbolically offer himself as a homosexual object to this parent.

5. A boy may be quite attached to his father, may resent all females who attract his father (particularly if the father is promiscuous or is strongly attached to some female), and may therefore turn away from all females and become homosexual.

6. A child who has a powerful attachment to his other-sex parent (or siblings) may, because of this attachment, come to identify with members of the other sex and may reject his own sex-role.

7. A child who has dislike for or hostility to his other-sex parent (or siblings) may acquire a general dislike or antagonism toward all members of the other sex and may turn to fixed homosexuality.

8. The child who fears his other-sex parent may come to fear most members of the other sex and therefore retreat to homosexuality.

9. A young male who is strongly attached to his mother (or sisters) and who thinks that it is wrong for him to be incestuously involved, may react against all members of the other sex, view them in an incestuous light, and therefore become attracted to other males instead of to females.

10. A male child who is ashamed of his mother's (or sisters') sexual promiscuity may retreat from heterosexuality into homosexual participations which do not remind him of this "shameful" activity.

11. A child who feels that either or both his parents will accept him better if he adopts the role of the other sex may be led to adopt this role to please them, and thus to become homosexual.

12. A child who hates either or both of his parents may (consciously or unconsciously) search for methods of degrading himself and them; and he may consequently adopt homosexual pathways of life.

13. The child who sees that his parents' marriage is distinctly unhappy, and especially perhaps that his mother dominates his father, may retreat from heterosexual relationships and become homosexual in order to avoid getting into a similar poor or dangerous marital relationship himself.

14. The child who feels that his parents favor one or more of his opposite-sex siblings may try to become identified with this other-sex and may turn to homosexuality.

For many reasons, such as the foregoing, it can be seen that family influences can be very important in turning a child away from endeavoring to fulfill his own-sex role and toward trying to identify with and to fill some inverted sex role. These are reasonably common family influences which may predispose an individual to become homosexual. In addition, of course, there may be uncommon influences, where the mother deliberately raises her son to be a "daughter" to her; where a father seduces his son to have overt sex relations with him; where a boy's brother is overtly homosexual, and directly seduces the boy into a homophilic direction; and so on.

In spite of these many ways in which early family life can prejudice a child away from his own-sex and toward the opposite-sex role, it must not be thought that there is anything magically automatic about the process of what often has been called the "family romance." For it must be remembered, in this connection, that practically every child undergoes some of the major family influences listed above; and yet, obviously, only a small proportion of those who undergo these "predisposing" influences actually become fixed, overt homosexuals. How come?

One important answer to this question—and one which the psychoanalytic writers almost invariably ignore—is that many children seem to have a *general* predisposition toward emotional disturbance that other children simply do not seem to have. Thus, millions of contemporary youngsters have a very weak father, whom they do not respect, and a dominating mother, whom they thoroughly dislike. But of these millions of children with weak fathers and dominating mothers, only a sizeable minority seems to become thoroughly upset about this kind of a family situation, while the majority somehow accepts the fact that this poor family situation exists and recognizes that it need not be repeated in one's *own* future marriages.

Moreover, even if we take only those children who *do* upset themselves, during their childhood and thereafter, because their fathers were palpably weak and their mothers were nastily dominating, most of them later turn out to be exclusively heterosexual, while only a small proportion becomes homosexual. Some of them who finally turn out to be non-homosexual do not marry at all; others marry but make sure that they select a non-dominating wife; and still others marry but make the same mistake as their fathers did, and select a bitchily dominating wife.

Clearly, then, the human individual, even when he grows up in a family milieu where conditions are distinctly inimical to his becoming heterosexually oriented and to his developing homosexual patterns of behavior, is not deterministically *forced* to become a sex deviant, as much of the analytic literature strongly states or implies. He does have something of a choice—even if that choice is limited by various physiological and psychological factors. Just because he *is* a human being, and is therefore able to *re*-assess the basic philosophies of life which he imbibes and develops during his childhood, he is to a considerable extent able to *change* or even *eradicate* these philosophies, and to replace them by other views of himself and the world.

Nonetheless, since the individual *is* predisposed to think crookedly, especially during his childhood, and since he also has the tendency *not* to reevaluate his basic assumptions about himself (even though he has the *capacity* to do so if he works at so doing), early influences on him are important. The Freudians, again, highly exaggerate the part that *family* patterns play in these early influences, and neglect the part that *general* culture patterns play. They neglect the fact that the child is not only, or often even mainly, taught by his parents and parent-surrogates, and that he is *also* trained by his peers, his school teachers, the books he reads, the movies he sees, and by various other institutions and means of mass communication.

For all this, family influences *can* be, and usually are, very important in early conditioning of the child. And when these influences are directed toward prejudicing an individual in favor of his own sex, biasing him against members of the other sex, or teaching him that heterosexuality is a dangerous state of being, he may easily—*particularly* if he has other innate and acquired tendencies that predispose him toward severe emotional disturbance—acquire and maintain patterns of fixed homosexuality.

Factors related to the desire to adopt the role of the other sex. For several reasons other than those specifically associated with their family upbringing, children may feel that it is more desirable that they adopt an opposite-sex role and may therefore become prejudiced in favor of that kind of homosexuality which goes with sex-role inversion (Kardiner and Ovesey, in Ruitenbeck, 1963). For example:

1. An individual may believe that members of his own sex are discriminated against in his community and that it would be more advantageous for him to adopt the role of the other sex. Thus, a male in our society may feel that he must assume too many socio-economic and other responsibilities, must work too hard to get ahead in life, must be over-courteous to females, etc. A female may feel that she is discriminated against in various ways because of her sex, that she leads an over-restricted life, that she is forbidden to enter or to make real progress in various "masculine" pursuits, etc. Both males and females who feel that they are held down or persecuted by their societies in these ways may give up their own sex identification and deliberately (con-

sciously or unconsciously) try to "pass over" and become, for all practical purposes, a member of the opposite sex.

2. Some individuals feel that they are personally too weak, too ungainly, too unintelligent, or otherwise too handicapped to succeed well at their own-sex role, and that therefore it would be better if they adopted the role of the other sex. Puny and physically weak males, in proportions significantly greater than chance, seem to adopt "fairy" roles; and girls with broad shoulders and unfeminine builds frequently become butch-type lesbians.

3. People who somehow come to think that their friends or associates will like them better if they adopt an opposite-sex role frequently ingratiate themselves by adopting such a role. Youngsters in a prison setup who are desperately in need of love and protection from the other inmates often become "punks" and take on female sex role in order to please their "protectors."

4. Some individuals in a given culture have pronounced interests—such as esthetic interests in males or mechanical interests in females—which do not harmonize well with the role usually adopted by their own sex in this culture, but which harmonize better with the role usually adopted by the other sex. Such individuals, in order to pursue their predilections more comfortably, may become homosexual.

Factors related to the real difficulties and dangers of heterosexuality. In a society such as our own, there are always real difficulties and dangers associated with being a full-fledged member of one's own sex; and rather than face and put up with these reality problems, many individuals (usually those who are generally predisposed to be seriously disturbed or weak-minded) will withdraw from the heterosexual rat race and adopt homosexual patterns of behaving. Thus:

1. Individuals may find that the maintenance of regular heterosexual contacts is an expensive and time-consuming process, and

that in many ways it is easier to engage in homosexual affairs. Males in our society may dislike the amenities of heterosexual courtship, the relative long periods of wooing, the expenses of dating, the difficulty of getting young girls to bed, etc., and may find that it is much easier for them to make out sexually in the "gay" than in the "straight" world. Females may dislike the necessity for dressing up, acting in a ladylike fashion, conforming to sexual restrictions of Western civilization, etc., and may therefore withdraw to an easier, freer kind of "gay" life.

2. Some individuals—particularly females in our culture—may have strong (and often highly exaggerated) fears of pregnancy in heterosexual relations and may consequently think that homosexual affairs are safer.

3. Some people have a genuine dislike or distaste for certain kinds of heterosexual relations and, rather than go through the hassle of insisting that they and their partners try other forms of heterosexuality, may withdraw from the field entirely. Thus, some males and females do not particularly favor penile-vaginal copulation, even though they immensely enjoy oral genital, hand genital, or other forms of sexuality. Rather than put up with the ceaseless explanations and discussions which they have to undertake in order to get what they want with a heterosexual partner, they find it more convenient to seek homosexual partners, who "naturally" tend to do what they prefer to do themselves.

4. Many people have little or no inclination to become emotionally involved with their sex partners and they find that, because emotional involvements are more expected in heterosexual affairs, it is more convenient for them to stick to homosexual, more casual encounters.

5. Sometimes there is an actual shortage of suitable members of the other sex—for example, a shortage of females in a frontier region or a shortage of males after a war has decimated the male population—and, rather than take the trouble of hunting up

some good heterosexual partners, the individual chooses to take the easier pathway and to resort to homosexuality.

Factors related to the need to be loved. The majority of homosexuals are monolithically tied to having affairs with members of their own sex not for purely sexual reasons, but for love satisfactions. They have a need—and, very often, a dire need—to be loved and accepted by others; and in one way or another they conclude that this need is not likely to be met heterosexually and that they have a better chance of its being met in the homosexual arena. Specific factors in this connection are these:

1. Some individuals have much greater love needs than sex needs; and, judging heterosexuality primarily as a *sex* area, they may withdraw from it into homosexuality, which they mainly define as a *love* area. Thus, females in our society often feel that males are mainly or only interested in them for their bodies rather than for their total personalities, and they sometimes become so revolted by this idea that they withdraw into lesbian relationships, where they can largely try for intense emotional involvements, often with a minimum of overt sexuality.

2. A great many people who have a dire need to be loved find that it is easier to get members of their own sex interested in them than to prove to be equally attractive to members of the other sex; and consequently, they accept the love of these same-sex members and turn to homosexuality. A mediocre-looking or low-achieving male, for example, may not go very far with girls when he competes with other males. But in the homosexual world he is likely to find partners who not only find him attractive but who will actively woo him. He may then, quite unconsciously, begin to find these males attractive himself.

3. Some people find it easier to love members of their own sex than to love members of the other sex because they have more basic interests in common with the same-sex members, or may

even be narcissistically attracted to them because they more closely resemble themselves.

4. In our society, there tends to be engendered a great deal of antagonism between males and females, largely because the two sexes are biologically different and are raised with conflicting goals. This sex antagonism prevents some individuals from easily loving members of the opposite sex and makes them more easily able to have good love relationships with members of their own sex.

5. Some people are so traumatized by an early love relationship with a member of the other sex—as when a boy's first girlfriend dies or cruelly rebuffs him—that they find it too uncomfortable to chance another deep love relationship with any member of this sex, and are therefore unconsciously biased toward forming deep love attachments for members of their own sex.

6. Young people frequently form crushes on members of their own sex, either from an older age group or from their peer group, because they admire the traits and activities of these others. Because they are so enamored, it is fairly easy for them, once their sex urges start to mount (especially soon after puberty) for them to confuse sex and love and to become sexually as well as amatively attached to those on whom they have their adolescent crushes. This may especially be true if the person on whom they have the crush happens to be homosexual himself and encourages them to have sex relations with him.

Factors related to secondary gains. Although it is by no means universally true that an individual who is seduced into having a few homosexual affairs early in his life will become a confirmed homosexual, it is also untrue that he will *ever* become one unless he was clearly being predisposed to being one from the start. Many human beings who are practically forced into an occupation, which they at first may hate or be indifferent to, later find that it has great secondary gains for them; and even though it may also have distinct disadvantages, they may stay in this occupation for the rest of their lives. Similarly, many individuals who for one reason or another give homosexuality a try, and who really are at first not at all predisposed to become confirmed homosexuals, later find that the rewards they gain from it are difficult to forego, and therefore never strongly try to give up homosexuality and to make a good heterosexual adjustment. The secondary gains of homosexual behavior may be unusually seductive and habit-forming in several ways:

1. The young boy who is induced to try homosexuality by an older male or by one of his peers may at first go along for the ride, even though his main sex goal is clearly that of sleeping with girls. But as he allows the homosexual "escapades" to go on for a while, he may find it an exceptionally easy, unrisky form of gratification; and when he starts to compare it to the time and trouble he must usually take to derive an equal amount of sex satisfaction with girls, he may come to think the game of hetero-sexuality is hardly worth the candle, and may become "addicted" to homophilism.

2. The individual who first engages in homosexuality on a prostitutional basis, only because he or she wants to earn money thereby, may eventually find that he gains sufficient secondary gains from the homosexuality itself to make it attractive on a non-prostitutional scale. As the saying in the homosexual world goes, "Today's trade is tomorrow's competition."

3. Individuals who first engage in homosexuality out of fear or ingratiation rather than out of desire, sometimes later acquire the taste for it and become fixed homosexuals. A weakling in prison who has homosexual relations with other prisoners mainly to pacify them and to stop them from persecuting him may sub-sequently learn to enjoy these relations in their own right and may continue to engage in them, mainly or exclusively, when he is no longer in prison.

Factors related to antisexuality and puritanism. A great many individuals in our society who resort to confirmed homosexuality are originally led to homoerotic activity mainly because they have been raised to be exceptionally guilty about heterosexuality, and therefore feel compelled to withdraw from this field of endeavor. Many orthodox religionists, for example, are told that it is very wicked for them to lust after members of the other sex and to engage in any form of premarital sex relations. But they are not equally warned against homosexuality, since *that* kind of behavior is considered to be so abominable by their parents and teachers that it is never even mentioned. In consequence, they fear heterosexuality enormously, are less fearful of homosexuality, and find themselves intensely lusting after members of their own sex, and eventually giving in to this lust. Some aspects of puritanism leading to homosexuality are these:

1. Heterosexual incest taboos are strongly emphasized in our culture, while homosexual incest taboos are practically never even hinted at. Consequently, when an Oedipus complex does exist, and a boy is afraid to have intercourse with girls because he strongly lusts after his mother and is thoroughly ashamed of his lust for her, our puritanical ideas about incest are the motivating ideologies behind his complex.

2. Puritanical teachings strongly state or imply that some actual physical injury will come to an individual if he or she engages in heterosexual coitus: he will, for example, acquire a venereal disease, or she will suffer sex injuries during intercourse or be the victim of a criminal abortionist. Such fears, which are by no means equally strong about homosexual acts, encourage homophilism.

3. Because of strongly instilled antisexual prejudices, males and females in our society are often exceptionally inhibited when they do have heterosexual relations, and consequently they do not thoroughly enjoy these affairs. At the same time, they may

somehow discover that they are less inhibited about homosexual acts, and may therefore come to enjoy these more completely and to become addicted to them.

4. Some individuals in our society actually hate themselves for having heterosexual desires or engaging in normal coitus. They therefore may actually try to degrade and punish themselves by engaging in homosexual activities, and they may ultimately only engage in these kinds of behavior.

5. The main act, of course, which is ranted and raved against in our antisexual society is penile-vaginal copulation. But this is the one act which cannot possibly be performed homosexually. Therefore, some individuals are encouraged to engage in non-coital acts, including homosexual ones, just because they are intensely conditioned against heterosexual coitus.

6. Many females in our society are particularly warned against losing their virginity, and therefore are motivated to stay away from all sex activities with males, since they realize that these activities could easily end up in hymen-breaking intercourse. Some of these girls therefore resort to lesbian activities, which they consider much safer, and to which they may then become obsessively-compulsively attached.

7. In an antisexual culture such as ours, great pains are taken to make the sex organs of one sex appear ugly or revolting to the members of the other sex. Thus, many of our males get the idea that female sex organs, menstrual functions, sex odors, etc. are disgusting; and many of our females are reared with the notion that the male penis is ugly, semen is nauseating, kissing a male member is horrifying, etc. Such anti-heterosexual ideas, naturally, encourage various males and females to become predisposed toward homoeroticism.

8. Judeo-Christian puritanism is especially anti-heteroerotic in many ways. Christians, for example, are prompted to revere the Divine Mother or Virgin Mary (and consequently to think of

copulating with a mother-figure as abhorrent), to go to parochial schools which emphasize sex isolationism, to lead as monastic an existence as possible (generally with members of their own sex), to forego pleasure for its own sake, to be in dire need of succorance from others, to be sexually masochistic, and to emphasize the sacrament and the great responsibilities of marriage and family-rearing rather than the joys of coitus. These kinds of basic anti-sexual attitudes easily induce millions of good Christians to abjure heterosexual participations, and at least indirectly help throw them into the homosexual camp.

Factors related to fixation and fetishism. The human being is born with strong tendencies to become fixated or over-channelized in various ways and obsessively-compulsively to stick to a certain path of behavior, even when it proves to be quite self-defeating. This is not an entirely unhealthy tendency on his part, since his devotion to a girlfriend, a business, or a scientific project may be a fanatic form of constructive fixation, just as his becoming obsessed with stealing or with a very limited form of sexual activity may be a destructive fixation. In any event, he easily can become fixated upon loving and/or having sex relations with members of his own sex; and he frequently does. Thus:

1. Some individuals engage in homosexual activities before they engage in heterosexual acts; and because they first gain sex pleasure homosexually, they may become channelized into these kinds of pathways and may never give heterosexuality a chance.

2. In some instances, the individual engages in both early heterosexual and homosexual relations, but he becomes much more guilty about the latter than about the former. Because of his guilt, he may dwell, in an obsessive-compulsive manner, on homosexual ideas, and may therefore become fixated on homophilic rather than heterosexual participations.

3. Some individuals become fetishistically attached to a particular form of sexual activity, such as oral-genital relations, and

favor this kind of activity over all other forms of sex behavior. If the sex act to which they are fetishistically attracted happens to be obtainable easier in homosexual than in heterosexual affairs —as, for example, is frequently the case in oral-genital relations— they may then become predisposed toward homosexuality.

4. Some young people acquire amative rather than sexual fixations. They unconsciously train themselves so that they are only able to love young boys, or strong-looking older males, or men with grey hair. Although these individuals may not at first become genitally attracted to their love objects, they are favorably disposed to do so later, or may even engage in homosexual acts which are not particularly tasteful to them (just as many heterosexual females engage in sex acts which they do not particularly enjoy) mainly in order to please the partners to whom they are homoerotically attached.

Factors related to inadequacy feelings. The most important causes of most emotional disturbances are the individual's severe feelings of worthlessness and inadequacy—which, in turn, are invariably related to his perfectionistic demands on himself and his grandiose requirements that he be as good as or better than other people in various ways (and sometimes in practically every way imaginable). Once he believes that he *must* perform remarkably well in certain areas or that he *has to* be accepted and approved by others, it is impossible for a human being not to be terribly anxious on many occasions and for him not to have underlying feelings of unworthiness (Ellis, 1962a; Ellis and Harper, 1961a, 1961b).

Although severe feelings of inadequacy do not *directly* or *necessarily* lead to fixed homosexuality in our society, they are usually the main predisposing factor. By no means all people who feel worthless turn in this direction—in fact, the great majority of them remain quite heterosexually oriented all their lives. But almost all individuals in Western civilization who become and who remain fixed homophiles do have an usually low estimation of themselves, and their severe feelings of inferiority are to some degree causally related to their homophilism. For example:

1. Individuals who have a specific sense of sexual inadequacy tend to fear failure in heterosexual relations (which they are raised to believe they *must* succeed at) and therefore to withdraw from this "dangerous" field of endeavor. This includes males who believe that they are ungainly, physically weak, or impotent, and females who believe that they are ugly, inept, or frigid. Such individuals often come to realize, sometimes by accident, that they will be acceptable to members of their own sex when they would not (in reality or merely in their own eyes) be equally acceptable to members of the other sex.

2. Individuals who have a general sense of inadequacy, even though they think they are sexually competent, may be sure that they will fail in heterosexual competition and therefore withdraw to homosexual affairs. Thus, males who have a low economic standing or females who come from a family with no social standing may feel utterly insecure and believe that they cannot succeed in wooing and keeping any heterosexual partner whom they would find desirable.

3. Individuals who feel exceptionally unworthy frequently engage in hero-worship and greatly admire members of their own sex who they feel are much more worthy than they. In their attempts to gain favor with, and sometimes magically to identify with, these admirable members of their own sex, they sometimes become homosexually oriented.

4. Some individuals feel so inept that they believe that they cannot get along in the world without an older or stronger protector, who will take care of them and run their lives for them. Males of this type, in our social system, sometimes find that they can obtain such a protector by themselves adopting a female role

and looking for a more dominant male to live with in a homo-sexual relationship.

5. Feelings of inadequacy are frequently shown in the form of shyness and lack of initiative-taking on the part of the person who feels insecure. If the shy individual happens to be a male, and if he resides in a culture such as our own where males are sup-posed to take the initiative in sex relations, he often finds that his feelings of unworthiness and extreme fear of failure prevent him from making any overtures toward girls. He also often finds, however, that in the homosexual world he may exist without taking any risks of refusal, since many of the bolder homosexuals will first make overtures to him. Consequently, he has a conscious or an unconscious incentive to participate in homosexual rather than heterosexual relations, even if he happens to be strongly sexually attracted to females.

6. People who feel inadequate, and who consequently with-draw from participation in a competitive activity, such as hetero-sexual dating, naturally fail to gain any experience or practice in this area, and they therefore actually *do* become relatively inept. They then falsely use their ineptness as "proof" that they really *are* worthless—when they really mean (if they were accurately perceptive) that *when* they consider themselves inferior, they are almost certain to act in a substandard manner. In any event, many individuals who use this kind of false circular thinking wind up by being heterosexually inept, and turn toward homosexuality— where they have lower standards for themselves and hence feel less inadequate.

7. As noted above, some individuals who feel imperfect and unworthy fear that, because of their failings, they cannot remain undominated by a member of the other sex, cannot accept the responsibilities of love or marriage, cannot be good fathers, etc. Consequently, they withdraw from heterosexual fields and stick

exclusively to homosexuality, where they feel that the demands on them are less onerous.

Factors related to hostility and rebelliousness. Severe psychological disturbance is usually compounded of two main elements: feelings of worthlessness, guilt, anxiety, and hurt (which we have just been discussing in the previous section of this chapter), and feelings of hostility to others and over-rebelliousness against social and other restrictions. These latter feelings often lead to homosexualism in the following ways:

1. Some individuals are so hostile to others that they find it very difficult to get along satisfactorily in the highly competitive kind of heterosexual relations that usually exist in our society. Their hostility, even when it is not directly aimed at their heterosexual partners, is soon discovered by these partners, who then tend to withdraw from these hostile individuals. Such continually angry persons often find it much easier to enter into homosexual than heterosexual relations, since many homosexuals are so emotionally disturbed themselves that they will make allowances for hostility in other homosexuals. In some instances, because homosexuals are frequently masochistic, they will even welcome hostile partners, and enter into prolonged relations with them.

2. Hostile individuals generally have low frustration tolerance, and will not accept imperfections in others. Consequently, they have a difficult time adjusting to prolonged, domestic-sharing relations, such as heterosexual marriage. They are, however, able to maintain sporadic, short-term relations, and therefore are more suited to the kind of homosexual life which exists in most of the large cities of Western nations.

3. Some people over-rebelliously refuse to conform to the restrictions of their culture, even when it would pay them, in terms of satisfaction gained, at least outwardly to do so. These people find the restrictions of heterosexuality in our society so intolerable

that they sometimes rebelliously give up heterosexual activities and confine themselves to homoeroticism. Frequently, such individuals cut off their nose to spite their face by adopting homosexualism; but it is the nature of their over-rebelliousness to do just that.

4. Hostile individuals usually love to put others down, so that they themselves can temporarily feel superior and can win the game of one-upmanship. Since the denizens of the homosexual world are usually terribly disturbed and easily upset, such angry persons find it more convenient for them to retreat to this homosexual world, where they can find victims more easily.

Factors related to severe emotional difficulties. As we have been consistently showing throughout this chapter, fixed homosexuality is largely the result of serious emotional disturbance. The confirmed homophile allows himself to be conditioned monosexually, even though he has it in his powers to fight this kind of conditioning and (especially when he is older) to vigorously counterattack it and *re*condition himself. He becomes thoroughly embroiled, in many instances, in negativistic, disorganized family relationships, and lets himself be unduly influenced by parental attitudes. He gives up on the difficult task of becoming a fullfledged member of his own sex, and often retreats into sex-role inversion. He runs away from meeting the real difficulties and dangers of heterosexuality and takes the deceptively easy pathway of refusing to work them through. He gives in to his dire needs to be loved, instead of fully recognizing them and concertedly fighting them, until he gains a good measure of true independence. He gets trapped by the secondary gains of homosexualism and thereby foregoes the much greater primary gains that he would normally obtain if he retained a heterosexual position in life. He kowtows to the puritanical sex attitudes and behavior patterns of his social culture, instead of reevaluating them and rejecting many of them as being obviously antihuman.

He gives in to his tendencies to become fixated or fetishistic, instead of working them through and attaining a more flexible, unfixated outlook and practice. He learns to live with his deepseated feelings of personal inadequacy and worthlessness, instead of concertedly challenging these and getting over them. He maintains his childish grandiosity, rebelliousness, and hostility, and makes little attempt to surrender them for more grownup, less hostile views of the world and others.

In numerous ways, then, the fixed homosexual is a goofer, a short-range hedonist, a self-hater, and a child who refuses to grow up and accept adult responsibilities and rewards. Once he becomes severely disturbed and makes little real effort to overcome his disturbances, he is propelled or compelled to become a confirmed homophile in several important ways:

1. As a neurotic or a psychotic, he becomes a less desirable sex-love partner than he would otherwise be, and frequently gets rejected by members of the other sex who simply find him too anxious or angry to tolerate for long periods of time. Consequently, he is sometimes practically driven to associate with those who *will* tolerate his disturbances—and to find these people in the gay world.

2. As a disturbed person, he will usually continue to live with some kind of serious symptoms which may well foster sex deviation. Thus, the phobiac who is afraid of social dancing in a public hall will tend to withdraw from heterosexual relations; and the obsessive-compulsive individual who is constantly ruminating about sex acts will find himself unsuitable for female companionship and may well be driven toward homosexuality.

3. Seriously disturbed individuals, especially psychotics and borderline psychotics, are frequently afraid of *becoming* homosexual, because they think that this is a particularly reprehensible form of behavior and that they would be utterly worthless if they *were* homophiles. Ironically enough, these sick people some-

times become so obsessed with fear of becoming overly-attached to members of their own sex that they finally drive themselves to do what they most fear and become homosexuals. Just as a seriously disturbed individual who terribly fears getting into an automobile accident will, likely as not, drive himself into exactly the kind of accident he fears, so do many irrational persons who desperately fear becoming homosexual actually drive themselves into fixed homophilism.

4. Psychotics are often so disorganized and disoriented that they have difficulty in adopting and maintaining *any* integrated pattern of behavior. Consequently, they try a wide variety of activities, some of which are appropriate and some of which are entirely inappropriate in their community. In this way, they may adopt a disordered sexuality which leads to all kinds of indiscriminate participations, including homosexuality; and they may in the process become addicted to homosexualism or may find that it is a form of sex play that they, in their disorganized way, can successfully follow in the equally chaotic gay world.

5. Many sick, and usually basically psychotic, individuals become what we generally label "psychopaths" or persons afflicted with a pervasive character disorder. These individuals tend not to have the usual responsible and self-corrective attitudes toward themselves that less disturbed people have, and consequently they engage in a variety of antisocial acts, including stealing, physical assault, and even murder. Moreover, they usually have long histories of careless or criminal activities and do not seem to learn by jail sentences or other forms of deterrence. Such individuals, frequently on a prostitutional basis or because they find that homosexuality is more easily available than heterosexuality in our repressive society, become homosexuals and remain fixed deviants as long as they remain generally psychopathic.

6. Alcoholism, drug addiction, and similar kinds of extremely sick behavior are occasionally etiological factors in homosexuality.

Alcoholics and drug addicts sometimes act quite uninhibitedly while they are intoxicated or under the influence of narcotics, and they may at these times experimentally engage in homosexual behavior which later becomes habitual. They also tend to become sexually inadequate, and sometimes completely impotent, as a result of their drinking or drug-taking; and they may turn to homosexualism because of their inability to carry on successful heterosexual relations.

7. Individuals with organic psychosis sometimes resort to aberrant forms of sexuality. Thus, men afflicted with arteriosclerosis of the brain may, after leading a normal pattern of sexual behavior for many years, suddenly take to having sex relations with either small boys or small girls, and may turn into confirmed sex offenders (Ellis and Brancale, 1956). Such individuals are generally (rather than just sexually) disorganized; and their sexual aberrations are a function of their severe psychotic states.

chapter 3

Are Homosexuals Necessarily Neurotic or Psychotic?

~~~~~~~~~~~~~~~~~~~~~~~~~~~~~~~~~~~~

It will be my contention in this chapter that a fixed or exclusive homosexual in our contemporary society is wrong—meaning inefficient, self-defeating, and emotionally disturbed—but that he has an inalienable right, as a human being, to be wrong and should never be persecuted or punished for his errors. Before, however, I establish the right of the homosexual to be wrong, it will be necessary for me to demonstrate, with data stronger than mere opinion, that fixed deviants are mistaken and self-sabotaging in their behavior.

For there also is some evidence that would at least partially indicate that the homosexuals are not necessarily neurotic or psychotic. Thus, several civilized and savage peoples of the world, especially the ancient Greeks, fully accepted overt homosexuality; and some of these peoples even seemed to believe that a man who did *not* engage in sex activity with other males was something of an anomaly. Moreover, as I and other writers have noted (Ellis, 1960, 1962e), there is nothing intrinsically immoral or wicked about homosexuality: because, instead of being innately born either a heterosexual or a homosexual animal, man is essentially a plurisexual creature, who easily can be conditioned to copulate with males, females, lower animals, and even inanimate objects. If anything, as many sex authorities have indicated (H. Ellis, 1936; Freud, 1938; Stekel, 1922), man is biologically inclined to be bisexual rather than monosexual; so that, theoretically, anyone who is fixated exclusively on heterosexual *or* homosexual relations is fetishistically deviated.

Why, then, do I and practically all other psychotherapists keep insisting that males and females who desire *only* members of their own sex as sexual partners are wrong or emotionally disturbed? For several reasons:

1. Whether we like it or not, we live in contemporary Western civilization, and not in ancient Greece nor in any other culture where homosexuality is fully accepted. However foolish it may be for our society to ban homosexual relations between consenting adults, the fact remains that it presently *does* punish homoeroticism. Consequently, homophiles are unfairly jailed, fined, fired from jobs, and otherwise ostracized for engaging in sex acts with members of their own sex.

In these circumstances, anyone who insists on practicing homo-sexuality, especially on a promiscuous, lavatory-haunting basis, is childishly and stubbornly defeating his own ends; and he is consequently seriously aberrated. Although many heterosexuals would love having intercourse with teenage girls, they sanely accept the fact that their benighted society will incarcerate them for statutory rape if they seek out such young partners; so they keep their hands to themselves when they are in the presence of "jail bait," and they thereby keep out of trouble. Homosexuals in our antisexual culture fail to calmly accept in practice, while vigorously fighting in theory, the restrictions of this culture; and they thereby almost always get themselves into various legal, social, and vocational difficulties.

2. Even if homophilism were not banned in our society, it would only be normal for an individual to be a fixed or exclusive homosexual if he had first open-mindedly tried a good deal of heterosexual activity, and then unprejudicedly concluded that he *preferred* relations with members of his own sex. This I have never actually heard of a fixed homosexual doing. I have seen

many of them (both as friends and as patients) who have had some heterosexual activity, and have even married a girl and had intercourse with her for years, but who still remain basically homophilic. All these homosexuals either never gave heterosexuality a full chance (never, for example, tried sex with more than a few girls); or else they did give it a chance and found that *sexually* it was as good as or better than homoerotic relations, but that the latter were more easily available or were more attractive for various *non*sexual reasons. The vast majority of fixed homosexuals, moreover, have had little or no heterosexual experience, and they *still* vigorously contend that they could not possibly enjoy such experience and must remain one hundred per cent homosexual. This kind of arrant prejudice and bigotry on their part is equivalent to antisemitism, anti-integrationism, and other kinds of racial and religious prejudice, and is distinctly a function of severe fetishism or anti-fetishism, and consequently of emotional disturbance.

3. Although it is theoretically possible for homosexuals to be accidentally conditioned to a strong attraction to members of their own sex and then merely to maintain this kind of conditioning, while leading undisturbed lives in all other respects, I have never actually found such an individual among the scores of fixed deviates I have seen for psychotherapy or among the many homophilic non-patients with whom I have been acquainted. In every case I have seen, irrational fear played the leading role either in inducing the individual to become homosexual in the first place or inducing him to maintain his early-acquired homophilic conditioning in the second place. The main fears homosexuals have include fear of rejection by members of the other sex, fear of heterosexual impotence, fear of intense emotional involvement, fear of marital responsibilities, fear of competition, among others. Basically, they are terribly afraid of failure and of what other people will think of them if they do fail in any way; and they consequently withdraw from hetero-

sexual relations which (peculiarly enough!) are relatively difficult to initiate and maintain in our society, into the "gay life,"
where sexual conquest, at least, is much surer and safer.

4. In addition to being exceptionally anxious, almost all fixed
homosexuals are short-range hedonists or "goofers"; and the
majority of them are not only doing things the seemingly easy
way in the sexual area, but are also avoiding responsibility, hard
work, and long-range planning in other important aspects of
their lives. That this should be so can be seen on theoretical
grounds: since even if an individual is accidentally conditioned,
virtually against his will, to become homosexually arousable during his early life, if he is not an avoider or a shirker, he will
grow up, perceive that homosexuality is exceptionally disadvantageous in this society, stop constructing rationalizations about
his being born a homophile and his having no ability to cure
himself, and work very hard, either with a psychotherapist or
by himself, to recondition himself to heterosexual enjoyment. I
am convinced, in fact, that literally thousands of homosexuals
do this each year, most of them without benefit of psychotherapy.
These individuals do decondition and recondition themselves,
largely by forcing themselves into having heterosexual affairs,
and ultimately make good heterosexual adjustments and completely leave the homosexual world in which they previously
were immersed. But short-range hedonists, of course, will do
nothing of this sort: since they shirk on their self-treatment or
their working in a psychotherapeutic relationship, just as they
do in most other aspects of their lives. Consequently, almost all
the fixed deviates who remain homosexual are short-range hedonists, or persons with low frustration tolerance, who are by that
very fact emotionally ill.

5. Although I once believed that exclusive homosexuals are
seriously neurotic, considerable experience with treating many
of them (and in being friendly with a number whom I have not
seen for psychotherapy) has convinced me that I was wrong:

most fixed homosexuals, I now am convinced, are borderline psychotic or outrightly psychotic. Freud (1924-1950) held that an individual's homosexuality or his defenses against his fears of being homosexual lead to paranoid schizophrenia, but I am inclined to hold the reverse: namely, that schizophrenics and borderline schizophrenics are not able to cope with the world successfully, and are particularly unable to achieve good heterosexual relations in our society; and therefore they frequently, though of course not always, turn to homosexuality. As I point out in Chapter I of this book, there is no scientific evidence that homosexuality is directly caused by constitutional or inherited factors. Nevertheless, there is an increasing body of data that suggests that serious mental illness *is* partly caused by physiological influences (Ellis, 1962b), and that this kind of illness, in turn, predisposes individuals to become fixed deviants in many instances.

Although I believe that most fixed homosexuals are basically psychotic, I certainly do not mean that *all* of them are. A sizable minority of exclusive homophiles (including many members of organized groups, such as the Mattachine Society and the Daughters of Bilitis) are reasonably integrated individuals whom I would classify among the normal neurotics of our society. They are somewhat but not too seriously self-defeating in their behavior; and there is little likelihood that they will eventually wind up in a mental hospital. Even borderline psychotics, for that matter, often are never hospitalized; so I am hardly contending that most fixed homosexuals, who I think are pseudoneurotic (Hoch and Cattell, 1959), are candidates for institutionalization. Most of them aren't; but they are still clearly in need of psychological treatment (C. Thompson, 1947).

What, precisely, is a borderline psychotic or pseudoneurotic? This diagnostic category, like any state of emotional disturbance, is difficult to define exactly, but let me list some of the main characteristics of the borderline individual. He tends to think loosely or slippery, or to have what Meehl (1962) calls cognitive slippage, and consequently to have great difficulty in making some of the finer discriminations that are necessary if one is to have adequate social relations. He has an exceptionally low opinion of himself, thinks negatively a good deal of the time, and constantly blames himself and/or others. He tends either to be consciously depressed and to feel himself on the verge of a breakdown; or else he may be exceptionally defensive, and have no idea that he is disturbed, even though most of his close associates realize that he is. He frequently has low energies, finds it hard to get through each day, is inefficient and disorganized in his activities, and tends to have a poor vocational history. He is frequently unspontaneous and anhedonic, and has little fun in life except when he is under the influence of alcohol, drugs, or some other stimulant. He is woefully dependent upon others, feels horribly depressed when he is rejected or ignored, and is often lonely even when he is with others. He is constantly upset over little things, often feels that the world is treating him unfairly, and creates one life crisis after another for himself. This, then, is the borderline psychotic; and this, if one honestly examines the fixed deviants one knows well, one will almost certainly see is the average homosexual.

6. Some authorities, such as Hooker (1957) and Westwood (1960), have presented evidence which purports to show that at least a few fixed homosexuals are just as well adjusted as are most heterosexuals in our society. This evidence is unconvincing, since it has largely been gathered through the use of projective techniques of personality assessment, which have no proven validity; or through naive questioning of homosexual subjects who had every incentive to say they were well adjusted. Let it be remembered, in this connection, that practically all studies of heterosexual marriage indicate that about ninety per cent of the subjects of these studies report that they are happily married; while even the most cursory examination of married couples by

objective observers shows that this is a terribly over-inflated self-estimate of marital happiness. What the studies of homosexual adjustment seem to show, at best, is that a highly selected group consisting of *a very few* fixed deviants may be as well adjusted as a randomly selected group of heterosexuals. Moreover, the so-called well adjusted deviants would appear to be adjusted *to their disturbance,* in that they are not guilty or upset about being homosexual. There is no evidence that they are truly non-anxious and non-hostile human beings. When I have had the opportunity to personally interview a few of the homophiles who have been found to be "non-disturbed" in some of the above-mentioned studies, I have found that, once their surface adjustment is scratched, a distinctly frightened or hostile individual, and particularly a sex-scared person, is revealed.

7. Clinical examination of exclusive homosexuals shows that the great majority, along with their being sexually and generally anxious or shirking, have various other symptoms of emotional illness. Thus, they obsessively-compulsively engage in cruising or other dangerous activities; or they become fixated on certain types of erotic objects, such as on young boys or on butch-type older males; or they superromantically idealize their emotional relationships, and perfectionistically demand the kinds of affairs that they never can possibly attain in the "gay" world; or they engage in a variety of highly sadistic-masochistic sex acts; or they become obsessed with the most superficial kinds of sex-love values, particularly those involved with physical beauty; or they surrender their entire roles as males and become "fairies" or "pansies," who try to ape females in the most outlandish ways; or they engage in a disorganized fashion in a variety of deviated sex acts, of which homosexuality is only one; or they participate in their homosexual relationships in such a bizarre, exhibitionistic, and disordered manner that they sooner or later get into some actual difficulty, such as loss of a job, blackmail, or arrest as a sex offender (Cory, 1963; Ellis, 1963a, 1963b).

So much for some of the main reasons why I feel that fixed homosexuals are almost invariably wrong or self-defeating. In fact, among the many kinds of disturbed people I have had close contact with for the last twenty years, they are among the most self-punishing and tragic. Only the severely depressed and suicidal patients whom I have seen have been sicker and more miserable.

If, then, homosexuals are, as I believe they are, weak and self-sabotaging, and if most of them refuse to do anything to help themselves even though it is well within their power to overcome their exclusive homophilism and to enjoy heterosexuality, should they not be forced to change themselves and be severely condemned and punished if they don't? No, I contend: no human being, the fixed homosexual included, should ever be blamed or punished for anything he does. For every man has the inalienable right to be wrong; and all sane humans should keep fighting vigorously to help him maintain this right.

Why has every human the right to be wrong? Because unless we unequivocally accord him this right, we will never help him to correct his mistakes or wrongdoings, and will in fact encourage him to be compulsively mistaken, immoral, or emotionally ill forever. I explain this seeming paradox in detail in my book, *Reason and Emotion in Psychotherapy* (Ellis, 1962a), which expounds a new system of therapy in which all the patient's sins are completely forgiven, and in which he is specifically taught that no one is ever to blame for anything, however wrong his behavior may be. Let me briefly restate some of my main theses here.

All human beings are fallible; in fact, fallibility or mistake-making or wrongdoing is synonymous with humanness. No man, therefore, can be *perfectly* moral or *absolutely* rational and sane, since to be so would require his being angelic; and no man, obviously, is an angel. If a man would be reasonably moral and emotionally stable, he should thoroughly accept himself (and others) as fallible; and whenever he tends to make a mistake, should tell himself: (*a*) "This deed that I may do (or have done) is wrong, erroneous, mistaken." Then he should ask himself: (*b*) "Now, how do I avoid doing it (or doing it again)?" A just and sane man, in other words, objectively and nonblamefully *accepts* his wrongdoings, and then calmly goes about trying to reduce or minimize them in the future.

A disturbed human being, on the other hand, notes his mistaken performances and then tells himself: (*a*) "This deed is wrong," and (*b*) "*I* am a sinner, a knave for committing it." By blaming himself in this manner, and translating his objective wrongdoing into a bigotedly evaluated sin, the disturbed person immediately brings about one or more of several most undesirable consequences:

1. He devaluates himself as a human being, identifies himself as a worthless individual, and thereby feels depressed.

2. He spends so much time and energy blaming himself for doing a wrong deed (or what he self-depreciatingly calls a sin) that he has little ability to focus on how to avoid doing a similar deed *next time*.

3. He keeps repeating to himself so often, "Oh, look what I have done! What a blackguard I am for doing this horrible thing!" that he frequently becomes obsessed with his doing this "horrible" act again; and he consequently becomes a compulsive wrongdoer, who actually keeps doing what he is most afraid of doing.

4. He convinces himself that because he has committed this awful crime, he is a *hopeless* sinner, who has no possibility of regenerating himself and *stopping* future wrongdoing.

5. He believes that he deserves to be severely punished for his so-called sinning, and he sometimes compulsively commits more misdeeds in order, sooner or later, to bring down upon his own head the punishment he is sure he merits.

6. He is so appalled at his sinfulness *in case* he should commit

a certain wrong act, that he frequently refuses to admit that he actually has committed it, even when he has palpably done so. Or he sometimes admits his act, but refuses to admit that it is wrong, even when it clearly is.

An individual, then, who blames himself for his wrongdoings, and thinks he should be punished for being a sinner, almost always winds up by becoming depressed and by compulsively doing even more misdeeds. Or else he finally stops his errors by going to the other extreme and adopting such an inhibited, life-constricting philosophy that he does the "correct" thing but leads a joyless existence. Similarly, when he blames others, he rarely helps them to correct their mistakes, but most frequently helps them to be depressed, constricted, and often more mistake-making.

This is what happens in regard to blaming homosexuals for their self-defeating, disturbed behavior. When they excoriate themselves and become guilty about their homosexuality, they rarely spend their time practicing heterosexual pursuits and thereby helping themselves to overcome their deviation. Instead, they usually become depressed; find that they then are even *less* able to make out well in the difficult, competitive heterosexual world; become even less able to get along in their homosexual relationships; then blame themselves more and become still more depressed; and then, as the vicious circle becomes larger, come to be *less* capable of good heterosexual or homosexual adjustment. When, on the other hand, homosexuals unblamefully *accept* the fact of their homophilic behavior, calmly *admit* that it is self-defeating, and firmly *refuse to punish themselves* for engaging in it, they have a much better chance of working at conditioning themselves to engage in heterosexual contacts and involvements.

By the same token, society does no good, as far as the prevention and treatment of homosexuality is concerned, by blaming and punishing deviants. For even if homophilism were intrinsically immoral, and should therefore be prevented, there is no evidence that excoriating and penalizing homosexuals for their so-called immorality actually helps them stop engaging in it. On the contrary, to the degree that they are made outcasts, they almost always become more emotionally disturbed—and hence more neurotic or psychotic.

Moreover, there is no reason to believe that, in itself, homosexuality is immoral or antisocial. The adult homophile who confines his sex activity to relations with other adults may well (as noted above) be harming himself and defeating his own best ends, but he is not needlessly and deliberately harming or taking unfair advantage of another human being. At worst, his behavior is a vice rather than a crime; and as Harry Benjamin and I pointed out several years ago (Benjamin and Ellis, 1954), any citizenry which socially or legally forces its members to surrender their vices is, by this kind of freedom-destroying suppression, doing much more harm than good. Certainly, cigarette smoking is a much more widespread and deadly vice today than is fixed homosexuality; but none of us, I hope, advocates that the government should therefore fine, jail, or otherwise persecute all smokers.

Homosexuality, again, is a vice that is partly created by our own social proscriptions against it, since it seems to have led to less self-defeatism and disturbance in ancient Greece, where it was not banned, than it leads to in the United States, where it is largely prohibited. It would seem to be, therefore, utterly unjust for a society such as our own to ban homosexuality, thereby to augment its emotional hazards, and then to condemn and punish those who are weak and undisciplined enough to practice it in spite of this ban. The persecution of homosexuals results in the same kind of social injustice that we perpetrate on millions of non-homosexuals by demanding that they perform outstandingly in life, by helping them become disturbed by inducing them to blame themselves when they are not remarkably achieving, and by then reproaching and penalizing them when they turn out to be neurotic or psychotic as a result of their self-castigation. It would make for far more sanity and justice if supposedly civilized communities established more reasonable standards of behavior and forgave their emotionally weak members who experienced difficulty in following even these moderate norms of conduct.

On many counts, then, I contend that every human has an inalienable right to be wrong; and that it is folly and cruelty to deny him this right. It would be lovely, perhaps, if we were all perfect, infallible creatures—though I, for one, would wonder about the advisability of living in such a boring kind of heaven on earth. Anyway, no fear: we are not, as long as we remain human, going to be ineffably faultless. All of us, heterosexual and homosexual alike, are going to continue to be weak, more or less undisciplined, irrational, and disturbed. And not merely during our early childhood, or for a few decades thereafter, but for all the long years of our lives.

The aim of corrective experiencing, then, as of that particular kind of reeducation which we call psychotherapy, is not to turn out an infallible, non-mistake-making person who will never have any sexual or general problems, but of helping the human individual *minimize,* without requiring that he ever *eliminate,* his overweening anxiety and his destructive hostility. To this end, we must continually, with objectivity and with firm kindness, point out the erring individual's errors, and show him how it is possible for him, with insight and much work and practice, to reduce these errors. But we must never, under any circumstances, blame him—that is, denigrate his intrinsic value as a human being —for being what he now is.

No one, I repeat, *is ever to blame for anything.* All of us are often *responsible* for our wrongdoings; but we are not lice, villains or subhumans for *being* responsible. *Everyone has an absolute right to be wrong*—even though, on occasion, he may have to be placed in protective custody, if his wrongdoing involves needlessly and definitely harming others, until he desists from palpably antisocial behavior. When humanity finally gives up the barbaric notion of an eye for an eye, a tooth for a tooth, and truly accepts the right of each of its adult members, however sick or vice-ridden he may be, to be forgiven for his wrongdoings, then and then only can serious emotional disturbance, including the symptom of fixed homosexuality, be minimized.

Homosexuals, then, are more sinned against than sinning. Contemporary American society most unfairly and uncivilizedly blames them, discriminates against them economically, jails them, and in numerous other ways punishes them. They are not understood and helped, as are many other emotionally disturbed persons. They are not looked upon merely with humorous tolerance, as are several idiosyncratic groups, such as the beatniks. Their beliefs are not respected and legally protected, as are the rigid, dogmatic, and often highly bizarre beliefs of many orthodox religionists. They are not even treated as well as are certain palpably antisocial groups, such as juvenile delinquents and hardened criminals, on whose behalf society frequently makes strong rehabilitative attempts. Our churches, settlement houses, charitable foundations, and other social institutions, which often come to the aid of downtrodden individuals, until recently have rarely had a kind word or deed for the homosexual.

This is most deplorable. Homosexuals, to be sure, often defensively claim that they are perfectly content to be the way they are, and that they don't need any help from anyone. But when they do, much more sanely and less defensively, ask for help in changing anti-homophilic laws or minimizing other forms of persecution (as organizations such as the Mattachine Society and the Daughters of Bilitis do), they still receive little support from heterosexuals. Indeed, it is precisely those heterosexuals who most vigorously contend that homosexuals are wrong and sinful who keep persecuting them most—and thereby, only help perpetuate and exacerbate the so-called sins.

If, therefore, this chapter would seem at first blush to be an indictment of fixed homosexuals, it is really a charge against heterosexuals who will not let the homophile be the way he is. If he is sick, as I strongly feel that he is, then he has the human right to be sick; and if he is not emotionally disturbed, as most homosexuals themselves feel he is not, then he of course has the right to be the way he is. Sick or well, right or wrong, he should be left to be himself, and only restrained from being so when it can be incontrovertibly proved that he needlessly is harming others than himself, or is unfairly taking advantage of a minor or other social incompetent. Even if the fixed homosexual is as wrongheaded and self-defeating as he possibly can be, the heterosexual who in any way denies him his right to be wrong is much, much wronger.

chapter 4

The Possibility of
Treating Fixed Homosexuals

~~~~~~~~~~~~~~~~~~~~~~~~~~~~~~~~~~~~~~~

It is generally agreed that the psychological treatment of sex deviates is a most difficult task—as, among others, Buckle (1949), de River (1949), Ellis (1960, 1961a, 1961b), Foster (1947), Gurvitz (1957), Rickles (1950), and the writers of the Wolfenden Report (1957) have pointed out. There are several reasons for this difficulty.

In the first place, many homosexuals and other deviates, in spite of their repeatedly being caught and convicted, are extremely loath to admit that they are psychologically disturbed. Either they feel that they are perfectly normal—and that society is at fault for not letting them behave in the manner they wish; or else they admit that they are abnormal, but prefer to believe that there are specific glandular or other physiological reasons for their abnormalities. Not a few of them, when apprehended, ask to be castrated, since they feel that some powerful hormonal factor drives them to their offenses. And other deviates are all too willing to undergo treatment with desexing hormone shots, tranquilizing pills, shock treatments, and even lobotomies.

Some of this willingness to undertake physical treatment results from severe guilt and concomitant self-punishing tendencies on the part of a good many of the offenders. But much of it also stems from the sincere conviction of many sexually troubled individuals—particularly, of course, the homosexuals—that they were born with a peculiar physical makeup, and that their constitution will somehow have to be altered before they can be cured.

Secondly, a large number of confirmed homosexuals receive so many "neurotic gains" or direct satisfaction from their aberrations that they have little or no incentive to work for basic changes. Whereas the average disturbed individual who is afflicted with phobias, anxiety attacks, or psychosomatic symptoms derives so much pain from his affliction that he is often only too willing to work to eradicate it, the average deviate *enjoys* his sex-love activity, and frequently fails to enjoy other, socially non-interdicted sex acts. Consequently, he has no great incentive to work at giving up his fetish or deviation.

Third, fixed homophiles are so seriously disturbed that it is doubtful whether they usually fall in the neurotic range. The majority—though by no means *all*—of them are borderline psychotics. They wear the "mask of sanity" that Cleckley (1950) rightly, in my estimation, attributes to nonsexual psychopaths; and they are consequently among the most difficult patients to treat. There is a good possibility, as I indicate in *Reason and Emotion in Psychotherapy* (Ellis 1962a), that borderline and psychotic patients are not merely raised to be sick (as the Freudians and many other psychologists and psychiatrists believe today), but that they are born with a clearcut predisposition to be adversely affected by poor environmental circumstances. Whether or not this is so, it seems well established today that individuals who are basically psychotic are much more difficult to treat with psychotherapy than are neurotics; and I think that there is little doubt that a high proportion of exclusive homosexuals fall in the psychotic range.

Fourth, many homosexuals are treated in a correctional or penal institution—which is hardly the best milieu for psychotherapy—and are reluctant to come for private treatment except when they are forced to do so by some court agency. In both institutional and private settings they frequently are not the most cooperative patients; and their progress is only partially that which they are theoretically able to make if they were more eager for and hard-working at treatment.

In spite of these almost insuperable difficulties in treating fixed homosexuals with psychological methods, the taking of a defeatist attitude toward their treatment is not scientifically warranted. The successful handling of homophiles and other sex deviants has been reported by a number of clinicians using a variety of psychotherapeutic techniques. Thus, successful psychoanalytic approaches to treatment have been reported by such therapists as Allen (1949), Bieber *et al.* (1962), Fink (1954), A. Freud (1951), Gurvitz (1957), Hadfield (1958), Karpman (1954), Lewinsky (1952), London and Caprio (1950), Poe (1952), Robertiello (1959), Rubenstein (1958), and Shentoub (1959).

Adlerian, Stekelian, deconditioning, and other non-Freudian approaches to psychotherapy have also been used with sex deviates; and distinct successes in this connection have also been reported by many clinicians, such as Buckle (1949), Creadick (1953), Deutsch (1954), Foster (1947), Nedoma (1951),Srnec and Freund (1953), and Stekel (1930). In view of the increasing number of reports of this kind which keep appearing in the professional literature, it should be clear that while the treatment of homosexuals is still difficult, it is by no means doomed to failure.

My own experience with the treatment of deviates started more than a decade ago, when I was Chief Psychologist of the New Jersey State Diagnostic Center, where all offenders in the state were mandatorily seen for diagnosis and some occasional psychotherapy. I was in training as a psychoanalyst at that time, and consequently used psychoanalytic free association and abreactive methods with some of the offenders I saw. I discovered that these techniques were of some value, but that most of the help derived by the patients was not from the insight they derived into the origin of their sexual aberrations, nor from the abreactivecathartic release they obtained from spilling out their past and present proclivities. I found, rather, that the guilt-attacking and blame-combatting influence of the therapist was the most therapeutic aspect of the contact I had with these patients.

I shall never forget, for example, the 17-year-old boy I saw who had been having sex relations with his 10-year-old sister and with older males. He was exceptionally self-hating—partly because he had been discovered in these relations, and partly because he knew that he had engaged in them because he did not have the nerve to pet with older girls, as many of his school friends had been doing. The more I allowed this boy to ventilate his feelings, the more depressed he seemed to become: since his associations only reminded him that he really *was* a skunk and he actually *had* fouled up in school, in his social affairs, and now finally in the sex area.

Although this boy had a tested I.Q. of 140 and had no difficulty in following psychoanalytic interpretations of his incestuous and homosexual relations, the insight he thereby acquired seemed to be of no help. He was willing to admit that he had always envied his father for being able to deprive him of his mother's caresses, and that he had quite probably become attracted to little girls because he had run away from competing with his father, and with other men or big boys, for the favor of older females. He also admitted that his attraction to older men stemmed from his needs to ingratiate himself with and safely identify with strong masculine figures. But this knowledge helped him not a whit to decrease his self-loathing. On the contrary, it seemed to make him hate himself more precisely *because* he now saw clearly that he was afraid to compete with males his own size. And, instead of becoming less sexually aberrated, he had to admit that he kept thinking sexually of the tougher boys in the Center where he was incarcerated, while he had little or no attraction to some of the comely teenagers who were also there (and who frequently tended to be attracted to him).

The first therapeutic headway I began to make with this patient was when I casually said to him one day: "So you screwed your little sister! My lord, what's so terrible about that? Do you think that there's practically any full-blooded boy of your age who does *not* think, and usually very often, of screwing his kid sister—not to mention his mother, his aunts, and—hell, if she's young enough, his goddam grandmother? What makes you think that *that's* so original?"

"You're only saying that to make me feel good," he said. "You don't mean to say that *you* ever did a thing like that, did you?"

"The devil I didn't!" I quickly replied. "Not that I actually made it with my sister, like you did. I guess I didn't have the guts to actually try. But I damned well thought of it a lot of the time—and about her young friends, too, who were only eleven or twelve when I was about seventeen. And about my mother. And my cousins. And my teachers. And every other damned female, practically, I knew. In fact, come to think of it, I was actually caught red-handed, when I was only six years of age, trying to get into the girl next door, who was then about a half year younger. A lovely blond wench she was! And most cooperative, sexually. Only our parents, when they caught me trying to pour a glass of milk—I think it was milk—into her genitals, didn't exactly wax enthusiastic. And her parents, naturally, raised a hell of a stink. But, after being in the doghouse for a short while, I somehow managed to survive—and to keep on lusting."

"You really did? And you didn't blame yourself for what you were doing?"

"Not a bit, that I can remember. And still don't. For what's *wrong* with good, honest lust? Naturally, when you do what you did, that's taking it a bit too far. There are laws against it—not against lusting, but against actually doing something with a young girl like your sister. And, like it or not, we have to obey such laws, in order to keep out of trouble. But if we make a mistake, as you have done, and not kept to the law, then it's just that—a mistake. But you're not necessarily a bastard for making it—just a wrongdoer who has made a mistake and who'd better see that he doesn't repeat it again. Blaming yourself, however, for making this mistake is not going to help you to stop making similar ones. In fact, if you keep on blaming yourself the way you're doing, and keep thinking that you're the kind of a louse who *must* keep making mistakes, then of course you'll keep on making them—because you *think* you must."

I saw, pretty quickly, that I had hit home with this boy; and the more I showed him, by my words and actions, that I didn't blame him for anything he had done, and that there but for the grace of my own cowardice I might just as well have been in his shoes, the less self-deprecatory he became and the more he began to see that one serious mistake didn't make him an inalterable villain. Within a few weeks from the time I actively started trying to reduce his self-blaming—or reduce the severity of his superego, as the Freudians would say—he began a remarkable comeback, stopped being depressed, became interested in esthetic and intellectual pursuits which he had previously lost interest in, and finally began to become attracted to a girl a little younger than himself. When he left the Center, he kept writing her warm notes; and he later made a normal heterosexual adjustment in his community.

This therapeutic experience caused me to do a good deal of thinking about the efficacy of the usual psychoanalytic methods for sexual and nonsexual offenders. Even though I for some years later continued to use such methods with my regular patients, I somehow modified them with my psychopathic patients and started to talk to them much more directly, to try to teach them a philosophy that, on the one hand, reduced their self-blame but on the other hand tried to get them to see that hostility, or blaming others, was equally wrong, and was in the last analysis self-defeating. In other words, though I was still psychoanalytically-oriented with my non-offender patients, I began to do much more and more character building, along educational or reeducational lines, with the sexual and nonsexual offenders whom I saw for treatment.

As my work in this area brought better and better results, and as I also became sceptical of classical psychoanalytic procedures when used even with run of the mill neurotics, I developed over the years my present system of rational-emotive psychotherapy. I have reported in several articles (Ellis, 1962b, 1962c, 1962d, 1963e, 1963f, 1963g, 1963h, 1964) and books (Ellis, 1957, 1960, 1962a, 1962e, 1963a, 1963b, 1963c, 1963d; Ellis and Harper, 1961a, 1961b; Ellis and Sagarin, 1964) how sexually and nonsexually disturbed individuals are treated with this method.

Let me briefly summarize the principles of rational therapy (called RT for short). It is a therapeutic technique that is based on the hypothesis that most significant human emotions and actions, including emotionally disturbed feelings and behavior, stem from basic assumptions, beliefs, or philosophies which the individual consciously or unconsciously holds. Neurotic and psychotic symptoms are caused and maintained by irrational or illogical ideas and attitudes, and tend to reinforce these irrational beliefs.

To accomplish effective psychotherapy, the basic irrational philosophies or value systems of the disturbed individual not only have to be brought to conscious attention, and their origins interpreted (as is done in analytically-oriented therapies) but, even more importantly, the patient must be shown how he is now, in the present, wittingly or unwittingly *maintaining* his irrational beliefs by continually reindoctrinating himself, through self-verbalization or autosuggestion, with the nonsensical philosophies he originally acquired. He must also be shown, most specifically and concretely, how to depropagandize or deindoctrinate himself from his self-defeating philosophies and how to substitute more rational value judgments in their place.

Depropagandization is taught the patient by the therapist

inducing him (*a*) to assume that all his exaggerated fears, anxieties, hostilities, guilts, and depressions are grounded in illogical beliefs and attitudes; (*b*) to trace these illogical beliefs to their basic underlying assumptions; (*c*) to question and challenge these assumptions; (*d*) to attack them, in action, with behavior that directly contradicts them; and (*e*) to replace them, ultimately, with rational, nondefeating values and beliefs which, when they are fully accepted, will automatically encourage undisturbed behavior.

One of the homosexuals I treated with rational-emotive psychotherapy came to see me several years ago after he had been arrested for having sex relations with another male in a New York City subway system toilet. He had also been previously in trouble for exhibiting himself, both to males and females, in public places. Actually, he had engaged in these homosexual and exhibitionistic acts on several occasions before he was first apprehended at the age of 24; and he had also masturbated in public places many times, but had never been caught doing so (although he had had some very narrow escapes).

I quickly determined, by some very direct questioning, that this boy was a fairly typical homophile and exhibitionist in that— as Ellis and Brancale (1956), Rickles (1950), and others have pointed out in the literature—he was unusually inhibited rather than over-impulsive in his general behavior, and felt inadequate and unconfident in various nonsexual aspects of his life. He was afraid to go to social affairs where he would meet new people; stayed on in an unsatisfactory job because he was fearful of being interviewed by prospective employers and rarely let other people know his true opinions, for fear they would disapprove of him for having them. Yet, he very much wanted to be in the limelight and had often done well in amateur theatricals—where, because he was playing a role, and consequently *not* being himself or risking his own views, he was able to get along nicely.

Heterosexually, this boy was not only a virgin, but had had no real petting experiences, in spite of attraction to some females. He masturbated daily, usually with homosexual images, but sometimes with fantasies of girls admiring his body and sex organs and begging him to have sex relations with them. When he actually dated a girl, however—which was rarely, since he was afraid that he would be rejected and made to feel ashamed for asking for a date—he made no sexual overtures, again out of fear that he would make the wrong move and be scornfully rebuffed.

"How come," I asked this boy during the first session of psychotherapy, "that you are so afraid to make a pass at a girl when you are out on a date, for fear she will reject you; and yet you don't seem to be afraid of having a homosexual affair in public, when there's a good chance that men you approach will reject you? Also, how come that you are not afraid that the females to whom you exhibit yourself at times will not turn you in to the cops? It seems odd that on the one hand you are so fearful and on the other hand supposedly so brave."

"I guess I'm not really that brave," he replied. "As for the males that I have sex with, I invariably wait for them to approach *me,* so that I take no risk there. As for the girls to whom I exhibit myself, I'm somehow convinced that they won't do anything against me. Something about her tells me that she won't. I just pick those kind of girls, I guess—not the type that looks like a lady, but the type that looks like something of a slut—who I am sure would want me to exhibit myself, and who might well invite me to go further."

"Perhaps so. But from what you've already told me, not one, not a single one, of these girls has taken you up and showed that she wanted you to go further. All of them, apparently, have run away. And the last two called the police. That's hardly a high rate of acceptance!"

"I know. I guess it's foolish to think that they accept me that way; and I sort of know they won't. But then, when they don't,

I can always quickly run to the nearest public john and get some man to accept me there."

"So in a way, you've got it made, and can't lose. If the girl somehow does accept you when you're exhibiting yourself to her, then that's great, and you think you're fine for having such good looks and such a large penis. And if she doesn't accept you, you can always have the alibi that you tried in the wrong, socially disapproved way and *that* is why she rejected you. The fact that you're desirable and OK is then bolstered by your quickly finding a man."

"Yes, I guess you're right: I've got it set up so that I simply can't lose."

"Ostensibly. Actually, you've got it set up so that you can't *win.*"

"How's that?"

"Well, from beginning to end you're always protecting your silly little ego, your false pride: by either staying away from making passes at the girls you actually know, for fear they may reject you; or by making impossible overtures to girls you don't know, and thereby giving yourself an advance alibi for rejection. Then, with the men, you stay away from those who might really be attractive to you and only allow yourself to be approached by those you are sure are attracted to you. But by 'protecting' yourself in this manner, you actually keep sustaining the false notion that if you *were* rejected, after a direct sexual overture to either a girl or a male, you *would* be a worthless slob. And as long as you retain that silly philosophy of life—or of *non*participation in life—you can't win and can only sow seeds of self-hatred."

"You don't think, then, that I really feel confident of any success whenever I exhibit myself to girls or even to men?"

"Maybe you do—but not of the kind of success you think you are confident of. You feel confident that you will startle a girl and arouse her acute attention. And you feel confident that you can't lose—because if, by any longshot of a chance, she does encourage you to go further, that's great. And if, as is much more likely to be the case, she runs away, you still haven't lost anything—because, as I said before, you've arranged the situation so that you have a built-in alibi. So, whatever happens, you feel confident that you will get *something* you want with the girl. What you don't feel sure of, however—and, in fact, will *never* feel confident of if you continue this kind of sex activity—is *yourself.*"

"But if I succeed at what I am trying to get—find out that some of the girls I exhibit myself to or men I pick up in johns *do* like me and do invite me home with them—won't I *then* gain confidence? Isn't that the way to get security, by succeeding at getting what you want?"

"No, that is the usual mistake of people, particularly males, in our society. They think that being successful insures ego-bolstering or increased self-esteem. But it doesn't—because, at best, it gives them a temporary boost, which will then subside as soon as they fail the next time. And, since they're not infallible, they've simply *got* to fail at some time in the future."

"How, then, can I get confidence in myself and keep it? If being successful at times won't do it, what will?"

"Only one thing will: and that is to like yourself *whether or not you are successful.* Or, in other words, define yourself as a perfectly valuable human being *even* when you fail. Not that it's good to fail; it generally isn't. Meaning, that it's *unfortunate* or *frustrating.* But no matter how unfortunate or frustrating it is, failure has nothing essentially to do with *you*—with your worth as a human being, as a person. Unless, by definition, you arbitrarily *connect* it with your self-worth."

"And that's what I'm doing, aren't I?—always connecting my opinion of myself with my self-worth, with my estimation of how good I am?"

"Yes, that's exactly what you're always doing, especially sexually. Instead of telling yourself, 'I would like to have girls accept me and to have enjoyable sex relations with me,' which would be a perfectly sane sentence, you're telling yourself the utterly insane sentence, 'I've *got* to have girls accept me and find me sexually attractive, because otherwise I'm a worthless individual who cannot possibly like myself.' This second sentence, which arbitrarily and nonsensically involves your ego, your personal *self,* with your sexual performance, seriously interferes with that actual performance: since it makes it too risky. For after convincing yourself that this sentence is true, and that you *do* have to succeed sexually to be a real *man* or a worthwhile human *being,* you forget that sex is an *enjoyable* pursuit, and that it would simply be too bad (rather than utterly catastrophic) if you missed out on it."

"So consequently I avoid it, with the girls I take out, by not trying with them, and I also avoid it by my homosexuality and my exhibitionism."

"Yes—and as I said before, you thereby fail with an alibi. For if you fail to get satisfaction while exhibiting yourself, you can always say to yourself, *'I'm* not so bad for having failed (especially in view of the dangerous and courageous chance I took) but those damned girls are ninnies for refusing me." And even if you fail in the homosexual relations—which is not likely to happen, since you wait till you are approached—you can always say that 'my blasted society's idiotic for banning homosexuality and making these men want to reject me out of their own fear of being caught in a banned act.' "

"I see. I blame the girls or I blame society instead of blaming myself. When I really should be seeing that *I* am evading the sex issue and that therefore *I* am to blame."

"No, not quite. You're evading the sex issue, all right; and you're *responsible* for your evasion. But you're not really to blame; meaning, you're not a louse, a slob, a worthless person for being responsible for this self-defeating behavior. That, in fact, is your main philosophic mistake in this whole business. By believing—

as you and most others in this culture unfortunately do—that you're personally condemnable—that is, that you're an incompetent bum—for your sexual inadequacy, you distract yourself from the real problem ('What should I be doing to overcome my inadequacy?') and preoccupy yourself with a false problem ('How can I punish myself for being such an inadequate no-goodnik?') By depreciating your ego or your self-worth for making sexual mistakes (such as your not making passes at the girls you date and your engaging in foolhardy homosexual affairs), you fail to work on the problem of how you can make fewer mistakes. Instead, you convince yourself that a louse like you must *forever* go on making similar blunders."

"That's precisely how I do feel. If I've done so many bad things in the past, how could I *possibly* do any better in the future?"

"You mean, 'How could a skunk, a slob like me, do any better in the future?' But that's only, again, your *definition* of yourself. For you're not a skunk or a slob—but merely a fallible human being, like all the rest of us poor mortals. And though your *acts,* of both sexual omission and commission, are wrong or mistaken, you are merely a wrongdoer or a mistake-maker, rather than (as you self-depreciatingly picture yourself) a louse or a worm for *being* a wrongdoer. If we can get you objectively to see, therefore, that even though your *acts* are bad (meaning inefficient, rather than horrible or sinful) *you* are quite capable of doing, in the future, less mistaken acts, the problem of your homosexual and exhibitionistic proclivities will eventually be solved. But as long as you senselessly believe, and keep convincing yourself, that *you* are a bastard for *performing* these acts, and that in consequence you never can possibly change (except magically, perhaps, by having some of the girls you exhibit yourself to or the males you approach accept and love you), you will never really work on the problem of your mistaken *acts* and thereby solve it."

"From what you say, then, the solution would seem to be for me to accept myself as a perfectly good human being—as one who is capable of changing his behavior no matter how bad it may currently be."

"Yes, for unless you stop condemning yourself for being disturbed, you will have virtually no chance to work against your disturbance. But if you stop condemning yourself and start accepting—not liking, mind you, but merely accepting—the fact of your present aberrant behavior, you will have the leeway to keep working concertedly against it."

"By tackling, you mean, my ego problem? By not defining myself as weak and unmanly if I fail with women?"

"Right. By taking definite risks of failing—making overtures with females you do know and who might well reject you to your face—and by showing yourself that when you actually do fail it is too bad, and certainly is quite frustrating, but that that's all it is: too bad. It has nothing, this kind of failure, to do with you as a *person*; it does not, unless you think it does, depreciate your self-*worth*. That's what you really have to see and work at."

"And if I do, you think I can really get over this sexual hangup?"

"Not only that, but over your fear of general social disapproval, your anxiety about going for job interviews, and all the other similar needless fears that you keep building up by telling yourself, convincing yourself that it *would* be catastrophic if you did try and fail."

"That sounds all right. But what do I specifically have to do to get over my anxieties and needless fears?"

"To take the risks, especially the sexual risks, that you have been avoiding all your life. Now let's see what we can first give you as a homework assignment in this connection."

At this point, the patient and I figured out a series of graduated exercises, in the course of which he would go out of his way to make dates with girls—particularly a couple of girls whom he had found very attractive but had not had the nerve to date before—and would then literally force himself, if necessary, to make sexual overtures to them, no matter what the chances were of their rejecting him. At first, he had a most difficult time carrying out this homework assignment, since he somehow managed to be very busy, to use illness as an excuse, and to do everything possible not to make the dates he was supposed to make. After several weeks of persistent prodding by the therapist, however, he did make dates with some of the girls he knew, including one to whom he was very attracted.

Then there was a battle to get him to try any sexual overtures with these girls. Even kissing them goodnight was at first a chore; and he often would find some reason why it was not appropriate to do so. When he got past that hurdle and began to enjoy kissing his dates, and to do some light petting with them, he next had the devil of a time going further. Peculiarly—or perhaps not so peculiarly—enough, the main thing that he found it virtually impossible to do was to bare his penis to one of the girls he was dating. He would go through heavy kissing and embracing, and even get the girl half undressed and do his best to give her a sexual orgasm through manipulation of her genitals. But he didn't try to get her to satisfy him, since that would involve her handling his penis, and he just "couldn't" bring himself to take the initiating steps that would lead to this activity.

I quickly showed him that what he was saying to himself, in this connection, was: "If I place her hand on my penis, she may shrink away in disgust, or think that I am too forward and hate me for it; and that would be terrible, since I would have to accept her disgust or her low opinion of me and make it my *own* view of how bad I am."

He was also telling himself: "Since I have got away with exhibiting myself to so many girls—as well as with my stupid homosexuality—without being punished, I don't deserve to 'get away' with the pleasure of having this girl satisfy me." And he was finally convincing himself: "If I do let this girl satisfy me sexually, I will become dependent on her for future satisfaction. And since girls are likely to be so unreliable in this regard, and may not be in the mood to fulfill my persistent sex drives, I will therefore be letting myself in for future frustration, which I just won't be able to stand."

I worked with this patient to get him to see that each of his self-indoctrinating chains of sentences had two parts, one sane and one insane. Thus, it was true that the girl he dated might be repulsed if he placed her hand on his penis; that he had usually got away with his exhibitionism and homosexuality; and that he might be subsequently frustrated if he became sexually dependent on any girl. But it was *not* true that therefore he had to think himself a horrible person, that he deserved to be punished for his wrongdoings, or that he was unable to stand frustration. These were groundless *assumptions* that he was adding to the facts of his actually or possibly making sexual mistakes; and he was only becoming upset—or, rather, literally upsetting himself—by needlessly making these assumptions.

I also showed this patient that his other neurotic symptoms, such as his fear of socializing and his reluctance to be interviewed for a new job, stemmed from exactly the same kind of definitional assumptions—and that if he *stopped* assuming that he would be a no-goodnik if he was not socially adept or if a prospective employer turned him down, his feelings of inadequacy, panic, and avoidance in these connections would soon vanish.

By getting this patient to vigorously question and challenge his own assumptions, and to force himself to pet with girls to orgasm, to risk social disapproval, and to go for several job interviews, I soon helped him to depropagandize himself in these vulnerable areas. About four months after I first started seeing him, he did take a chance with one of the girls he dated, and did assertively induce her to pet him to orgasm, even though she herself was at first loath to do so; and a few weeks later he had enjoyable intercourse with the same girl. He went to several cocktail parties and made himself meet new acquaintances there. And finally, he actually got a new job, as a result of three interviews that he faced and fought his way through.

As he was making progress in overcoming his fears of failure and his low frustration tolerance, this patient became able to control his exhibitionistic and homosexual urges; and a few months later, they seemed to disappear. As he said to me in one of our closing sessions: "The more I try to assert *myself* with females, and see that it actually can be enjoyable, the less I feel urged to assert, by exhibiting myself to girls or making a homo-sexual conquest, that I am super-manly. I see now that girls *do,* though perhaps with some persuasion on my part, want to give me approval and sex satisfaction when *I* think I am worth receiving this from them."

"You mean," I asked, "the more you *are* you, and take the risks of being yourself, the less you find that you have to *display* a false or symbolic you-ness, a sham manhood, by exhibiting yourself or making homosexual conquests?"

"Yes. The more I stand up for myself, I guess, the less I have to show anyone, girl or fellow, that my great penis is standing up for me."

After 42 sessions of rational-emotive psychotherapy, extending over a year and a half, this patient began to have a steady sex-love affair with a girl, whom he later married. He has now been satisfactorily married for four years and has no strong exhibition-istic or homosexual tendencies. In fact, in the privacy of his own bedroom, with his wife, he obtains little satisfaction from her looking at his genitals or his body, but finds the sensual and caressive aspects of sex more enjoyable than the exhibitionistic or voyeuristic aspects.

I have treated, in my private practice in New York City,

scores of homosexual patients during the last 10 years, and I have found that the rational therapeutic approach is much more effective with these kinds of patients than was my previous psychoanalytic approach to therapy. Some of these patients have overcome their basic sexual problems in from five to 20 weeks' time; and others have required two or more years of therapy. In most instances, as soon as the patient begins to admit that it is his irrational philosophies of life, and not any external events, that are creating his sexual disturbance, and as soon as he begins consciously and actively, in theory as well as in overt practice, to contradict and challenge these irrational philosophies, he tends to make steady improvement in a manner that is so consistent that it can almost be graphed on a steady upward slant. When he refuses to admit that he and his *own* disordered thinking are causing his "emotional" disorder, or when he admits this but refuses to do any work or practice at combatting this thinking, he then makes little or no progress.

That is not to say that only rational-emotive or other highly active-directive methods of therapy will benefit sex deviates. As noted earlier in this paper, other techniques have also reportedly led to good results in this connection. But after working for a good many years now in this field, I would hypothesize that the more active, forceful, and direct a psychotherapist is with the sex offenders he sees, and the more objective and non-blaming he himself is in regard to aberrant sexual behavior in our society, the more success is he likely to have with these normally very difficult types of patients.

chapter 5

*The Most Important Factors
in the Treatment of Confirmed
Homosexuals*

~~~~~~~~~~~~~~~~~~~~~~~~~~~~~~~~~~~~~

The fact that fixed homosexuals are exceptionally difficult to treat is not phenomenal, since *all* seriously disturbed individuals resist getting better, even when they do come for psychotherapy and are willing to spend a considerable amount of time and money on it. It is conventionally assumed by Freudian and related therapists that resistance to change is largely a function of the patient's not wanting to get better, of his unconsciously fighting his therapist, of his deliberately trying to defeat his own ends because of his masochism, or of his having great difficulty in seeing the deeplying unconscious roots of his disturbances and therefore truly accepting what he is and why he is the way he is.

Most of this theory of therapeutic resistance is psychoanalytic mythology and is not backed by any appreciable amount of confirming data. The real reasons for the patient's resistance to change are probably rooted far more in his inherent biological makeup than in any rationalizations for the ineffectiveness of psychoanalysis. As I explain in detail in the last chapter of *Reason and Emotion in Psychotherapy* (Ellis, 1962a), man seems *naturally* to be the kind of animal who easily thinks crookedly, and therefore easily establishes and maintains self-defeating patterns of behavior (which we label as neurosis and psychosis);

and he also, unfortunately, seems to be the kind of individual who, once he does begin to think irrationally and therefore to become "emotionally" upset, has enormous *difficulty* in changing his disordered thinking and emotions—*even* when he has reasonably good insight into what they are and what he must do to change them.

Millions of human beings, for example, know very precisely *that* they smoke, eat, or drink too much; they almost fully accept the fact that this *is* self-sabotaging behavior, and they often even know exactly what they must do to cut down on their smoking, eating, or over-drinking. But their insights in these connections are of slight help to them in actually stopping; and not merely many but the great majority of these self-hurting individuals either do not appreciably stop their insane behavior, or else they stop it for a while and then soon fall back to their old nefarious ways.

The same thing goes, of course, for millions of individuals who have non-physical symptoms of severe disturbance, such as phobias, obsessions, compulsions, and temper tantrums. Although many of these individuals are very bright, have years of therapy, and presumably pretty well understand the origins of their disorders, they at best temporarily reduce them but never really undergo cures. Psychoanalytic methods of treating such individuals are notably inefficient and unproductive; but other methods of psychotherapy are also of dubious or limited value.

Homosexuals are even more difficult to treat than most other psychotherapy patients for several reasons. They frequently do not admit that they are basically disturbed, but insist that only society is disturbed for persecuting them. They often enjoy their homosexual acts immensely and therefore cannot look upon these acts as disabling symptoms. They wrongly believe that they were born to be homosexual and that there is nothing unusual or aberrant about their being fixed deviants. When they come for therapy, they usually want to tackle their other symptoms—such as their anxieties, depressions, and guilts—but want to leave their homosexuality alone. They are usually evaders or goofers, and tend to work very little on their therapy, just as they work little at many other aspects of their lives. They are mostly (as pointed out in Chapter 3) borderline psychotics or outright psychotics, rather than psychoneurotics; and individuals who are that seriously disturbed are notoriously difficult to treat and cure.

In spite of these difficulties, it is possible to treat homosexuals with psychotherapy and often to achieve excellent results. This is especially true if the following principles of treating them are observed.

The Setting of Realistic Goals of Treatment. As far as the cure of fixed homosexuality is concerned, it is unrealistic to try to eradicate the homosexual's *desires* for members of his own sex. Firstly, these desires are not especially abnormal, as man is born with a plurisexual disposition and there is nothing unusual about his seeking satisfaction with males as well as with females. The homosexual's abnormality is not that he *wants* sex relations with members of his own sex, but that he erroneously believes that he *must have* such relations, and those primarily or even exclusively. It is this irrational premise of his which is his sickness, and it is this of which the therapist must help him rid himself. He is cured, therefore, not if he never has any homosexual desires for the rest of his life, but if he is easily able to handle those that he does have, refuse to give in to them compulsively, and keep them within the bounds of a *generally* well-ordered sex life that would also include his having the desire for heterosexual participations.

The same thing could be said, of course, of various heterosexual inclinations which are catered to in an emotionally sick manner. Thus, if a male compulsively lusts after 12-year-old girls and tries to have coitus only with such girls, he is definitely fixated on this kind of sexuality, is often phobiac in relation to sex affairs with older girls, and is therefore disturbed. If, through psychotherapy, he loses his reluctance to have intercourse with older girls, and if he can easily keep his hands off 12-year-olds, we would normally consider him "cured"—even though he still had some amount of attraction to younger girls and sometimes *thought about* copulating with them.

So the realistic goal in the treatment of confirmed homosexuals is not the complete eradication of their desires for members of their own sex but the placing of such desires in their proper perspective: as a relatively *minor* part of the general sex drives of the treated individual. Even more important, in many instances, would be the goal of helping this individual to tackle his general, and often nonsexual, problems with himself and others: as, for instance, his feelings of inadequacy, guilts, depressive tendencies, and childish hostilities. Here, again, however, it should be sophisticatedly acknowledged that since *all* humans have a tendency to feel inferior, anxious, depressed, and overly-hostile, and since psychotics and borderline psychotics probably are born and reared with greater self-defeating tendencies in this respect than are "normals" and neurotics, there is not very much chance that a homosexual patient will be *completely* cured of his underlying propensities to worry and rage. If a therapist helps him to be considerably improved in these connections, that is all that we may usually hope for.

Nonetheless: it should be emphasized that the main goal in treating confirmed deviates should not be the removal of their homosexual symptom, but at least an appreciable amelioration of their general emotional upsets that have caused and are maintaining this symptom. I have had some "successful" treatments of homosexuals that were actually misleading. I treated, for example, a paranoid schizophrenic young man who had never had any heterosexual relations whatever, although he was 33 years of age when I first saw him. I had a very rough time trying to induce him to date girls and make any overtures of a sexual nature toward them; and for a year and a half I got absolutely nowhere with him in this respect, since he had all kinds of rationalizations for staying away from females. In one instance, where a charming girl was obviously enamored of him and would have gone to bed with him in a minute had he made any attempt to show sexual interest in her, he finally stopped seeing her entirely, just when I thought that he would make a pass at her and surrender his heterosexual virginity.

Almost by accident, however, this man later met an older, and not particularly attractive, woman, with whom he was able to have long, heart to heart talks, and who did not seem to threaten him sexually. He eventually, when under the influence of alcohol, made some sexual overtures to her—and at first he got roundly rebuffed. To my surprise, however, he persisted, and soon was having a steady affair with her. Then, to my even greater surprise, he gave up all his homosexual interests, fell madly in love with this woman, and became exclusively heterosexual. Even his masturbatory fantasies were entirely of women, and he seemed to have lost all desires for males. He was very happy with this result and considered himself totally cured of his fixed homosexuality. Unfortunately, however, I had to admit that at the close of therapy he was just as schizophrenic as he had been at the beginning, and was merely involved with his inamorata in the same sick way that he had previously been homosexually involved with a number of different boys.

The main therapeutic goal that is often sought by therapists who take a pessimistic view of the possibility of curing homosexuals is that of adjusting them to their homophilic existence, particularly by helping them rid themselves of guilt and anxiety about this kind of life. Such a goal is practical enough, in that it frequently works; but it achieves only a very limited therapeutic success, because the patient is still compulsively attached to homosexuality and erroneously believes that he cannot engage in a satisfying heterosexual relationship. He therefore is less sick than he was at the beginning of therapy, but still definitely neurotic or psychotic.

As an interim goal, however, this therapeutic pathway may sometimes be quite helpful. In many instances, with my own homosexual patients, I *first* show them that there is no need for them to be guilty about their homophilism, since at worst it is a self-defeating form of behavior (rather than a heinously immoral act) and there is no good reason why they should totally condemn themselves for making this kind of a mistake. Once, however, I help these patients to engage in homosexual acts in a nonguilty manner, I go on to show them that they should never condemn themselves for *anything*—for any kind of error or wrongdoing that they may perform. If they see this, they are usually also able to see that rejections of all kinds by other human beings, including by females, at most prove that they have been mistaken in their approach to these others—and that this kind of a mistake, too, is hardly reprehensible, even though it is unfortunate. As, in this wise, they begin to lose their fears of failing, they are much easier able to entertain the thought that they might be able to approach females sexually, and I frequently am able to help them do so. Inducing them, therefore, to give up their guilt about their homosexuality is employed as a stepping stone toward the goal of inducing them to give up all aspects of self-denigration, and thereby be enabled to take the risks and responsibilities of heterosexual involvements.

Active-directive methods of treating homosexuals. One of the main reasons why psychoanalysis has proven in the past to be of little value in the treatment of homosexuals, and why classical analysts, especially Freud himself, took a dismal view of the possibility of curing homosexuals, is that orthodox analysis is a rather passive method of treating all kinds of patients. The analyst, for a long period of time, does little more than listen to the endless free associations and dreams of his patients; and when he finally does begin to make interpretations, he largely makes them about the causes of the patient's *past* behavior, particularly his mixed-up relations with his parents, siblings, and other individuals who were important to him during his early days. Even when the analyst interprets the patient's present behavior, he still does so largely in terms of the past—and explains, for example, that the patient's present fear of having sex relations with women stems from his mother's chastising him for his sex curiosity, and his playful looking under her own skirts, when he was a child. These kinds of interpretations, even when they are valid (which, of course, they frequently aren't!) usually prove to be quite unhelpful to the patient, who is *right now* struggling with feelings of great disgust when he even thinks about women's genitals and who perhaps feels compelled to follow attractive men into public urinals and to make sexual overtures to them.

What is really bothering the homosexual patient is not the fact that he had an Oedipus complex as a child, nor that he has transferred to his analyst some of the feelings that he may have had long ago for his parents, but that he is a self-talking animal who tends to repeat to himself endlessly, with very little critical evaluation, the same kind of irrational ideas that he picked up (and was even sometimes born with a tendency to acquire) during his early life. No matter *why* he originally became a fixed deviant—and, as we have seen in Chapter 2, there are many reasons why he may have first gone in this direction—he only *remains* one because he in some way still believes in, and is currently reconvincing himself of, the validity of these early-acquired doctrines.

In consequence, the homosexual patient not only has to be shown exactly *what* he is now illogically thinking in order to remain a fixed deviant, but he must somehow be induced to vigorously challenge and question his own erroneous thinking, until he finally changes it. Moreover, since this thinking has led to emotional and sensory-motor habit patterns, some of which are quite enjoyable (or, at the very least, temporarily anxiety-reducing), he must be encouraged forcefully to keep interrupting and reorganizing these habit patterns and to replace them with opposing and inhibiting modes of behavior.

This is exceptionally difficult for any human being—and particularly for an emotionally unbalanced one—to do. Even "normal" and unrigid thinking and motor habits—such as, voting for a certain political party for a number of years or holding a tennis racquet in a given manner—are hard to break, no matter how clearly the individual who has these habits sees that it would be wise to change them. Pathological habits, such as extreme fears of women or the taking of great pleasure in masochistic homosexual acts, are even harder to tackle and to uproot. The person who sees that these pathological ways of behaving are unwise, and who tries to force himself to modify them, either has little luck at first in his attempts at reformation, or else he temporarily succeeds—only to fall back to his original maladjusted position, and then to become convinced that he just *cannot* change.

Human beings, moreover, are simply wonderful rationalizers. They easily find scores of reasons why, just because it *is* difficult for them to change their modes of thinking and acting, they should not attempt to do so. Homosexuals, in particular, "reason" that they were born the way they are and can't change; that they are engaged in a better, more esthetic and more human, way of life than are heterosexuals; that homosexuality is good because it is a bar to the population explosion; that they *should* rebel against society, because it has no right to make homophilism illegal; that they are only emotionally disturbed because they are socially persecuted; that it is utterly *impossible* for them ever to enjoy heterosexual relations; that they are too weak to compete in the heterosexual world; etc., etc. These kinds of rationalizations bolster their goofing and give them good "reasons" for giving up their attempts at heterosexual adjustment whenever the going gets a bit rough.

Homosexual resistance to change, again, is frequently bolstered by most of the denizens of the gay world. Whereas the average neurotic or psychotic will be greatly encouraged by his friends and associates, especially if they themselves are emotionally disturbed, to go for therapy and to try to help himself, the homosexually disturbed person will usually find that his friends and paramours greatly discourage his going for help. Many of them seem to feel that if *he* is successfully treated, *they* will have to surrender some of their last last-ditch stands against becoming more heterosexually-oriented. Rather than risk *this* possibility, they frequently try to get him out of treatment and to drag him back to a full homosexual existence.

Because of the unusual intensity and variety of roadblocks to psychotherapy that arise when the homosexual patient does come for psychotherapy, it is usually necessary for the therapist to take a distinctly active-directive role. He must not only show this kind of patient precisely what are the irrational philosophic premises that he holds that cause him to become and to remain a fixed deviant, but must persist in attacking and challenging these premises, and in getting the patient himself to carry on this attack. Time and again, in many instances, the therapist must go over the same ground—until he has ruthlessly shown the patient that *there is no other way* than his seeing and counterattacking his own self-sabotaging ideas.

Thus, one of my confirmed homosexual patients kept bringing up, as if it were an inalterable fact, the point that whenever he dated girls he would not have any sex feelings for them, while he spontaneously would become aroused by merely seeing males walking on the street. I equally persistently kept showing him that, each time he went with a girl, he specifically kept telling himself that he *wouldn't* make a good impression on her, that he *couldn't* make any overtures to her, and that he *never would* be able to succeed sexually with her, even if she indicated that she wanted to have intercourse with him. Under *these* circumstances, when he was focusing so strongly on the negative aspects of having sex relations with a girl, he naturally felt no desires for her. In addition, I kept actively knocking down this patient's excuses in regard to not calling or dating this or that girl; kept persuading him to give certain girls another chance, after he had cavalierly decided that they were not for him; and kept encouraging him to hold hands with, to kiss, and to fondle some of the girls whom he did reluctantly date.

Only after many active urgings and cajolings on my part was I able to induce this patient to engage in sufficiently prolonged petting with a girl that he finally did, much to his own surprise, become fully aroused, and was even able to have an orgasm while vigorously embracing her. As he remarked at this point, "I never would have made it with her had you not kept after me the way that you did." With still more proddings on my part, he was then able to have intercourse with a girl, and soon after that lost most of his compulsive homosexual tendencies.

Active-directive therapy with homosexuals frequently includes actual instruction in sexual technique. For fixed deviates not only have failed to gain the knowledge and practice of petting methods that most heterosexuals gain during their adolescence and early adulthood, but they also use this lack of knowledge as an excuse for not making any sexual overtures. They are so certain that they will be inept when they make love to a girl that they rarely make any attempts to do so. Not only, therefore, must their perfectionism and fear of failure in this respect be ideologically revealed and tackled, but it is often also advisable to show them exactly what they can do in caressing a girl, getting to her erogenous spots, removing her clothes, giving her an orgasm, and so forth. The more prepared that they feel that they are in these respects, the greater is the likelihood that they will start some sex play.

Even many of the nonsexual aspects of heterosexual dating have to be taught to some shy, inexperienced homosexuals who have managed to avoid this kind of dating previously. How to meet a girl, how to behave when he picks her up, where to take her for dinner, what to do when he is in the movies with her, how to make sure that he is alone in her apartment with her—these are some of the various things in which specific instruction must often be given if the therapist is realistically to expect the homosexual patient to get along reasonably well when he is dating girls.

Although much of this material is covered in books, such as *Sex and the Single Man* (Ellis, 1963b), which may be used as recommended reading, I find that homosexuals just cannot be trusted to read this material with the same interest as heterosexuals do, and that therefore much of the teaching that they require in this respect must be given to them personally by the therapist. Moreover, when they have started dating, the therapist must often check, in minute detail, exactly what they *are* doing with the girls that they date, and must patiently and uncondemningly show them how to correct the mistakes that they usually make in this regard.

Homework assignments, which are a special feature of rational-emotive psychotherapy, are exceptionally useful in the treatment of fixed homosexuals. Left to their own devices, they will usually find ways to avoid doing anything that they consider dangerous, notably in the areas of heterosexual engagements. It therefore behooves the therapist to give them specific projects to do and to keep checking on them to see if they carry out these assignments. If they do carry them out, considerable progress is usually made: since the assignments generally consist of doing something that they are afraid to do, and the accomplishment of such feared things not only tends to get the patients over major practical hurdles and enables them to do things that they previously thought that they could not do, but also (and sometimes more importantly) helps depropagandize them as far as their *general* anxiety-creating philosophies of life are concerned.

Many of the assignments given to homosexual patients are, as is to be expected, specific sex assignments about dating girls, making overtures to them, and having intercourse with them. But they are also given nonsexual homework as well. A case in point is that of Peter J., 26 years of age, who had been completely homoerotically oriented since the age of nine, when he had begun having overt sex relations with his older brother and a few of his brother's friends. Since that time he had always worshipped older males, particularly those who were tall and strong and who were athletically proficient. Peter himself was short and slim and had never excelled at any sport, and had avoided almost all physical activity, because he was terribly afraid that he would do poorly at it and make a fool of himself in front of any spectators.

One of Peter's first homework assignments, when I saw him for psychotherapy, was for him to learn how to dance. He was entirely uncoordinated in this respect, he insisted, and he had no sense of rhythm; therefore, when he had tried to dance, on several occasions, he had done exceptionally poorly, and had convinced himself each time that he just had no ability in this area. I showed him, when he explained to me what had happened in regard to dancing, that he really had no good evidence for his belief that he could not dance, since every time he attemped to do so he began with the clearcut prejudice that he would not be able to succeed, and he viewed his initial attempts with enormous suspicion and scepticism. As soon as he made even a minor error—which he always quickly did, because he was over-anxiously *watching* his performance instead of trying in any way to *enjoy* it—he immediately concluded: "There I go again! I *knew* I couldn't do this. What a fool I'm making of myself even trying!" And, of course, with this overwhelmingly negative feedback, he then made more and more errors, and he gave up dancing after only a few minutes.

I insisted that, at the gay bar where he sometimes went, and where the males danced with each other (or with an occasional lesbian who frequented the place), Peter keep dancing and dancing and dancing. He also took a few lessons with a regular dance teacher, who himself was homosexual; and finally took a course in modern dance, also with a male homosexual teacher. I tried to get Peter to take some dancing lessons with a female partner and to practice his social dancing with some "straight" females that he knew; but he at first was too shy to do this, and would only engage in dancing with male partners. Nonetheless, he did carry out his homework assignments—even though on several occasions he was tempted to call the whole thing off, and conclude once again that he was hopeless in this area and that he would never become a proficient dancer.

Much to his own surprise, Peter not only became an adequate social dancer after several weeks of lessons and practice, but he then began to get into the full swing of things and became better and better, until even he was willing to describe himself (about four months later) as "you know, a damned good dancer; in fact, I think I'm really becoming one of the best around. I don't think I'll ever make it as a truly good modern dancer, since there's some of the guys in my class who I'll never come close to. But even there, I'm getting to be not bad, not bad at all; and I must say that I thoroughly *enjoy* the classes, and expect to go on taking them, though I know I'll never be a real professional."

The successful completion of this homework assignment clearly convinced Peter that he had been unnecessarily putting himself down, and that he obviously could do many things, such as dancing, which he had previously stubbornly held that he was not able to do. On his own, he decided to study French, which he had also convinced himself in the past that he had no aptitude for, and he did so well in his French course that he then made up his mind to go back and finish college—which he had dropped out of several years before, largely because of his continual failures in language courses.

Finally, Peter was able to take on the additional homework assignment of dancing with females, and found that this, too, became enjoyable, and that he began to have erections while on the dance floor with some of his pretty female partners. He then went on to heterosexual dating and, about a year and a half after he began psychotherapy, had what he called a "wild affair" with a girl, and surrendered his heterosexual virginity. He was very happy about this and later had affairs with other girls. At the close of therapy, he still had a tendency to become emotionally involved with strong, athletic-looking males; but this tendency was much less than it had been when he began treatment, and he was easily able to handle it. He also was becoming attached to some of the girls he dated and he felt that it was only a matter of time when he would meet one that would really send him and with whom he would want to live and later possibly marry.

Just as significantly, Peter at the close of therapy had much greater general confidence in himself than he had ever previously had, was looking forward to finishing college and getting a higher-level job, and could clearly see that his former negative attitudes toward himself had no foundation in fact, but had stemmed only from his terrible fears of failing, and his conviction that unless he did perfectly well at some activity right from the start, he would never be able to master it at all, and would make a fool of himself in the eyes of others. He was considerably less other-directed at the close of therapy than at the beginning;

and he specifically credited his first homework assignments in the field of dancing as being of immense value in helping him see that he could do many things that he previously had been afraid of doing, and that it was not terribly important if he tried such activities and failed miserably at them.

Other active-directive methods are also of great use with confirmed homosexuals. It is usually assumed by Freudian, Rogerian, and other therapists that it is the relationship between the patient and the therapist that largely serves as the vehicle for intervention into and cure of the patient's basic problems; but there is little evidence that this is actually true. Rather, as I noted in a paper given at the American Psychological Association annual convention a few years ago (Ellis, 1962b), there is some reason to believe that the principles of basic personality change can be directly *taught,* and that didactic presentations, either by the therapist himself or in the form of the printed, spoken, and recorded word conveyed to the patient from other sources, may be very helpful.

In my own work with fixed homosexuals, I find that direct teaching is of tremendous importance. I show my patients, during therapy sessions and by referring them to suitable printed literature, that homosexuality is not directly inherited, that it usually stems from and is maintained by some forms of irrational anxiety and/or hostility, that it invariably has a philosophic basis which can be understood and challenged, that it is the result of unconscious self-training on the part of the fixed homosexual and always can be eradicated by conscious re-training, and that it is part of a general emotional sickness that unnecessarily restricts the individual's life space and grossly impinges on his *joie de vivre* and flexibility.

I also teach the patient precisely what simple exclamatory sentences he is telling himself in order to maintain his one-sided homosexual patternings and how he can logically parse these sentences, and vigorously question them, until he gives them up and replaces them with a saner, less self-defeating set of philosophic assumptions. Finally, as noted above, I teach the patient, in many instances, exactly what he can do to help himself to abet his heterosexual dating and sex overtures, and how he can succeed at penile-vaginal copulation.

This is not to gainsay the fact that in rational-emotive psychotherapy, as practiced by me and my associates, a certain amount of relationship or transference therapy takes place. It inevitably does: since therapy *is* partly a human encounter between the patient and the therapist, and much learning transpires as a result of this encounter. The therapist, however, can also be a direct as well as an incidental educator; and the better he understands what fixed homosexuality is and how it can be modified, and the more effectively he directly as well as indirectly communicates this knowledge to his patients, the more effective in the treatment of homosexuals he is likely to be.

Group therapy with homosexuals. Group therapy is often used with confirmed homosexuals today; and frequently they are treated in special all-homosexual groups, where they can feel comfortable with each other and can work through their problems. I have personally found this to be an ineffective form of treatment, because when a few members in a homosexual group begin to get better, and to be able to look forward to heterosexual participations, the other members of the group, who are not yet that far advanced in giving up their disturbances, frequently become jealous or insecure, and do their best to drag the improving members back into the fold.

I therefore make it a practice, in my group therapy, to place only one or two homosexuals in with a group, the rest of whose members are heterosexual. I find that the first thing that usually happens in such a setup is that the homosexual patient, once he is able to speak out frankly about his sexual problem, derives immediate benefit just *because* he is able to discuss it frankly with several straight individuals. He usually finds that the risk-taking he is thus able to pursue demonstrates to him that it is *not* so terrible if he is different from others, and even if some of these others disapprove of him for being different. Actually, he also discovers that most of the members of his therapeutic group do not condemn him for being homosexual, but act in such a manner as to convince him that he need not condemn himself for having this kind of a disturbed symptom. Rather, the group members look upon his homosexuality objectively, as a trait that is to be seen as a problem and then vigorously combatted; and he tends to take on the same attitude toward his homophilism as they do.

While accepting the fixed deviant, in a non-blaming manner, *as* a homosexual, the group members generally try to show him that he *need* not remain deviated, and that he *can* have successful adventures with members of the other sex. They indicate to him that he *is* to some degree sexually desirable; and that even if he at first fails in his heterosexual attempts, that will not prove anything negative about *him*, as a total person, but will merely indicate that so far he has not learned how to go about these attempts in a more efficient manner.

Best of all, to some degree, the members of a therapy group generally keep after the homosexual patient, give him concrete homework assignments that will direct him toward heterosexual affairs, and check up on him fairly regularly to see whether he is carrying out these assignments. They therefore serve as a constant reminder to him that he is still goofing, and that if he wants to help himself he'd better work persistently and hard at trying to overcome his fixed deviation. In this respect, the prodding of a patient's group can be even more effective than the prodding of his therapist, since the therapist is only one individual, and a special kind of person at that; and it is relatively easy for many patients to edit out the messages he is trying to convey to them, while it is more difficult for them to ignore the messages of eight or nine members of their group.

In the therapeutic group, moreover, at least in the kind of a group that is made available to the patient in rational-emotive psychotherapy, the patient, under the direct supervision of the therapist, learns to be an active-directive therapist to all the other group members. When they bring up their problems, he not only tries to show them what is really bothering them, but actively tries to talk them out of the nonsense that they keep telling themselves to create their emotional upsets. In so doing, he consciously or unconsciously begins to realize, in most instances, that *he* is telling himself the same kind of philosophic balderdash that the other members of the group are constantly reinfecting themselves with; and that *he* can challenge and question this nonsense just as he is trying to get them to do. Just as most professional therapists seem to improve considerably in regard to their own deepseated problems as they continue to help others to effect basic personality change, so does the participant in rational-emotive group therapy seem to help himself appreciably as he vigorously tries to help the other group members. Homosexuals in particular, if they can be led to be active members of a therapy group, are able to attack the fundamental passivity (or passive-aggressiveness) that is so frequently theirs, to take chances that they rarely took in life before, and to radically change many of their modes of thinking and behaving.

Acceptance of the patient but not of his symptoms. Perhaps the main thing that has to be accomplished in treating almost any kind of neurotic or psychotic patient is to induce him to accept him*self* fully while, at the same time, he is realistically

facing the fact that his *symptoms* are inefficient and self-sabotaging and that they simply must be worked against and given
up. For, as is specifically taught in rational-emotive psychotherapy, and as is more indirectly demonstrated in various other
types of therapy (especially Rogerian and existential treatment),
the whole *person* is never to blame for his ineffective, and sometimes even immoral, *acts*. All human beings are essentially good
and worthwhile—meaning, that they deserve to continue to
exist and to find some kind of happiness for themselves—even
when their *performances* are clearly substandard. Although it is
highly *desirable* that the individual behave well and effectively,
and it is most unlikely that he will be *maximally* happy if he
does not, he still does not *have to be* a fine performer in order
to like himself and to consider himself worthy of future existence
and pleasure. To the degree, in fact, that he *unconditionally*
accepts himself as worthwhile, and tries to enjoy himself and
better his lot in life just *because* he is alive and human, he is
likely actually to be a better performer and to act satisfactorily
in his relations with his fellows; and to the degree that he likes
himself *only* because he achieves and impresses others, he is
likely to wind up by being terribly over-anxious, and hence a
poor performer and relater.

Homosexuals in our society tend to consider themselves notably
worthless, because they are failing to achieve the heterosexual
relations that they are told they should effect, and because they
are usually condemned, persecuted, and sometimes severely
penalized by the heterosexuals with whom they come into constant contact. Accepting, as they do, the low estimation of themselves which their fellowmen usually have of them, they then
tend to believe that it is absolutely impossible for them to change,
and if anything they become more fixed to deviant ways of
living. It is therefore most important that their therapists accept
them fully as worthwhile human beings, and that they do not

exacerbate the bitterness by repeating society's mistake of condemning homosexuals for being what they are.

As I indicated in a paper on interrogating offenders some time
ago (Ellis and Brancale, 1956), it is not difficult to win the confidence of deviants if the therapist himself is non-moralistic and
if he is able, without any embarrassment on his part, to use the
kind of language and concepts used by the deviants themselves.
This, however, can be taken to some extremes—as is frequently
done, today, by some therapists who are themselves confirmed
homosexuals. These therapists, as might well be expected, are
highly sympathetic toward their homophilic patients, and get
along very well with them as far as acceptance is concerned. Unfortunately, however, they lean over backward and not only
accept the *patient* but his *symptoms* as well. They indicate to him
that there is nothing wrong with his being a fixed deviant; that
as long as he is not guilty about his homosexuality, he might as
well continue unquestioningly to enjoy it; and that if he fully
accepts himself *as* a homosexual, all will be right in his world.

Moonshine! As emphasized throughout this book, the fixed
homosexual definitely *is* disturbed, and his confirmed deviance
is an integral part of his disturbance. Consequently, accepting
his symptoms is *not* equivalent to accepting *him*. *He* is a good
person *in spite of* the fact that his sexual fetishism and inflexi-
bility are self-defeating and mistaken; and when he is helped to
get rid of his sexual (as well as his nonsexual) errors, he will
still be a worthwhile individual, but he will also be a more
effective and happier person.

The competent therapist, therefore, should be able to fight the
patient's symptomatology without fighting *him,* and should be
able to show him the error of his *ways* without demonstrating
that he is a no-goodnik for *displaying* these erroneous ways.
Preferably, therefore, the therapist himself should be a relatively
undisturbed (or what Rogers calls a self-congruent) person—as

he is most unlikely to be if he is a fixed, inflexible homosexual. This does not mean that a confirmed homoerotic therapist is not able to help a homoerotic patient *at all,* but just that he is likely to help him in limited ways; and that the more he himself is effectively heterosexual, the more he is likely to be of maximum helpfulness to the fixed homophilic patient.

The therapist, in other words, should be able to be a good model as well as a good teacher for his patient; and the healthier, more flexible, and better-rounded an individual he is, the more he is likely to be able, nonsexually as well as sexually, to show the patient the road to greater sexual and general healthfulness.

chapter 6

*Verbatim Transcript of
Recorded Interviews with a
Young Homosexual Treated
with Rational-Emotive
Psychotherapy*

~~~~~~~~~~~~~~~~~~~~~~~~~~~~

[The two cases that are included in Chapters 6, 7, and 8 of this book are presented in the form of verbatim transcripts of tape recorded interviews between the patients and the therapist. Each of these patients was seen several years ago and has maintained the gains made in the course of the rational-emotive psychotherapy sessions. It is most important that this kind of material be presented, even though at times it appears to be repetitious, ungrammatical, and inelegantly stated, since only in this manner can the reader fully see what the therapy process is actually like. Accounts by the therapist of what he *supposedly* did are notoriously bowdlerized and often (consciously or unconsciously) fictionalized. Only tape recordings, and the verbatim transcripts taken from such recordings, are likely to tell the truth, and nothing but the truth, about what transpired between the patient and the therapist.

[Homosexuals themselves are always demanding that cured individuals be shown to them in person, so that they can interrogate such patients and determine if they are truly changed in their sexual orientation and behavior. Such a procedure is almost always impractical, because cured homosexuals would very rarely want to publicly confess their previous inclinations or to submit themselves to an attack—and, unfortunately, it inevitably would be a decided attack—from still practicing homosexuals who are defensively convinced that cure is not possible, and who would have strong motivation to demonstrate that the rehabilitated homosexual was not really cured; or who (as Cory

131

points out in his introduction to this book) would tend to insist that he was not truly a fixed deviant before he went for treatment. Under the circumstances, perhaps the most convincing thing that can practically be done to show homosexuals that other confirmed deviates definitely have been helped, through psychotherapy, to overcome their sexual fixations, and to truly enjoy heterosexuality after a lifetime of aversion to it, is to present verbatim transcripts such as those which are printed in the next three chapters. It may be predicted that even this kind of material will by no means fully convince homophiles who are determined to go on thinking, no matter what evidence to the contrary is presented, that fixed homosexuality is completely incurable; but some of them, at least, may be shaken in their prejudiced beliefs.

[In any event, here are some verbatim transcriptions which show, in tape recorded detail, how one exclusive homosexual of 31 was helped to succeed at and distinctly enjoy heterosexual relations with several girls; and how a married bisexual of 51 who was compulsively running after men with large penises and getting into trouble with the law and with his wife for doing so, was enabled to overcome his compulsion and to be satisfied with heterosexual relations. Other verbatim transcriptions, one of which shows even more remarkable changes from exclusive homosexuality to predominant interest in heterosexuality are too lengthy to be included in the present book but will be published later in *The Encyclopedia of Homosexual Behavior,* which I and Donald Webster Cory are now engaged in editing.

[The patient with whom the following recorded interview is held is a 31-year-old freelance copywriter who has been a fixed homosexual since the age of 14. He has had only a few heterosexual experiences, when girls have taken the initative with him; and these have not turned out very well, since he has shown himself to be too passive, effeminate, and "campy," and the girls therefore quickly sought other lovers. He has been very promiscuous homosexually; but even in this area has tended to be unaggressive and passive, and never to make the first overtures himself and thereby risk possibly being rejected.

[The recorded interview comprises the fifteenth session with the patient, who has been seen irregularly for individual psychotherapy over a period of seven months at the time it occurs. However, he has more regularly attended group psychotherapy for the past five months. He first came to therapy largely because he wanted to do creative writing but did not have the courage to try, even though he was competent as a copywriter. After a few months of therapy, he did actively try some creative writing and has been steadily progressing at it ever since. He also considerably improved his general working habits. At first, however, he made no attempt to work on his homosexual problem; and only in the few weeks before the fifteenth session has he shown any inclination to do so. Both the therapist and his therapy group have been encouraging him to try going with girls, and he now seems ready to make a serious attempt to do so—though, as the contents of this interview show, he is resisting heterosexual participation in several subtle and obvious ways.

[The technique of therapy employed with this patient is rational-emotive psychotherapy. Rational therapy (or RT) is based on the assumption that human beings normally become emotionally disturbed because they are born with biological predispositions which make it easy for them to think crookedly or irrationally; and because they biosocially acquire illogical and nonsensical thoughts, philosophies, or attitudes. Human emotion itself is conceived of as largely being a certain kind—a biased, prejudiced kind—of thought; and it is held that people can be taught to change their negative and disturbed feelings by changing the thoughts that almost invariably underlie these feelings.

[The rational-emotive therapist believes that people literally talk themselves into neurotic states by telling themselves illogical and irrational sentences, or ideas, which they have previously learned from their parents and their culture, and have internalized and keep ceaselessly repeating. The main emphasis of the therapist who employs rational technique is on analyzing the patient's current problems—especially his feelings of anger, depression, anxiety, and guilt—and concretely showing him that these emotions arise not from past events or external situations but from his present irrational attitudes toward or illogical fears about these events and situations. Thus, a patient is shown that it is not his Oedipal attachment which made and keeps him disturbed, but his self-perpetuated illogical ideas underlying this attachment—for example, his groundless beliefs that he is wicked for lusting after his mother, that he cannot survive without his parents' love, that he will be castrated by his father, that it is horrible to have others think of him as incestuous, etc.

[Where, in psychoanalytic techniques, considerable time is spent on showing the patient how he originally *became* disturbed, in rational-emotive analysis much more emphasis is placed on how he is *sustaining* his disturbance by *still* believing the nonsense, or illogical ideas, which first led him to feel and act in an aberrated fashion. RT differs from psychoanalytic procedures in that (*a*) not merely the facts and psychodynamics of the patient's behavior are revealed but, more to the point, his underlying philosophies or ideas which lead to and flow from these historical facts; (*b*) a concerted *attack* is made on the irrational beliefs that are disclosed in the course of the therapeutic process; (*c*) emphasis is placed far less on the disclosure of the individual's unconscious drives or feelings than on revealing his unconscious and irrational *attitudes* which underlie these drives or feelings; (*d*) the therapist literally *teaches* the patient how to observe his (unconscious) illogical thinking and how, instead, to think straight; and (*e*) the patient is usually encouraged, urged, or commanded into emotionally *reeducating activity*.

[The recorded session that follows is a fairly typical interview employing rational-emotive technique, except that the patient, probably because of the previous individual and group sessions he has had, is more accepting than many other patients are, and requires relatively little counter-attacking and annihilating of his irrationally-held positions. But he does give considerable lip-service, as so many patients do, rather than true allegiance to sane views and actions; and the therapist consequently keeps trying to induce him to question and challenge his lip-service and to think and act in a manner that will lead to truly rational convictions, and hence thorough-going emotional and behavioral changes.]

[First couple of minutes of the session consists of joking about making the tape recording.]

T-1   How are things?

P-1   Oh, pretty good. I'm, uh, haven't been too well. I can't say I haven't been too disturbed. I've been keeping pretty busy, but I'm on that going to sleep routine again.

T-2   Yes?

P-2   And I don't, you know, I don't, I don't think I really need the sleep but I just sleep.

T-3   How much have you been sleeping?

P-3   Uh, well, like last————. I've been making it a point to get home at midnight and usually if I'll go to, you know, if I, if I go to sleep at midnight I feel that I should wake up around eight or nine, you know eight-thirty in the morning————

T-4   Yes?

P-4   And it's to my advantage to wake up then 'cause I can get a day started. And I'm discovering that I'm waking up at nine-thirty and ten and eleven [*laughs while saying this*]————

T-5   Yes, yes?

P-5   And then in the afternoons, if I get tired————. Like yesterday afternoon I went in and I thought, "Well I'll flop down." I was sort of, I'd been writing all day; my eyes were tired; and I thought, "I'll sleep for an hour because, um, then I'll go out to dinner." And this was at five and I woke up at eight-thirty. And this is just too much sleep, you know. I'm just wasting too much time sleeping [*laughs while saying this*]————

T-6   Yes?

P-6   And I don't, uh————. You know, if, if I were physically exhausted it might make sense, but I'm not.

T-7   Are you sleeping past an alarm, or anything like that? Or are you not bothered with the alarm?

P-7   Uh, no, I haven't. I haven't bothered with the alarm except that I know for a fact last night I slept through a phone call, the phone rang and it didn't wake me up. And the messenger boy from the desk had a package and he came up about, he said about six, and said he knocked and knocked and knocked on the door and I didn't wake up. So evidently I'm really going out, you know. I'm not waking up to noises.

T-8   Yes, really sleeping right through them————.

P-8   Yeah, yeah. And you know, and it, like an unexpected noise. I would, I should think I would, wake up, you know, more rapidly. At least I used to be a very light sleeper. Anybody walked through the room, I'd wake up.

T-9   Yes?

P-9   And if somebody [*last part of sentence inaudible because of T's interruption*]——

T-10   Well, why don't you have an alarm on?

P-10   Well, up until just recently—oh, the last year—I've always been able to flop down and say I'm going to sleep for an hour, and I'd sleep for an hour and wake up.

T-11   Yes?

P-11   And now I'm getting, you know, like——. I don't know, an attitude of "I can sleep." Or, or I don't, I don't respond to what I'm telling myself: that I'm gonna wake up.

T-12   You don't have that internal alarm clock going——

P-12   No, which I used to—could count on.

T-13   Yes?

P-13   You know, if I'd say, "I'm going to wake up at seven," I'd be up at, you know, five minutes 'til.

T-14   But isn't the thing, then, if your internal alarm isn't working, to use the——

P-14   Yeah.

T-15   ——external until it does work?

P-15   But it's, uh; it's just that I, you know——. If, if I have to get up, I suppose I could, you know. I would use an alarm——.

T-16   Yes?

P-16   But just the——. What bothers me is this idea of, of why am I wanting to sleep so darn much [*laughs while saying this*], you know, when I know it's physically not necessary for me now, because I'm getting more sleep than I ever have——.

T-17   Yes.

P-17   Unless it's, uh, you know: just a hiding kind of habit——.

T-18   And then you think it possibly might be that you're trying to evade work, or evade life, or something like that?

P-18   I think that probably that's the only thing I can figure. But one thing: since I told you I was, you know, I was quitting with the boys———

T-19   Yes?

P-19   I've, uh, you know, seen some of the, the, the boys that I've known———.

T-20   Yes?

P-20   They have come to dinner and things like that. But this is where I've made it a point to be home by twelve o'clock. And I hadn't, I ain't had no sex at all for two or three weeks, 'cause I haven't made it with any of the girls I've met yet.

T-21   Yes.

P-21   And, uh, you know, I have the feeling that maybe I'm sort of hiding behind sleeping, you know. I know, I know I'm not getting the sex I would like, so I go to sleep and sleep it off, you know. [*Laughs while saying this.*]

T-22   Yeah.

P-22   That's the only reason I can, thing I can figure. Of course, I don't feel frustrated in any———. Particularly in any other areas.

T-23   But when you're awake, do you feel sexually frustrated?

P-23   No. Now this is also the strange part. I was noticing this morning that since this, you know, since I said I was going to try really working at getting girlfriends and things, I haven't been at all, uh, particularly desirous of sex. You know, I haven't, uh, just felt like, gee, you know, I've gotta go out and, and, and find something or somebody.

T-24   Yes?

P-24   Of course, for one thing, frankly, the times I have felt I wanted to have some, you know, have sexual relief, it's just too easy to masturbate. You know, I can always take care of myself that way [*laughs while saying this*]; which isn't, you know, doesn't really solve the problem particularly except———

T-25   Yes?

P-25   ———it is a relief.

T-26 Well, again: do you think that your lack of sex desire is an evasion for———?

P-26 Yeah, I do. I think that on one, in one hand, uh, I'm, I'm thinking, you know———. I say now, you know, I want this and logically this is what I want to do; and still I'm some, you know, more subconsciously then and, and sort of sneaky subconsciously [*sort of laughs*] I must be fighting it to dodging it, ducking it, not, you know———. Taking the easy way out———.

T-27 All right, now. Let's ask ourselves———. Let's assume for the moment that this is true, that you are "sneaky subconsciously," as you say, fighting it. Let's ask ourselves exactly what you would be saying to yourself, sneaking subconsciously, in order to fight it? What would you be afraid of with, let us say, the girls, that would induce you (*a*) to sleep more, which you are doing, and (*b*) when you're awake, not to have that much of a sex desire?

[Up to this point, the therapist has waited, somewhat more patiently than is often done in the highly active-directive method of rational-emotive psychotherapy, for the patient to bring out some material that would show that he is not yet acting on his resolve to go with girls instead of, as in his whole previous life, with boys; and then, when this material is brought up, to be able to use it to illustrate to the patient exactly what he is telling himself (consciously or unconsciously) to *create* his inactivity and his indecision. He now tries to get the patient to see that his lack of sex desire and his greater demands for evasive sleeping do not exist in their own right, but *are* related to concrete, simple exclamatory sentences with which the patient is indoctrinating himself.]

P-27 Now that's the, that's the hard one, frankly, 'cause I don't think I'm afraid, in the sense of being afraid of girls———

T-28 Yes?

P-28 ———I mean, uh, of a sex relationship. I think what I'm afraid of is probably just the going out and the, and the first———. I'm really afraid of the first contact, the, the, how to get in to it.

T-29   Of the encounter——

P-29   Yeah.

T-30   Yes, of the encounter, the meeting——

P-30   Yeah, yeah.

T-31   That you do have to go out first and get to meet and know the girl——

P-31   Yeah. And, and that's, that's when I, you know, I get terribly shy and I get all, you know, messed up. And I think probably what I'm doing is, is, you know, well, if you oversleep, then you don't have to go out.

T-32   Yes, that's true. And if you don't have the sex desire, you don't have to go out.

P-32   Yeah, yeah!

[The therapist solidly nails down the circumlocuting patient, and gets him to admit that his sleepiness and his lack of sex desire are both excuses for his not wanting to go with girls because he is afraid of rejection, especially during the first contacts. But, not being satisfied with this admission or insight on the patient's part, he still tries to get him to see the exact self-sentences he is employing to create his fear: so that he can then logically parse and attack these internalized sentences.]

T-33   All right, now. Let's assume that, for the moment, that you're afraid of the contact. Now let's get the exact sentence which you're saying to yourself to make yourself afraid of this contact. What are you saying is *dreadful?*

P-33   Well, it sounds too simple to say, "They won't like me," you know——

T-34   In oth——

P-34   —and I'm sure that's the bottom of it.

T-35   Yes. In other words, you're saying, "If I go——"

P-35   But I'm inventing a lot of crap to say [*sort of laughs*]. "I won't——. They won't like me," I guess.

T-36   Well, let's get that a little more specific. You're saying, "If I go out and meet the girls or a girl," let us say, "then there's a good possibility that she won't like me and that would be *dreadful*———"

P-36   Yeah.

T-37   "———if she didn't!" Is that the sentence you think you're saying?

P-37   I don't, I don't, I can't say that that's just it, though.

T-38   Yes?

P-38   It's, it's like, uh, you know. I defeat myself before I go out because pretty, half the time I just said, "Well, I'm gonna go somewhere and I'm———" You know, like, you know. I joined the Museum of Modern Art and I've gone a couple of times and I walk in and I look around and immediately I don't e—, I don't even see a girl I, that, that is appealing looking to me.

T-39   Yes.

P-39   You know. So already before I, you know, I'm, I'm, I'm cutting myself short before I even start.

T-40   Yes, but again———

P-40   And I don't know whether———

T-41   ———is that just another technique for the fear again? You, you've given two techniques so far: one, you stay———

P-41   [*Interrupting and answering T's first question*] It probably is, it probably is.

T-42   ———asleep; two, you lose the desire. And three is you're saying, "The girl isn't goodlooking enough."

P-42   Yeah.

T-43   But we still get back to the proposition that if you did have the desire, if you did get up early, and if she were goodlooking enough, and you did make some kind of an overture, that she then wouldn't like you?

P-43   Yeah.

T-44   And that would be *terrible*?

P-44   Yeah, I guess. Yeah, uh, I, I, I'm, I mean, that, that's, that's right――

T-45   Uh-huh?

P-45   But I don't even think I've got to the stage of finishing it out and saying, "That would be terrible." [*Laughs while saying this.*]

T-46   But you don't say it――

P-46   [*Interrupting*] I mean, I'm, I'm, you know, I'm not rationally saying, I mean, I'm not letting, openly saying it to my-self――.

T-47   You're not consciously saying that. Right. But doesn't your behavior show *by inference* that you must be saying something like that? Because if you were saying just (*a*) "If I went out and did these things, didn't sleep, had the sex desire, and liked the girl physically, she might reject me"—just that; if you were saying that, would you then start going into these evasive dives of yours? If you weren't saying, "It would be terrible if she did reject me," because if she rejected you, you'd still get the lovely *experience* of being rejected――

P-47   Yeah, yeah.

T-48   So on some level you must be saying, "It would be terrible, it would be awful! I couldn't take it; look what a crumb I would be if she rejected me!"

P-48   Also involved in there is that, uh――. As we talk I'm realizing that I think I'm still very, I'm too much on my own terms. Like when I go out to the, to the Modern and I want to meet a girl and I don't meet her in the first ten mi-nutes――

T-49   Yes.

P-49   Then, you know, it's a bad deal; and I walk out and go home. [*Laughs while saying this.*]

[Although the patient keeps talking in a slippery, somewhat over-cavalierly accepting and yet evasive manner, the therapist keeps try-ing to pin him down; and insists that his behavior, if not his words, *show* that he must be telling himself that it would be awful if he were rejected by a girl. Instead of becoming defensive about this persistence on the therapist's part—which, according to many psychoanalytic and client-centered theories he is definitely supposed to do—the patient is partly driven from his lair, and makes an even more incriminating admission: namely, that he not only goes to sleep and downs his own sex desires, but that even when he finally drives himself to the museum to look for girls, he doesn't really give them a chance, but rejects them during the first ten minutes and gives up the search. This often occurs during rational-emotive therapy: the therapist's active persistence brings out more confirming material from the patient, instead of leading to classic resistance.]

T-50   Is there a little————?

P-50   You know, uh, I'm, I'm sort of making the effort but not really the effort, at least, uh————

T-51   Yeah. Now is there a little grandiosity here? Really————

P-51   Yes, unfortunately, I, I, you know, I'm looking for somebody good enough for me, not me good enough for them [*sort of laughs while saying this*].

T-52   Yes, and is this————?

P-52   And I think it is part of the problem————.

T-53   Is there another sentence?—that "If John goes out and does these kind of things————"

P-53   "————they ought to come flocking and they don't!" Yeah.

T-54   That's right. "And they don't and this is terrible!"

P-54   I think that's even more than the fear————.

T-55   Yeah.

P-55   I mean, the fear of the fact that they're not going to come flocking. [*Laughs while saying this.*]

T-56   Yes.

P-56   You know, more than the physical fear————

T-57   The fact that it's so unfair that they're not flock————

P-57   Yeah, yeah!

T-58   And they should!

P-58   Yeah. Because, you know, I get, it's, uh, it's a crooked thing. I get all this shit from everybody about, you know, "You're a goodlooking guy and————" you know————

T-59   Yes?

P-59   "You shouldn't have any problems about meeting peo-ple————"

T-60   Yes?

P-60   And I do! [*Sort of laughs.*] You know, I just flat out do. And I go out with this great feeling of, gee, you know, "I'm God's gift to women." And then nothing happens [*laughs while say-ing this*], you know————

[Again, the therapist, by his insistent, direct interpretation, has smoked out the patient a little more. Rather than wait for the patient to see that, in addition to being overly-fearful, he is also grandiose (which he might or might not finally see) the therapist directly questions him about this, and he admits that there is a grandiose element mixed in with his fear. In fact, as the patient goes on to see, his feelings of grandiosity then lead to his becoming still more fearful: since, when he starts out with the idea that he's God's gift to women and, largely because of his own quick withdrawal or lack of full participation, nothing happens to help him meet suitable girls, he then becomes *more* afraid to make overtures and thereby prove that he is *not* so great as he assumes he is.]

T-61   Yes. But isn't that notion that you're a goodlooking guy and you shouldn't have any trouble meeting people, isn't that rather unrealistic? Because, no matter how goodlooking you are and how bright you are and how well educated, don't we *all* have trouble meeting people?

P-61   Well, I don't know about the rest of the world; but *I* do! [*Laughs while saying this.*] No, really, you know, it's————

T-62   But, but don't you think that most people have some degree of trouble—even though they have relatively less than others who are not goodlooking or are stupid and uneducated? Don't they always have some trouble? And don't they have to do some work to overcome that some degree of trouble?

[The therapist emphasizes here one of the main ideas of rational-emotive therapy: namely, that insight into one's disturbances is not enough; and that after gaining such insight, one must *work* to counteract one's self-defeating philosophies and to *do* what one is afraid to do.]

P-62   Yeah, that's it. I think that really, you know, a lot of the problem is that I, I, it's, it, I finally made up my mind that I would work at it and————. But I'm not performing.

T-63   Yes.

P-63   You know, up here I'm, I said it once————. I'm going to work at it; but then I'm ducking it by going————

T-64   But, that is, what is it you're, what is————?

P-64   ————at, at, at meeting people: at, at pushing myself a little more into walking up and saying, you know, "What's your name?" [*Laughs.*] Just that simple————.

T-65   That's fine. But isn't that the *second* thing you have to work at? You do have to work at that. But don't you also have to work at that crap you're telling yourself?—"They should————"

P-65   Yeah, yeah.

T-66   "————they *should* do this for dear old John. And wouldn't it be *awful* if they didn't!"—and so on? Now isn't *that* where the work may *first* be required, before you can secondly get off your ass and go out and actually talk to girls————

P-66   Yeah.

T-67   ————and meet them and so on? So you're seeing it, number two, as your————

P-67   The goal. But I'm not seeing the, uh—

T-68   Yes. But are you seeing the *more important* goal, which has plagued you all your life in so many other respects, in your work and so on? The number one, that I must work on *me,* on John————

P-68 Um hm [*barely audible*].

T-69 ———on what *I* tell myself. Now are you seeing *that* very clearly?

P-69 Not really. That's where I get bogged down.

T-70 Yes.

[The therapist, again as an integral part of the rational-emotive therapeutic approach, wants to make sure that the patient just doesn't jump in, without any real understanding of the basic issue involved, to approach the girls he wants to meet. Instead, the therapist insists, he must first tackle problem Number 1: the basic philosophic nonsense, that he is telling himself to create his fear of girls (and to create difficulties in his work and other aspects of his life). If he tackles this Number 1 problem, and sees what irrational sentences he is telling himself to create his anxiety and his inertia, then he can more easily and logically tackle problem Number 2, the actual making of overtures to the girls.]

P-70 And, and that, that was where the other day, I was, uh———. I no—, I, I noticed after I'd been talking to the whole group [*that is, his therapy group*] that I kept talking about things; and that in the sense is my thing.

T-71 Yes.

P-71 Is, I mean———. The, the goal is, I'm substituting the goal as a thing rather than, than working on *me* as a thing [*sort of laughs while saying this*]———

T-72 That's right, that's right; you got it with the others in the group———

P-72 Yeah.

T-73 You could see it with Susan the other time in the group, but are you really seeing it with *you*———?

[The patient, in his previous group therapy session, pointed out to some of the other members of the group that they were not really working on *themselves,* but on changing certain things about their external lives. He now begins to see that he is doing exactly this, himself: trying to change his overt behavior with girls, but not trying to change his own basic catastrophizing philosophies which create his fearful behavior.]

P-73   I mean, now————. Like that first date is the thing I'm shooting for; and it really shouldn't be that important to me.

T-74   Yes. Oh, it should be important————

P-74   I mean, it should be important. But it shouldn't be the————. It's for *later*. [*Laughs*.] That it happened————

T-75   The main, right————. The main thing is changing *John*.

P-75   Yeah.

T-76   What *he's* telling himself: *his* ideas, *his* philosophies. Which have kept you back, as we just said a minute ago, in lots of other respects, including and especially this one with the girls. Now shouldn't most, or a great deal, of the work, at least, be *there?* Then, finally, you still will have to do the work of————

P-76   Yeah.

T-77   ————getting up, as I said, off your ass and going out and meeting the girls. But you never quite get to that when you're doing the counter-work, we might say, of falling asleep————

P-77   Yeah, yeah [*barely audible*].

T-78   ————so much; of not having sex desire; of seeing that the girls are ugly; and so on—which is John. That's *John*.

P-78   Yeah, yeah [*barely audible*].

T-79   There: *that's* what you're telling yourself at what I call point *b*.

P-79   At the, yeah. At the same time I must, I must, ah, ah, just out of sheer fairness to me and the discussion [*sort of laughs*] admit that I *have* been noticing pretty girls more lately————.

T-80   Yes?

P-80   I mean, uh, occasionally on the subway, I haven't had, haven't had—have yet to get the nerve to walk over to a pretty girl I'll see on the subway—

т-81   Yes?

p-81   ————and say, you know, you know, "I'd like to call you or something" [*sort of laughs*]————

т-82   But the defenses are going down somewhat————?

p-82   But I'm seeing a lot prettier girls than, than I have, and————

т-83   Yes?

p-83   ————discovering that I'm no—, that the, the prettier girls I'm seeing are younger————

т-84   Yes?

p-84   ———— than me. Which is, I never noticed people, girls that were younger than me————.

т-85   You didn't notice all————?

p-85   They were always my age, or a little older.

т-86   Yes, because you edited out————

p-86   Yeah, yeah.

т-87   ————the most eligible and best-looking ones————

p-87   Yeah.

т-88   ————so you wouldn't have to do anything about it.

p-88   I'm, I'm, I'm sure that's it. But I, I really am noticing that there is an awful lot of younger, prettier girls around————

т-89   All right. So that, that, that fearful and that grandiose sentence at point *b*, of "Wouldn't it be awful if I failed or they should do this to me!" seems to be going down a bit and giving you leeway.

p-89   At least I can *look* now! [*Laughs.*]

т-90   That's right. At least you can look. But it's still there————

p-90   Yeah.

т-91   ————and it requires more work. Apparently, you have done some on it, because you have asked yourself, *"Would* it be so awful?" And in your copywriting and work and all, you are doing things now————

p-91   Yeah.

T-92   —which you've never done before in your life. Isn't that true?

P-92   Um hm. And I've even, I've even been active enough that I have made a couple of passes at people and, you know, been refused. But at least I'm, I'm sort of trying even there.

T-93   Yes.

P-93   Granted I, the, that, one, one of the gals I made a pass at is as sick as I am, I think and this is her problem, too. [Laughs]. But, uh, you know, at least I tried in some way, to make known what I wanted to happen. [Sort of laughs while saying this.]

T-94   And you weren't too afraid?

P-94   No.

T-95   So you're contemplating the fact that maybe it isn't so awful?

P-95   No, actu—, and, and it was, uh, as I say. I, I, uh, uh, you know, it was———. It's a girl I, I know, Jane; and I know she's, she and I have known each other for a long time and sort of been, you know, just good friends for years. I, I find Jane very appealing———

T-96   Yes?

P-96   And, uh,———. But I don't think I'd ever get anywhere with Jane, 'cause a, she's, she's just a little too, uh, too hip on being a big businesswoman and one of the editors of Harpers and Vogue. And her career's going to come first and all that kind of stuff———

T-97   Yes.

P-97   ———so that she sort of builds the wall out, too.

T-98   Yes.

P-98   And we had dinner the other night and she invited me up for a drink after dinner. And I went and, uh, I made a pass and she said No and that was that. But at least I tried. [Laughs.] Although granted I was, it was in pretty safe territory, because I must, I, you know, I, it was, I, I guess, in a way, I felt that I probably would be refused anyway. It was like practice time. [Laughs.]

T-99   I see. Yes. So you were able to do it easier than with some girl that you wouldn't be sure of———?

P-99   Yes, that I had no idea of.

T-100 Yes. But still it was an advance; and the practice *is* good, isn't it?

P-100 Yeah, yeah, and I found, and I really did find, that I could, uh, could make a pass without being embarrassed myself———

T-101 Yes.

P-101 ——— at having, you know, made an improper approach or something.

T-102 Sure.

P-102 And, uh, I didn't get hit, so I guess I came out on top! [*Laughs while saying this.*]

T-103 And you did get some experiences, too———.

P-103 Yeah, yeah. I mean, I came out more plus than minus, I guess. [*Still is sort of laughing.*]

T-104 Right. How many girls have you made a pass at in your whole life?

P-104 Four or five.

T-105 So this was one of the four or five.

P-105 Um hm. I've been very reticent in that area, I will admit it. [*Laughs.*]

T-106 Yes.

P-106 No. In fact, uh, even, even carry it further back. I don't think I've ever made a pass with a guy, it was always, you know, they chased me———.

T-107 Yes.

P-107 And I'm sure that this has a lot of bearing on it. I want the women to chase me, too.

T-108 Yes, that's right, too———.

P-108 You know, it's an old habit pattern as well as, yeah———

T-109 Yes, and isn't that one of the main reasons for homosexuality:

that boys find that other boys will chase them, while women won't?

P-109   Yes.

T-110   And it's much safer; and it wouldn't be so terrible, because they won't get rejected that often——

P-110   Yeah. You can say yes without being the villain of the piece.

T-111   That's right.

[As usual, the therapist tries to go a bit beyond the immediate conversation, and to make the educational point that the patient is much like many other homosexuals: that he has been afraid to be assertive with girls, and to risk rejection thereby; so he has found it easier to be passive with males. Fear of rejection will naturally lead to non-assertive behavior, the therapist is saying; and only by tackling this fear and seeing that it is *not* terrible to be rejected will the patient become truly non-homosexual and otherwise more assertive.]

P-111   You know——

T-112   You refuse them, but they're not going to refuse you——

P-112   Yeah.

T-113   Unless you make the overture; and you don't have to.

P-113   Yeah, that's, that's very true, because——

T-114   Let's get back to changing John. *Would* it be so terrible if you got refused even by a girl you didn't know that there was a good chance beforehand she was going to refuse you, and you didn't know at all what was going to be? Or *would* it be so terrible if you grandiosely *didn't* get exactly what you wanted without any effort and without their selecting you?

P-114   No, it, it, uh, it wouldn't be bad. This I, you know, I, this I can, I can logically believe this.

T-115   At *times.*

P-115   Yeah, at times.

T-116   But *most* of the time, more strongly, you still believe the other things——

P-116 Yeah. And somehow I, I don't catch myself saying it to myself.

T-117 That's right.

P-117 It's, it's an old habit pattern of————. I, I mean, you know, I
don't even really know when I say to myself, you know,
"Duck and dodge!"————

T-118 And yet isn't that the value of the symptoms, such as the
sleeping too much————

P-118 Yeah.

T-119 ————and so on: that if you track them down, you'll find that
you must be saying————

P-119 Yeah.

T-120 ————these things to yourself if the symptom is still there?

[The therapist points out that even though at times the patient believes that it is not terrible if he gets refused by a girl, most of the
time he still believes that it *is,* and he is concretely telling himself that
it is. The patient agrees, but points out that he does not clearly see
that he is telling himself catastrophizing sentences. Persistently, however, as is common in this form of psychotherapy, the therapist shows
him that his symptoms prove, behaviorally, that he *must* be telling
himself something along these catastrophizing lines.]

P-120 But the, what I'm saying is that I see it *after* the fact————

T-121 Right.

P-121 After I've gone to sleep [*sort of laughs*] and wake up, I think,
"Oh, oh, it's eight o'clock! You've shot the whole evening,
you know————"

T-122 Yes, but if you————

P-122 "————you goofed!" [*Laughs.*] But————

T-123 All right. But if you clearly see it *after* the fact and keep admitting completely after the fact even, that, "Yes, I still do
have this horrifying idea," won't you get it back to *before* the
fact, in time?

P-123 I guess I will.

T-124 We must perceive that we have the negative notions—the fears and the hostilities and the grandiosities—before we can really get to work on them. And if you can perceive and perceive and perceive them through these symptoms—the lack of sex desire, the oversleeping, and so forth—then you can finally get back and clip them, contradict them, challenge them, kick them in the teeth.

P-124 And also, I must admit, too, that on, on this thing, it's not just the, uh———. Work wise, I'm still working, but not as, uh, it's like in the last two or three weeks there's———. Just everything has sort of like got soft-pedaled.

T-125 Yes.

P-125 Uh, I've done some good work and I haven't. I haven't had too much commercial work coming in, so I've had time to do samples. But, uh, I really haven't done as much work, much samples as I sh—, as I feel that I should for the time I've spent. I haven't found the apartment that I've been saying the, to myself, that I want to get; and I, you know, I don't know how, how much of this is involved with this general, you know, turning off. I think it's a lot of, it's probably just re-sistance in want—, in change. I, I logically know I want to change and, and I'm just not.

T-126 In other words: because you're resisting the change in the sex area, you think you're also resisting doing much in the other areas———?

P-126 Yes.

T-127 A little sit-down strike!

P-127 I'm sort of, yeah———. I'm sort of, you know, uh, just in general procrastinating or even blaming one area for another.

T-128 Yes.

P-128 You know. Like, well, I didn't get the work today, done to-day. So I have to work tonight. Or if that's not the excuse, then I worked too hard today and I'm gonna take a nap or [*laughs*], you know. And it, it, it, I'm, I'm ma—, making a vicious circle I think of, uh———

T-129 So the work and the apartment hunting become another excuse———

P-129 Another dodge, really.

T-130 Yes, for not going out more———

P-130 Um hm.

T-131 ———and encountering the girls and taking the risks—committing yourself.

P-131 That's right.

T-132 But again: What is there to be afraid of? What is John saying to John?

P-132 Basically, I, I think there's, uh, it's a real shy———. I, I, I think———. Or, or not basically, but part of this is that, that when I start thinking about, well, the idea of, you know, going out and meeting people, I start getting (a) financially afraid———

T-133 Yes?

P-133 Because, uh, you know, it's, uh [*sort of laughs*], you know———. So if I might find somebody, I do fall in love and I should wanna get married, who can *afford* it? [*Laughs.*]

T-134 Yes?

P-134 Which is also an excuse and a smoke screen. Because I know a lot of people have afforded on a lot less than I have.

T-135 Right!

P-135 But, uh, and right now something occurred to me———

T-136 Yes?

P-136 Occurs to me is one [*sort of laughs*], I think one of the few pieces of motherly advice I ever got was, "John, don't ever get married, it's a drag!" [*Laughs.*]

T-137 From your mother, literally, you're talking about———?

P-137 Uh huh, uh huh, uh huh. Literally.

T-138 Yes, yes? At, how old were you, do you think, when you got———

P-138 Ah, thirteen or fourteen.

T-139 And was it repeated several times over the years?

P-139 Yes———.

T-140 Um hm.

P-140 This was her general attitude that———. You know, she wasn't real happy with, uh, being a Hausfrau, and she, and she———

T-141 Yes?

P-141 Well, I was told this several times.

T-142 Yes?

P-142 "Don't get married."

T-143 Yes?

P-143 Of course, then they reversed it. And when I got grown and the sud—, then suddenly they decided they wanted grandchildren. It was all reversed and the pressure was on and the———

T-144 Yes?

P-144 My little brother provided the commodity———.

T-145 But the question is: whether her telling you not to get married in itself started souring you, or whether you got soured for other reasons and the entity———

P-145 I think I just grabbed that as something to use.

T-146 Yes.

P-146 Really, that was a good excuse. Mama said it so it was all right———

T-147 That's right. "If it came from the horse's mouth———"

P-147 Yeah.

T-148 "———the mare's mouth, then it must be so. And she didn't have such a great life———"

P-148 Yeah.

T-149 "———so why should I?"

P-149 And also I must, must admit, this is one of the reasons, I think, that so much———. Really, I'm very financially oriented in that sense. Or, or I'm scared shitless [*laughs*] of poverty. Let's face it.

T-150 Maybe that was the more important doctrine they taught you, rather than———

P-150 Yeah.

T-151 ———not to get married: never be bloo———

P-151 But that was involved with it, you see, at the end. I'm sure that at the time that was what, what Mother's bitch was, was, you know. "Don't get married, because I got married and look how poor I am."

T-152 Yes, I see. Yes.

P-152 You see?

T-153 Yes. But then in other respects the—

P-153 And somehow marriage and poverty go together [*laughs*], to me.

T-154 Yes.

P-154 I'm sorry: they just do. [*Still laughing.*]

T-155 But in other respects, too, they would teach you, or she would teach you, that poverty was an awful business———

P-155 Oh, yeah.

T-156 And by all means do everything possible not to be poor, and so on.

P-156 Yeah. and this is why somehow, uh, well———. And even in the, when, when I was growing up, I couldn't date because I never had money, I mean, you know———

T-157 Yes. Right.

P-157 And, and it was very, uh, and we were, you know, sort of in that unfortunate position of being one of the old families in the town with no money.

T-158 Yes.

P-158 And you were expected to take your date to the Country Club or———

T-159 Right.

P-159 At least, I was taught that was what you were expected to do——

T-160 Yes, isn't this the——

P-160 And I couldn't afford it.

T-161 All right. But isn't this the same again: "How, what a shit I, John, would be——"

T-161 Yes.

T-162 "——if I took my date not to the Country Club and took her on a cheap soda date——"

P-162 Yes.

T-163 "——or something like that." Which again is what you were taught: that John should be——

P-163 Yes, yes.

T-164 —the right kind of person.

P-164 That it was going to be all or nothing, and I didn't——

T-165 Yes.

P-165 ——have the all and, but maybe if I, you know, if I saved my money and never got married, I might someday be able to afford [*laughs while saying this*] to take somebody out, you know——

T-166 Yes. It's interesting that, from the beginning to the end of the sequence, the fear exists, that is inculcated. Because it's terrible to take the girl out; to encounter her; to have a date; and not do it right, at the beginning. And at the end of the sequence, it's terrible to be married to her, and be poor, and so on.

P-166 Yes.

T-167 And all along the line, it's terrible, it's awful, it's catastrophic: economically, socially, sexually, and otherwise. What awful things would happen if you didn't do everything just right——

P-167 Yes.

T-168 ———from the beginning to the end of the———

P-168 And the only tra, traps, uh, the trap that I see to that is that you put everything off until you're too old to enjoy it!

T-169 Yes, but you see———

P-169 But you——— [*barely audible*]

T-170 That's exactly the illogic of this position: that it's awful to do this and do that; but they never say that it's awful *not* to do———

P-170 ———what you do do! [*Laughs.*] Yeah, yeah. They don't tell you what it's wonderful to do; that's the problem, you know———

T-171 That's right. And if, assuming it was quite disadvantageous to take a girl out, not be able to take her to the right place, and to marry her and not have enough money, and so on, look how disadvantageous it is to sit on the sideline and to become———

P-171 Yes—

T-172 ———a homosexual and so on. *That* they don't paint the picture of!

P-172 No.

T-173 And as one of my patients keeps saying, in one of my groups: When you do get some of the advantages, it's a bargain, even though you get the disadvantages of life. Because otherwise, without that bargain, you will just get these disadvantages: the lack of———

P-173 Yeah, yeah.

T-174 ———participation which they don't tell you about, they don't emphasize.

[As is usual in rational-emotive psychotherapy, the therapist acts as a frank propagandist for a wiser, saner way of life, and points out that, yes, it may be disadvantageous to take chances, but without risks one is not likely to get some of the main advantages of living. Where other therapists frequently resort to this kind of wise propaganda, too, they often have no proper theoretical grounds on which to do so.

Rational-emotive therapy, however, does contain theoretical constructs which make it appropriate for the therapist to include wise philosophies of life in his reeducating of the patient. This particular patient, incidentally, has half-learned many of the views that the therapist has been previously pointing out to him; and that is partly why he interrupts so frequently with a "Yeah, yeah" response. He sometimes knows what the therapist is going to say before the therapist finishes making his point.]

P-174 That's right. Because, uh, now I think, and that's, that's what, uh, I'm still fighting, you know. I, I've, I've come to realize that, you know. So I've wasted 15 or 20 years————

T-175 Yes.

P-175 On, uh, you know, not wanting to be alone, but being alone definitely.

T-176 Yes.

P-176 But I'm still having to fight the other one: about the economic crap and the "You wouldn't be so good" mess "if you didn't have it." [Laughs.]

T-177 Yes. And it would be disadvantageous. We're not denying that————

P-177 Oh, sure. But—

T-178 But would it be so disadvantageous as your mother made it out and you're making it out to be and so on? It would have—

P-178 No, logically now I realize it wouldn't————.

T-179 Yes?

P-179 I've just got to be able to accept it.

T-180 That's right. Because again, as we said with Susan the other day————

P-180 Yeah.

T-181 She sees logically————

P-181 I'm having that same trouble. I can tell myself the right sentences at the right————

T-182 Yes?

P-182 At the right time, sometimes———

T-183 Yes?

P-183 But I don't really accept them 100% that that's *really* right.

T-184 Yes. And it, and it is true that, as you just said, you tell your-self the right sentences at times. But what are you saying the *other* times?

P-184 Yeah.

T-185 You're saying just the opposite sentences, aren't you? "Oh, my God, isn't this terrible? I can't stand it!"

P-185 Yeah. I'm not even saying the sentences. I'm getting so busy in other areas or mak, or making like I'm so busy, that I guess, uh, you know, back here somewhere I'm saying it———

T-186 That's right.

P-186 But I'm expressing it in work or in, uh, you know, running around———

T-187 Yes, you, we can say the sentences instantaneously———

P-187 Um hm.

T-188 A split second. And then immediately we go on to go to sleep or avoid sex—avoid sex desire in your case, or something like that. But the sentences still seem to be there. The *philosophy* is fundamentally there; because, if it weren't, why would you have to go to sleep? If you really weren't afraid, weren't———

P-188 Yeah. [*Barely audible.*]

T-189 Telling yourself: "Oh, my God, if I encounter the girl, look what'll happen. She may reject me; and finally, if I marry her, I may be poor!" And so on. If you weren't saying that, why would you *have* to use these dodges?

P-189 I wouldn't, you know. [*Laughs.*] This I know: I wouldn't ———.

T-190 Yes.

P-190 If I weren't saying that.

[The therapist, not content with the fact that the patient seems to see that his current sleepiness and his lack of sex desire are dodges to keep him away from the girls he fears, and not content that the patient also now seems to see that he has been using his mother's warnings about poverty as an excuse to stay away from girls, wants to make sure that the patient is most concrete about these insights: That he literally sees the exact sentences that he is telling himself to *cause* this evasive behavior. Because, according to the theory of rational-emotive therapy, if the patient merely sees the effects of his self-sentences, he will have great difficulty changing his behavior; while if he sees the exact sentences that lie behind and cause these effects, he will have a simpler and more definite task in contradicting and challenging these sentences. Then, *while* doing this challenging of his own philosophies, his own internalized sentences, he will find it much more feasible to push himself into action—that is, to force himself to meet girls and to make overtures toward them.]

T-191 Not that the lack of action itself, or the symptom itself, is not important: because you see that repropagandizes you further. You say the sentences, then you start———

P-191 And then I say, "I'm not doing anything!" and that makes it worse.

T-192 That's right. You start blaming yourself for falling asleep or evading the sex desire, or so on. And round and round you go! [*Bell rings and T starts taking off the microphone that is held by a cord around his neck, so that he can answer the doorbell*]

P-192 Don't pull your head off! [*Laughs while saying this.*]

T-193 Yes. I got to take this lavalier off and go answer the bell.

P-193 You need a longer string! [*Laughs.*]

T-194 [*Says something inaudible, because he is away from the microphone; then returns and puts on the microphone again.*]

P-194 Now that's the upsetting thing about———. Somewhere I can, I can see logic or illogic, when other people are talking sometime, you know. Not, not infallibly; but I can talk myself into the most delightfully logical circles [*laughs*], you know; and I can't catch the flaw.

T-195 You *don't* catch it; not you *can't* catch it.

P-195 I don't. Well, yeah, I don't catch the flaw. I don't see it. Yeah——

T-196 And isn't that where the work mainly gives up——?

P-196 Yeah.

T-197 ——where you don't go after catching the flaw? You know something is wrong pretty quickly, because you go to sleep or something like that too much. But then, instead of doing the work at *John,* as we said before, you start saying: "Well, let's see, what am I going to do about the other kind of work?"——

P-197 Yeah. And "I'd like, I ought go out tonight. But where am I going to go?" This is——

T-198 Yes.

P-198 ——this is one of my standard sentences——.

T-199 Yes.

P-199 That I, that I've got to learn how to say: "Well," you know, "go anywhere!" [*Laughs.*] You know: "Go ride the subway for two hours if you want to go out——"

T-200 But that "I *ought* to go out tonight, where am I going to go?" is what I call against the grain, because the grain is still underneath——

P-200 Yeah.

T-201 "Jesus Christ! What a horror it would be if I *did* go out——"

P-201 Yeah.

T-202 "——and did finally marry the girl!" And so on. And that grain has to be worked on. And it's more important, in many respects, to work on that grain than the second grain of "Let's see the actual technique of going out," and so on, which you still have to do.

[The therapist is still doggedly trying to get the patient to tackle his basic *philosophy,* his self-sentences, that create his block against seeing girls, rather than merely to help him acquire techniques of seeing them.]

P-202   Yes. Well, actually I, you know————. I, I suppose, you can't————. The prob, part of the problem, too, is you can't just say, "Well, I'm going to do this and then I'm going to do that." You have to be doing them both at the same time and being sure that, that what one is and what the other is.

T-203   Yes. And as you said————

P-203   Grain one and grain two in, in this case, for me I think have to come at pretty much hand in hand.

T-204   Right, that's right. And, and————

P-204   I've got to work at it, while I'm, I'm thinking about it. But I have to start thinking more logically about which is, which is which————.

T-205   Yes. And be aware, as you just said a minute ago, to be aware, to become aware, to perceive what you're doing on *both* levels: on the inactivity with the girls and the inactivity with *John*— the not looking at your own internal verbalizations, your own sentences, which are so, so important. The goofing, most of it in a sense, is right there.

P-205   Yeah.

T-206   And it isn't an *inability* to look at it. It isn't that it's deeply buried and unconscious. You *could;* but you're not making the effort there. You're slurring it over and saying, "Well, I fell asleep again. Isn't that fascinating!"————

P-206   Yeah. [*Laughs.*]

T-207   Something like that.

P-207   "I wonder what causes this?" [*Laughs.*]

T-208   Yes, but no real attempt to *find out!*

P-208   Yeah, yeah, yeah.

T-209   And, on theory, you should *know* what causes it. Because there must be some crappy internalized sentence there: some fear or grandiosity or something like that.

P-209 I think it's more in terms of grandiosity than fear; although they, I'm sure, they mean the same thing when you really work it back.

T-210 Yes. They're the other side to the same coin sometimes.

P-210 Yes. But I, I have much more of a tendency to take the grandiose side than, than————. Like I really basically, I don't think I feel that I'm a pretty shitty individual. I think I have more of a tendency to think, "I'm the grandest little thing that, that ever hit the earth." I mean————.

T-211 Yes?

P-211 You know: "Why doesn't everybody recognize me?" [*Laughs while saying this.*]

T-212 Yes, that's right.

P-212 You know. Like somebody asked me one time, "What would you like to do?" What would I really like to do? And I said, "I'd like to, if I were completely honest, the thing I would like most to be would be sort of the darling of, of, of the social world." You know————

T-213 Yes.

P-213 This is a very grandiose attitude. And I, you know, it's, it's not going to happen just by wanting it.

T-214 Yes!

P-214 You know, and I————. And I, I, even looking at it, I, I know it's a pretty crappy thing to shoot for. But if I just, you know, if wishes were horses, and that was the wish I would make up, that would probably be it! [*Laughs while saying this.*]

T-215 Right.

P-215 Until I learn how to; or until I catch myself and, and change.

T-216 Yes. But the two are related. Because the reason you have to be the darling of the world is because you————

P-216 Is to prove that I'm not bad! You know————

T-217 ————you're not. Yes, you're saying, "I'm a piece of shit."

P-217 Yeah.

T-218 "Either I'm the darling of the world. Or I'm utter zero, crap!" See? and are *either* of those things true————?

P-218 No.

T-219 Are you *really* a piece of shit, if you're not the darling of the world?

P-219 No. But you see, what I'm, the————. When I'm alone, just working with myself, I cannot worry about whether I'm being accepted or not accepted, because I can get very absorbed in what I'm working at.

T-220 Yes?

P-220 And that, that is, it's a very pleasant little dodge: get busy so that you don't have to think about it————

T-221 Yes, it has advantages in its own right————.

P-221 Yes.

T-222 If it weren't *all* of your life.

P-222 Yes.

T-223 But if you intend to make it all of your life————

P-223 Yes. I don't turn it off after the first eight hours, and then go out and do something else————.

T-224 That's right. There are other aspects—such as the social relations, the girls, and so forth. And they would become rewarding, these other aspects, if you gave them the chance as you've given the being alone.

P-224 Um hm.

T-225 Which, incidentally, several months ago you weren't giving that much of a chance————.

P-225 No, no. I didn't, I didn't like that so much. Now, now I've gotten to where I even fight to be alone a lot.

T-226 Yes.

P-226 Uh, very selfishly. I have one friend, Wayne, who, I must admit, he's a divine friend to have because he's, he's loaded. He loves to take you out and spend all the money———— [*laughs while saying this.*]

T-227 Yes.

P-227 ———take you to the best restaurants and the theater and all this, because he's scared shitless of being alone.

T-228 I see.

P-228 You know, and, and when I first met Wayne it was through Carl. And, and, uh, uh, he knew that Carl and I had had several fallings out. He liked me, and I said, "Look, Wayne, there's, you know, I'm through with guys [*laughs*], no hanky-panky involved. I know your game, but if you want somebody, go pick on some other little boy———"

T-229 Yes.

P-229 "———I'll be glad to see you on occasion." And, uh, it's gotten to the point where Wayne calls every night and wants to go somewhere and do something. Got divine plans. And I've just had to learn how to say, "No, I'm sorry." He can help me very much business-wise, too, which is one of the reasons that I, I really feel I, I don't want to drop that contact———.

T-230 Yes.

P-230 But I'm not interested in him sexually, and he knows it. And as long as he wants to buy my company, that's fine and dandy by me———. [*Laughs while saying this.*]

T-231 You have———

P-231 It does take away from the time of going out and meeting girls, I must admit.

T-232 But you have learned to say, "I'm sorry," and not feel———

P-232 Um.

T-233 ———"Oh, my God, this is terrible! He may not love me!"

[The therapist emphasizes that the patient is improving in this respect, since this has been one of the patient's main problems, with all kinds of people: that he has not been able to say no to them when they have asked him to do various things for or with them.]

P-233 No. In fact, uh, last night or night before last, he had invited

me to dinner and, uh, I thought we were going out to dinner.
And I—he said, meet him at the apartment, and I was there
and there were four or five people there. Boys. And the party
got to looking like it was going to wind up with everybody,
you know, going to bed with each other. And this wasn't for
me. So I just calmly got up and put my coat on and said, "I
have to be at home by midnight, because I've got to get up
early in the morning." Which was, you know. And I found
this very easy to do————.

T-234   Yes. You weren't catastrophizing————

P-234   And I'm finding that I can, can, uh, you know————. So that
it's *their* problem, if, if, if they can't accept the fact that I'm
going to do what I wanna do!

T-235   All right. There you were *not* saying, "If they can't accept it,
I, John, am, am a piece of shit!" You *weren't* saying that this
time————

P-235   No, no. And I found that in that area I've been, you
know————. That's an area that I know well enough that I
know I can turn my back on it, and to heck with it!

T-236   Now, why can't you do the same thing with girls? If you
could say, "If she doesn't accept me————"

P-236   Yeah. Well, this is exactly what I keep saying: "Now why
can't I reverse the procedure?" [*Laughs while saying this.*]
But I'm not doing it.

T-237   But obviously *in theory* you're able to. Because————

P-237   Yes.

T-238   ————if you used to be afraid of people like this—what they
thought of you if you refused them something; and saying,
"Jesus Christ, that proves I'm no good!"—and you're not doing that now, you can certainly do exactly the same thing with
girls: where you still are afraid, "If they reject me————"

P-238   Yes. [*Barely audible.*]

T-239   "————or if they ask too much money or something from me
and I can't bear up, I'm a piece of shit." That's the same basic
thing, isn't it————?

[Educationally, as is often done empirically but without theoretical rationale by other kinds of therapists, the rational-emotive therapist logically tries to show the patient that if he can change his internalized sentences and thereby conquer his fear of what other people think of him in one area, where he had previously had considerable trouble, then he can certainly do so in this other area, his relationships with girls.]

P-239 Yes, it really is. Well, as, as a lot of it has to do with practice, in the area with them I'm getting the practice of saying no.

T-240 You're beginning to.

P-240 I'm beginning to.

T-241 You weren't a few months ago?

P-241 No. But I mean within the last two or three weeks.

T-242 Right.

P-242 Or since this Carl thing. And I decided I was through with all that crap.

T-243 Yes.

P-243 I'm finding that it's very easy to do, or not. But it's not difficult to say——

T-244 Right.

P-244 ——exactly what I want and what I intend to do.

T-245 Yes.

P-245 And, you know, let the *world* adjust to it! [*Laughs while saying this.*]

T-246 Now if you can do that with, with them, why can't you do it with girls? And you'll find some who get high, highly insulted and won't take you the way you are. Which is tough! But you'll find others who will.

P-246 Now, I'm sure that's true. I don't, I guess there's basically, there's always been this thing, too: that I, I've never really accepted that females were, that girls were, were not different from men——

T-247 Yes.

P-247 Very different————

T-248 Yes.

P-248 You know, it's, it's, the————. I've always assumed that women reacted to everything differently————

T-249 Yes, I see.

P-249 I've never taken the trouble to really find out that they don't————

T-250 They're all human beings————

P-250 That they want sex as much as men want sex————

T-251 That's, that's right————

P-251 And that they, you, you know————

T-252 And they are human beings at bottom.

P-252 Yes. And I've never accepted that. It sort————. They were always like a little goddess somewhere. [*Laughs while saying this.*]

T-253 Yes, that's right.

P-253 And, uh————

T-254 Which is probably what your mother tried to get you to believe, or something along that line.

[The therapist brings up the past, from time to time, not to dwell on it in a psychoanalytic manner or to over-emphasize its influence, but merely to show the patient that his present beliefs originally were imbibed from his parents and others in his past life, and that he now can see this and question and challenge these beliefs.]

P-254 And even now I find that difficult to, to, uh, just be myself—in the sense that, that it's just another human being————

T-255 Yes.

P-255 I'm talking to, not something special and big, you know————

T-256 Yes.

P-256 ————big deal.

T-257 It *is* possible.

P-257 Yes. I, I can see———

T-258 Accept on that level———

P-258 Logically, that it's possible for me to work on being———

T-259 To *work* on, you say.

P-259 Yeah.

T-260 Yeah!

P-260 To really work on! [*Laughs.*]

T-261 Yes, to really *work* on.

P-261 On, on just accepting women as people and not women as some special thing.

T-262 Want to hear some of this [*tape recording of the session*] back?

P-262 Yes.

[In sum: The therapist, using material that the patient brought up during the session, quite deliberately tried to structure the interview so that the patient would see and admit (*a*) that he was evading really going with girls, even though he said he wanted to give up his homosexual behavior and to have a try at heterosexuality; (*b*) that behind his evasions lay a clearcut catastrophizing philosophy of life, concretely embodied in the internalized sentences, "Wouldn't it be terrible if I made attempts to relate to girls and they rejected me! What a thoroughly worthless individual I would then be!"; (*c*) that some of his attitudes toward going with females were originally indoctrinated by his mother, who was herself somewhat embittered against marriage; (*d*) that, because of his general fear of failure, he has been ceaselessly reiterating his early-acquired attitudes and using them as an excuse for his continuing avoidance of heterosexual relationships; (*e*) that he doesn't have to be afraid of standing up for his own desires and saying no to either males or females, and that if he keeps making progress in being decisive with males, as he has been doing, he will help himself to be more daring and more decisive with girls; (*f*) that there is nothing very special about females, in that they are a regular part of the human race, and he can be just as easy-going and relaxed with them, and accept possible rejections by them, as he is now learning to be with males; and (g) that there is no magic about his tackling his social-sexual problems and becoming less of a patsy and more of an individualist: the main thing is that he must keep working and working, by challenging his own internalized sentences and by taking active plunges into new patterns of behavior, until he begins to find it easy to think and act in the heterosexual and uncatastrophizing ways that he is aiming for.

[Following the fifteenth session, the transcript of which has just been reviewed, the patient was mainly seen for once-a-week group therapy sessions. He came in for the eighteenth individual interview seven months later, largely to report that he had been having regular intercourse with a girl for the previous two months, and at first had done very well, but more recently was not always able to get an erection. Quite obviously, this was because, after a couple of failures, he began worrying about failing again; and, like any normal heterosexual male, the more he worried, the more he failed. When this was explained to him, and he began to examine his own catastrophizing sentences, he quickly saw how he was defeating himself, and immediately thereafter he began to be unusually potent. He later stopped seeing this particular girl, but he started an affair with a married woman who had previously had a good many lovers, none of whom proved very satisfactory to her. She found John exceptionally satisfying sexually, since he was able to copulate for an hour or more at a time and to maintain an erection even after he had had an orgasm. Excerpts from his eighteenth session follow.]

T-1   It is very obvious that you are quite capable of getting an erection and maintaining it; there is no question about that, but when you think you are not, then you are not.

P-1   Yes.

T-2   And it is the thought, "I'm not, I'm not, I'm not, I'm not," which is killing.

P-2   Do you think I need to concentrate on the object and not on the method?

T-3   That's right—on *what* you are doing, instead of *how* you are doing. This is the essence of success in almost any motor task because, here, just think of a guy driving an automobile and he starts thinking of something, you know, "Am I driving this well, am I going to hit that car over there?" You know, "I might get into an accident———"

P-3   This is a part of my life, I do this in everything I do.

T-4   Well, all right, that's the point.

P-4   In dancing, today in ice skating, everything I've ever tried.

T-5   Well, that's the point. It's *how* you are doing instead of *what* you are doing that you are focusing on, and that kills it. Almost any motor task will fall apart at the seams.

P-5   Well, at least, you know—well, good, at least I don't feel as if I'm absolutely, you know, an oddball about this.

T-6   No, the only thing we can say is maybe physiologically you have less of a tendency to get easily erect than somebody else, but more of a tendency to stay erect once you are erect.

P-6   Yes. Once I'm erect, you know, actually I have gone all night without losing an erection and being pretty active, you know, the whole time.

T-7   All right, that's rather phenomenal, that's very unusual.

P-7   But as I say, sometimes it takes forever to get me there, you know.

T-8   Well you're not really trying to get there. You are trying to watch yourself get there, worrying about getting there. And if you can see how you are worrying and say, "Look, none of this shit, back to the issue which is—look how enjoyable this thing is." Not—"Look, what a great guy I'll be if I satisfy her; but how enjoyable it is." And I don't see any doubt whatsoever that you will remain quite potent.

P-8   I don't think it's even that, the panic isn't the fact how great she is going to think I am. At least I don't think it is, well consciously. "Look, if you don't perform you are going to lose this whole situation." You know.

T-9   You either do this or you lose it.

P-9   That's what panics me more than really thinking whether she thinks I'm the greatest lover she has ever had, because really I couldn't care less.

T-10   That's right. As Laura [*a member of his group*] said tonight, it's still the P.O.S. [*piece of shit*] in back of it all.

P-10   At least I've made a big step forward. I feel as if I've made a big step forward since, you know, a year ago.

T-11   Yes, there's no question, you are going steadily with this girl and generally you are enjoying her. And most of the hassle that you thought would exist has not really come to bear—has it?

P-11   No. I feel fine. Sometimes I put myself in the position, you know, ultimately, like forcing her to be aggressive at times, and this is an old trick.

T-12   Yes, the old trick. You used to do that even with boys.

P-12   Yes, always. I don't think I ever in my life approached a guy, except putting myself in the location where it was obvious the guy was there to be picked up.

T-13   Yes, so you are still up to some of your old tricks, but there has been considerable improvement.

P-13   Yes, I think so and I feel better about it. Also in this funny relationship—I took a few nights ago, not a few nights ago but a week before Christmas, during the week before Christmas. Carol and I had gone to a backers' audition and had dinner and came to my house; and we got there and Don was there (this boy who is staying "temporarily" with me and I finally told him the other day to, you know, find an apartment). Don was there and you know we spoke to him and he was watching TV in the living room and we quietly went into the bedroom and sat and talked for a while, you know, thinking that Don would get the hint and go back to his room and he can take the TV 'cause its portable. But it didn't seem to make any difference and he stayed there for about half an hour and finally, you know, I feel good about this, I finally walked into the living room and I said, "Don, Carol and I are going to bed, and will you please go into the bedroom," which I don't think I would have been able to do a long time ago, you know, at least I've gotten over this, especially since the fact that he is gay, you know.

T-14   That's right. So you were able to face that.

P-14   Yes. I think now I've gotten to the point where, you know, what other people do is their business and I've got to worry about me.

T-15   How are you doing as far as the boys are concerned—do they bother you? Do you have trouble?

P-15   No. I really haven't. I still see quite a few of the boys, you know, people who were particularly friends (T: Yes), but maybe at one time had a little sex thing with but it never built up. (T: Yes). And I've made no bones about it, that I'm interested in meeting girls and I have a girl that I am going with and for this reason I'm not being bothered. It has made a, I noticed at Christmas I wasn't invited to nearly as many Christmas parties because all the gay ones were no longer inviting me to their parties, which is good. I was really glad of this, it sort of automatically removed its own temptation to go to the party. But it's never a problem here, you know. Just by opening my mouth and saying the wrong word, I've fought that. But they can either like me or not depending on their personality, but it's not my problem whether they worry about what I do in bed.

T-16   And as long as you keep making it with Carol or some other girl you are not going to go around being obsessed with making it with boys.

P-16   Well, actually, you know, as I say, I think, really to be perfectly honest, I think it was a combination of what was the easiest target and habit.

T-17   Yes, the one that you had to be less aggressive with.

P-17   Yes.

T-18   They pick you up and they take the role, and there was nothing much to be lost.

P-18   Because, let's face it, you know, in fact it was very funny———. Carol knows this background and she knows a lot of my friends and she knows I've gotten through this gay bit; and fortunately, I'd come out and tell her. But at one point she asked me, having met some of the guys I knew and wondering, and I didn't lie about it and I told her the truth. Anyhow the other night, well Carol was in her period and we were, you know, making love and wanting to go to bed and she said, "Well, I don't know whether you'll want to," and I said "Why?" And she said, "Well, I'm in my period." Well frankly, I've never had any experience with anybody in her period and I said "Does that mean you can't screw," because I didn't know, honestly. And she said, "No, silly, usually when a woman is in her period she is hotter than other times, but it is messy," And I said, sort of laughing, "I've gotten covered with shit, who cares about a little blood?" So, fine and dandy, we went to bed and frankly I felt that was one of the most pleasurable evenings. It really didn't bother me.

[The patient, John, was seen for several months more in group psychotherapy, and then quit the group because he wanted to try things on his own. He had continued, up to this time, to make considerable progress with his work; was much less passive in his business and social relations; and was making steady progress in his heterosexual relations. A year after he had finished with psychotherapy, his current girlfriend was seen by the therapist, since she had some problems of her own. She reported that the sex relationship with him, as well as their general relationship, was quite satisfactory, and that he was proving to be a much better lover than any of her previous boyfriends had been.]

chapter 7

*Verbatim Transcript of
Recorded Psychotherapy
Sessions with a Married Male
Compulsively Addicted to
Homosexuality—Part I*

~~~~~~~~~~~~~~~~~~~~~~~~~~~~~~~~~~~

First Session

T-1 Make yourself comfortable. What is your problem?

P-1 I've got a terrible problem right now. The one before that was
the cause of this, I guess. I'm out on felonious assault and on
bail of five hundred dollars. And I'm really very innocent, and
I've got to find some way to think because I'm going crazy
about what's happened. The cause of this is homosexuality.
I've been that way all my life and I've been trying to treat it;
but I guess I've been treating it in the wrong manner. I
thought I could do it by myself—I was a pretty strong person.
I got in trouble once before and my wife said that I ought to
get some male hormones. So I went to this Dr. Josephson, and
I went through a whole operation. He laid me down and his
nurse was there, and I went through this operation. And he
talked to me, and that seemed to help me. The whole thing is,
I've been trying to fight it and I haven't. I'd get this little
quirk which I couldn't control. That's what I'm really here
for: so when I have the urge, how to control it. I don't feel
like I'm in my right mind. I feel like I'm insane.

T-2 Who referred you to me?

P-2 Well, do I have to tell you?

T-3 No, it isn't necessary. I just normally like to know.

P-3   One of your patients. And I don't like them to know. Nobody
        knows I'm this way. I've been married twice. I've always
        wanted to live a normal life, but I always felt there was some-
        thing wrong with me. I always felt immature and not under-
        standing.

T-4   How old are you now?

P-4   Fifty-one. [*Pause.*] I'm in terrible trouble. I've caused my wife
        such anxiety. That's what it is. I don't care about myself.
        [*Sighs.*] She's not a very well woman. She has diabetes. I'm
        afraid she's going to have a heart attack.

T-5   How long have you been married to her?

P-5   Nineteen years.

T-6   How long were you married to your first wife?

P-6   About two years. She died of tuberculosis. We were very
        happy. I wasn't so bad while my first marriage lasted. Then a
        lot of trouble started. But I can go back, and I was always
        kind of effeminate. I was always attracted to men's bodies.
        When I was a young boy I used to look at men's penises, when
        I'd go swimming or something. And I just didn't pay any
        attention to it. I didn't want to accept it—that I was that way.
        [*Sighs and pauses.*] Now, even, I never look at a woman. Well,
        sometimes I do look at a woman, if she has a good figure; or,
        but now the first thing I look at———. It's like a habit now:
        the first thing. But since this time, I've been fighting it; I
        don't do it. Oh, I know if I can just get out of this, I think
        I'll be helped so much! I feel I've been punished so greatly for
        it.

T-7   I'm sure we can get you out of it—if you *work* at it. Now,
        what do you look at first? You said the first thing you look
        at—is what?

P-7   You mean, passing in the street?

T-8   Yes.

P-8   Passing?

T-9   Yes.

P-9   Oh, a man's penis; the shadow of his penis. [*Sighs.*] Then, when I did have these affairs with men, I really didn't enjoy it. I very often didn't get an erection; I was scared of it.

T-10   Where did you meet them—in bars and all?

P-10   No, I never go to a bar. I don't drink. I'd meet them in the street or in a subway. Somebody would look at me. I'd never try to force anybody. If they would like me, I would. Believe me, Doctor, I'm telling you the absolute truth. It's very hard for me to come here and pay you all this money. I'm a remedial reading teacher, and I'm in terrible debt already with my lawyer. So I want you to know I'm telling you the exact truth.

T-11   All right. Now when did you first get into trouble?

P-11   [*Pauses.*] Oh, it was about two years ago.

T-12   What happened then?

P-12   Well, I was walking in the park, and there was a young man there and we both were attracted to each other. And we were looking for a place. And then two plainclothesmen got a hold of us, and they said, "Why don't you go home? Why do you do it out here in the open?"

T-13   Did they book you for anything then?

P-13   Yes, they arrested me; and I was just in jail overnight, and they let me go. I just paid a five dollar fine.

T-14   All right. Since then, there have been no difficulties until the present time?

P-14   Oh, I had one the time my wife—. She never knew about this one.

T-15   When did she find out?

P-15   [*Sighs.*] Well, one time I was walking along with some young fellow that I know—like me, a homosexual. And we happened to see some man sitting there, and he was very attracted to him and he said, "Let's go over and talk to him." He seemed to be lonely, sitting alone; so we went over and the other boy said, "Do you want to come with us?" and all that. I don't remember exactly what was said, but that was the idea of it. So he came with us. And then I had my car with us; and then we drove uptown; and then he went with the other fellow and I went home. I didn't think he cared about me; I was too old.

The next day I received a phone call from him. He said he wanted to see me. I said, "Oh, you want to see me? I didn't think you cared much about me. You seemed to be much more interested in my friend." He said, "Oh, I don't like young boys; I like men like you." So we made a date and he invited me in for a drink; and I went in, just to be sociable. And he said, "What will we do?" And I said, "Well, let's go do it." He said, "Shall we go to a hotel?" And I said, "O.K." And he professed to be very tired and all that; and I was tired and I said, "We won't do anything; we'll just lay in bed and play around." I was attracted to the man's body. And I said, "Let's go have something to eat; then we'll go to a show or something." I felt I was glad to be with somebody. I don't know if I was feeling lonely or I just like to feel close to a man for a particular time. And just as I was getting dressed, he said, "You're under arrest."

Now this is very important, Doctor, because it's the basis of what happened this last time. I said, "Please don't." I said, "I've got a wife and if she ever finds out, she'll feel terrible." I said, "Of course, I should have thought of all this before." [Sighs.] He took out my wallet and he examined it and looked at it; and I said, "Please, you can have everything I've got; but please give me this one chance." He said, "Well, my friend needs a suit." I said, "I'll give you the money for that." I saw what he meant, and we went into my drug store. This hotel was on 96th street; and we walked over to my drug store, where I dealt, where they knew me very well. And I asked them if they'd lend me twenty dollars, which they did. And all the time he was standing outside; and all this time I thought he was a cop. And he said, "Now, don't you say anything about this or you'll get killed. Don't you say anything." He took me around the side. "Now come on, I'm going to take you in the car." Much later I said, "I'd appreciate it if you'll let me go."

Then five days later I received a call from him. It just happened, we had this apartment where I taught remedial reading; and my wife was in the back, and we had an extension phone. And he said, "I understand you told all about me." And I was so embarrassed—I was teaching at the time—and I said, "I did not." And he said, "Well, I'm coming up and I need some money; I'm broke." And I said, "What do you mean, you need some money? I gave you all I could." And I was so frightened by it, my wife finding out. All the time she was listening. And she came in and said, "What's this all about?" And I told her about it; and he came up, and she came after him, and she said, "You get out of here!" And he got scared and ran away.

T-16 All right; now how did that relate to the present situation?

P-16 Well, I was on my way home and I had to urinate. Very often I don't go; I try to stay away from things that———.

T-17 When was this? How long ago?

P-17 Last Wednesday. It was a little after four, or a quarter to five. And I went into the urinal and there were two men standing there. There were three urinals, one on the right and one on the left. There was the man on the right, showing his penis; he had an erection. And after I entered he left. And I urinated; and I saw this man still standing there, and he was a very attractive, strong-looking man. So after this I said———. I don't ordinarily do a thing like that. I don't really like it, believe me. I just feel like I want to touch it. I don't know if it's what I want to do or what.

So I said to him, "Would you come to my place? I'll suck you." I thought, "I don't like to do that, believe me." But I do it. I just play with it a little while and I give them some money and I run. And I said, "Do you want to come?" And he just looked around. And I just finished up and went over to wash my hands. And I saw he was still there, and so I thought he was interested. He struck me as being one of my kind. So I said, "Come on; come on." And as I touched his penis, and as I was just about to go, he came back and he said, "You're under arrest." I said, "Let me go, let me go!" I mean, I got hysterical. He was holding me up, because I never thought———.

For a moment, as I say, when I get that way I'm not in my right mind. Something happens to me. I love my wife, we have a beautiful home. My wife couldn't have any children. My students all love me; they're all my children. I love people. When he said that to me, I said, "I'll give you all my money; don't hurt me!" I was just resisting him. It was fear. It was a shock. And he kept thinking I was trying to fight him. In fact, in the case he said that I scruffed him. I was scared to death of him. Believe me, I was horrified. So after he turned me loose, another one came along and he punched me and twisted my arm.

Of course, I may have aggravated this condition by just resisting them, and they thought that I was trying to fight them. And so they just hurt me more and more. And the more they hurt me, the more I thought that they weren't policemen. So they pulled me out, and as they pulled me out I kept yelling for help. I thought I was being mugged and they were kidnapping me. And they pulled me out and they had my hands in handcuffs. Even though he showed me his badge, I didn't believe it was a real badge; I just thought it was a fake. I mean, after all, I didn't do anything. The man I thought was like me—I didn't try to seduce him in any way.

I kept resisting; and as we came on the cop on the beat there, I was in such a state of mind I even thought he was a fake. He didn't look like a policeman to me. So he said, "All right!" He stood there, and when they tried to get me into a car, and I saw a police car, I started yelling for help. And the men—there was a little garage across the street, and they all said they heard me—so they took me into the car and I said, "So they didn't believe me. Now they're calling me pickpocket and all that." So the other one, not the one who arrested me, but the other one, punched me so hard that he knocked me on the shoulder of the other fellow. He said, "I suppose the handcuffs aren't tight enough. Do you want me to tighten them more?" I could barely move my wrist. So I said, "I'm sorry. I really thought you were."

I was apologetic and I was as nice as I could be; and they took me in the police station. Oh, yes: and while I yelled for help the cop came along and got into the car with us. And by that time I became fully convinced, so I just gave way. Then when we came into the police station, he said, "Get up there!"

And he kicked me and I fell down and hurt my knee. And he kept pushing his thumbs in my temple, near my eyes. And I said, "I'm a teacher; these are my life to me. I can't work again if you gouge out my eyes." And they were very humiliating. They said the most awful things to me. They called me sissy and all that. Just like when I was a boy, I'd get with the boys and I'd get so beaten up, just to be a boy.

Then they put me in jail; and I got this lawyer. And he said that my wife—he was sympathetic—he said my wife was all wrong. She said, "Why don't you get a nice boy?" And I said, "I don't want that." I said, "If I want that, I could easily have it." But instead I had this quirk; I was a tramp, I was a pervert.

T-18 How have your sex relations with your wife been?

P-18 Well, recently they haven't been too good. At one time, they were very good.

T-19 You enjoyed your sex relations with her?

P-19 Yes. My wife was pregnant; she had a miscarriage. We were looking forward to having a baby. She has had a very hard life.

T-20 How old is she?

P-20 My age.

T-21 What does she do?

P-21 She was a school teacher, and now she teaches remedial reading. We both do the same thing.

T-22 Do you get along all right in your work?

P-22 Oh, very well. We love each other.

T-23 Do you have friends?

P-23 Everybody's my friend.

T-24 Well, you've had this quirk—as you've rightly called it—for a long time; and probably the quirk relates to your feelings of inadequacy about your manhood. I don't think it's necessarily sexual—because sexually you seem to enjoy your wife. And did you have good sex relations with your first wife?

P-24   Yes.

T-25   And you don't seem to get much pleasure out of the sex with
these males. But your problem is that you hate yourself so
much. You feel inadequate, and you believe erroneously that
getting close to some strong male with a big penis or something will make you more adequate. And it won't, of course,
do anything of the sort. Ironically enough, you're pursuing
the path of weakness, and you're construing or believing it is
strength. But it's not strength; and this idea that you have in
your head—this completely irrational idea—is the thing that's
motivating you, and that's going to make things much worse.

The thing that's made it completely worse is the second idea
that you have—after you've done the first thing—that you're
a louse, that you're no goddamn good, for doing this sort of
thing. And you're blaming yourself all the time for doing it;
and the blame is causing you to become compulsive. The reason you do it compulsively is *because* of the blame. Whenever
a person blames himself for anything he does, then he starts
doing it more rather than less. Blame does *not* stop you from
doing things. You're horribly guilty, and have been so for
years about this thing. And there's nothing to be guilty about.
You should have gone years ago—as your lawyer said—and
just got cured of it, which would have been relatively easy at
the time. It's merely an obsession now.

[The therapist jumps in, just as soon as he can with this verbose and
highly upset patient, to try to show him what some of the roots of his
homosexual compulsion are. Although he at this point knows relatively little about the patient, and may therefore be guessing wrongly,
his therapeutic theory tells him that when people behave the way in
which this patient has been behaving, they normally do so because
they have deepseated feelings of inadequacy that drive them in this
direction. Then, when their self-condemnation produces a negative
symptom, such as compulsive homosexuality, they berate themselves
mercilessly for having this unpleasant symptom—and they thereby
become more compulsive. The therapist sees no reason why he should
not quickly show this to the patient, in the hope that giving him this
kind of an understanding of his problem may work, and he may
rapidly be set on the road to recovery.

[If the therapist proves to be wrong about the cause of the patient's problem, or if he proves to be right and the patient does not accept his interpretation, he may then change his interpretation, or at least drop it temporarily. But since he is trying to save the patient's time and money, and to save him as much misery as possible, he takes the chance that his therapeutic theory is correct, and he makes direct interpretations immediately. What is more, he directly starts *teaching* the patient what he is doing to upset himself, so that he can then swiftly teach him how *not* to do what he is doing. The therapist also feels that a good deal of repetition may be necessary before his interpretations, if correct, sink in and are used by the patient; and sees no reason why this repetition should not start right away.]

P-25   Believe me, Dr. Ellis, it finally reached me. It hit me on the head that what I was doing————. [*Pause.*]

T-26   That what you were doing was *what*?

P-26   Well, first of all, it was against the law—the way I was doing things.

T-27   Yes, it was silly. It isn't that you've done anything wicked.

P-27   But I've done things stupid.

T-28   You've done things stupidly—that's right. You've screwed yourself.

[The therapist is trying to make the point that the patient's *behavior* has been silly and stupid; but that *he,* as a total individual, is not necessarily stupid. Also: that even if the patient has behaved stupidly, he is not wicked, not a louse, for so behaving, and need not excoriate himself—again, as a total individual—for this ineffective activity. The patient, however, verbosely tends to sidetrack the therapist from vigorously making these points.]

P-28   The trouble is that I was too unintelligent about it. Another thing that happened. After my wife died I was—my first wife was killed in an accident—I got a terrible shock. And we were married fairly young. I was teaching reading at the time, but my lessons were all falling down. I don't know whether it was because I wasn't putting in the enthusiasm that I should, or

what. I got into this school, where all teachers were, and I got
into it big. And my first experience was some man that invited
me down, another teacher invited me down for a drink. He
took me to his place.

T-29 How old were you at the time?

P-29 Oh, I must have been about 23 or so.

T-30 Yes.

P-30 All this time, I felt there was something missing in my life.

T-31 Well, there is something missing in your life—that is self-
respect.

P-31 Yes.

T-32 Yes, and you've gone after it the wrong way. You've gone
after the love of others, rather than your own self-respect.
That's what this is: it's a seeking after approval, after love.

[Again, the therapist tries to interrupt the patient's facile flow, to get
in some interpretation of the philosophic *basis* of his disturbance, so
that he can then induce the patient to *attack* his underlying irrational
ideas that he *needs* the love and respect of others before he can possibly accept himself.]

P-32 Why is it in just only this particular thing? Because I think
I'm a very excellent teacher. I've gotten some excellent results.
People have commented on me, and how much I've helped
them in their lives and————.

T-33 Well, what happened when this fellow took you to his place?

[Probably an error on the therapist's part here. Instead of following
up on the patient's question about why he particularly showed his
feelings of inadequacy by trying to win and identify with strong-
looking men, when he could have compensated much better by convincing himself what a great teacher he was, the therapist goes back
for more information and asks about the specific first sexual encounter. Actually, in rational-emotive psychotherapy much historical
information can be dispensed with; and asking it of an over-talky
patient, such as the patient in this case, is often a risky and wasteful

procedure. But the therapist thinks that perhaps he can get some useful information to use later by finding out about this first homosexual encounter; so he encourages the patient to talk about it.]

P-33   He took me to his place and we laid down, and he had given me a few drinks. And at the time I started drinking, I didn't care. I took a few drinks to relax. So I just laid down and relaxed and all that. And he started playing with my penis; and I thought, "I don't know. He just likes that." And then he went down on me and I was horrified. "How can he do that sort of thing to me?" I was so horrified. I was so—he disillusioned me so. You may not believe me, Doctor, but that's what I said. He said, "Oh, no," he said, "I'm just wetting it, before I jerk it." Then after that he never came near me; and we were friendly, we were nice and friendly.

I know his name, but I won't say it. I see him occasionally, and all that. And then I was in there, and I got more and more intimate. But even before that, I was always searching for something. I used to get these math lessons, away out in Brooklyn. And I'd walk and walk for miles, searching for something—I don't know what. I remember once, when I walked about, I was so alone when I was a kid. My mother had too many kids; and my father never cared much for me. He must have instinctively felt that I wasn't a real man. I don't know what it was.

T-34   No, it was probably because he was a disturbed guy himself.

P-34   And he made fun of me. In fact, he wanted me to be a doctor, and I wanted to be a doctor; but I also wanted to be a teacher. And he fought with me so much about being a doctor.

T-35   What was he? What was his profession?

P-35   Well, he was a poor, hard-working man. He had a small store, and we lived on the lower East side.

T-36   Yes. So he wanted you to make up for him.

P-36   Well, I didn't have any brothers; and I was the only one who could do it for him. But he never showed any interest in me; he liked my sisters more than he liked me.

T-37   You took that seriously!

P-37   Oh, yes!

T-38   Yes, that's your problem! You've been taking all this nonsense seriously, all your life.

[The therapist tries to show the patient that his father fought with him not because he, the patient, was lacking in manliness, but because the father himself had serious problems of not being manly and wealthy enough. He also tries to show the patient that it wasn't merely the *influence* of his father that originally made him disturbed, but his taking his father's propaganda seriously. This is a central tenet of rational-emotive psychotherapy: that it is not the individual's early environment, *per se,* that negatively affects him: but his *allowing himself* to be affected by it, and his later *continuing* to take the negative views of his fathers (and others) overly-seriously.]

P-38   All my life—until I grew up. And then I realized he's an ignorant man; he doesn't know any better.

T-39   That's right!

P-39   Because I keep giving people advice all the time—like a psychiatrist. I had a student who was married to a very famous actress. You know, Mr. Zerox. His wife studies with me, and I've helped her more than he could ever think of helping her. I help people tremendously.

T-40   Yes, I'm sure you do. But not *yourself!*

P-40   Not myself.

T-41   Because you still believe the same crap that you're trying to get them out of. And you've been blaming yourself for years and years for not being a man—for not doing the right thing; for being homosexual; and so on and so forth. And this blame has done you in enormously. You're still doing it, right now.

[The therapist tries to point out that even during this session the patient is harshly condemning himself; and that his need to keep showing how tremendously he helps people is also an indirect form of blame, since it shows that he only estimates himself highly when he does fine things and others approve him for so doing. But the therapist only gets to mention this briefly, since the patient rushes on compulsively.]

P-41   And I had one thing that hurt me a lot, too. There was this woman, this very old teacher who taught at the same school I was in. And she said, "If you have an urge, go ahead and do it and get it out of your system." I don't know; I thought that maybe that would help. I thought I'd just do it and then I'd forget about it and all.

T-42   Yes,

P-42   Yes.

T-43   Well, you've got to have something more than this. You have to have a different philosophy of life. If you have a different philosophy, you won't get into this mess: it will be impossible. You only get into messes or are unhappy because of something that you believe or think. And you've believed a lot of nonsense all your life, even though you've helped others. If you get rid of this nonsense that you believe, you can't possibly get into messes. Because the nonsense is what causes you to do it, the homosexuality. It's nothing magic that pushes you to do it. The urge is led by an idea. You can't have any urge, except impelled by an idea. Even a tennis player doesn't really work with his hands—he works with his head. If he's not directing his hands with his head, he could be as dexterous with his hands as a juggler, and yet he wouldn't do anything well, as you probably know.

P-43   Oh, yes. I know all that definitely.

T-44   Yes. Now consequently, the same thing goes for anything else—any so-called emotion that people have is led by an idea. Now your main emotion all your life has been one of self-depreciation and upsetedness. You just mentioned a minute ago that it hurt you very much, when these things happened. And right *now* you feel hurt, don't you? Well this hurt *you're* doing to *you*. Nothing can hurt you from the outside. It's only your *attitude* toward the things that happen that hurts you.

   Right now, you're unhappy; but you're *not* unhappy because

of what has happened. That's a myth. You're unhappy because of your attitude toward what has happened. You think it's *horrible* that you have done these things and got into this situation and hurt your wife; and so on. And it *isn't* horrible—it's too goddamn bad, but it's not horrible. And when we convince you it's too goddamn bad, then you'll do something to stop it. But as long as you think it's horrible and awful and terrible, you won't do anything to stop it—you'll just go deliberately and punish yourself, as you've done to a large degree.

You've been masochistic, because you've said, "I'm just no goddamn good; therefore, I deserve to suffer." And therefore you haven't taken any precautions; you've been rash in several instances, such as the last one; and so on. And you unconsciously *deliberately* get yourself into trouble, because you think you deserve to be punished for doing these "horrible" things. Now, you haven't done *anything* horrible in all your life. You've done a few idiotic and stupid things; but even when somebody has done something idiotic and stupid, the thing to do is say, "Now, look. I did this today; now what am I going to do *tomorrow?" That's* the issue. But you're not saying that. You're saying, "I did this. Oh, my God, this is terrible! This is awful! How could I have done this?" And this will make you do the same thing tomorrow.

Now you have to focus on the problem. Again: you're a teacher; and you know perfectly well that if your students, or you or anybody else, get in front of an audience and start worrying about that audience, they're not going to recite or act well. Because they're being distracted. The only thing you can do in a case like this is to concentrate on the problem; and the problem is, "How can I interpret this material?" *That's* the problem. The audience is *not* the problem; the director of the play is *not* the problem. Nothing is the problem but, "How can I interpret this *material?"*

But you get distracted from that problem and worry about everything else under the sun: whether your mother or wife is liking it, if she's listening, or about something like that. Then you're not going to recite or act well. You can't do it: you can't do two things at once. You have to focus on the problem. Now, you haven't been doing that: you haven't been focusing on this simple problem—and it's really a simple problem you have—that you admire males and that you'd like to see their genitals, and so forth and so on. "Now, how can I stop this crap, this problem?" Because it *is* crappy: it isn't doing you any good; it's getting you into trouble.

Instead, you've been focusing on, "Oh, my God! Look at this horrible thing I did! What would people think if they found out? What would my wife think if she found out?" And so on. And this is irrelevant nonsense. This has nothing to do with the case. In fact, it *creates* the problem—this "What would people think if they found out?" This has probably been your main problem all your life. You've worried about what would people think of you: Are you a sissy? Are you a man? And so forth. And this crap has driven you into this kind of behavior.

Then, once you get into this kind of behavior, you start worrying about the behavior itself; and then it gets worse— it's a vicious circle, you see. And the more you do it, the more you blame yourself; and the more you blame yourself, the more you do it.

Now, we have to get you to see, for the first time in your life, that there is a simple problem here. And the problem is, "How do I not defeat myself in life?" That's the real issue— that I would like to do *x;* and if I do *x,* I'm going to knock myself off; therefore I can't do *x.* Not because *x* is wicked or wrong, or people wouldn't like me for doing it, or all kinds of irrelevant things; but because I just would knock myself off.

Suppose, for example, you had no homosexual urges what-soever; but suppose you just adored 16-year-old girls; the one thing you wanted to do was get in bed with a 16-year-old girl; that was your greatest preference (which lots of people prefer). Well, if you got in bed with a 16-year-old girl, you'd be an idiot, because it's against the law. Sooner or later, one of these 16-year-old girls would complain to her mother, or get pregnant, or something; and you'd end up with a charge of statutory rape.

Now, it really isn't vicious to get in bed with a 16-year-old girl. The law is a little off; it's an antiquated law. Girls of 16 are really not that much different from girls of 18. And yet you'd be acting like an idiot. Just as if you rode on the left-hand side of the street instead of the right. It wouldn't be wicked; but you'd be behaving idiotically. You'd get arrested or you'd get into an accident very quickly.

P-44   I wouldn't do it.

T-45   That's right. Even if we disagree with the law, then the thing we should do is to try to get the law repealed: go down to Union Square, and talk against the law, and so on. Such as I do. I write books. I don't happen to be homosexual in the least myself, but I think it's unfair for homosexuals to be arrested and prosecuted, and so on. So I write articles and books saying this. Now, I don't go out and protest by *being* homosexual. That would be idiotic; I'd defeat my own ends. Then they'd say, "Hell! No wonder you write these books: you're homosexual." I'm not in the least homosexual, but I think it's unjust, unfair to ban it. Now if you really think it's unjust and unfair, then go fight the law. There's nothing to prevent you from getting on committees and doing all sorts of things to stop the law. But to go out while the law still exists————.

P-45   It's stupid!

T-46   That's right. Now, we got to get you to see that it's stupid in the sense that it's self-defeating.

[The therapist rather longwindedly and lecturingly keeps making the point that, whatever the patient has done, he has merely acted self-defeatingly, and is not wicked or horrible for having acted in that manner. And he should try to stop behaving badly, not because he is a worthless louse if he continues to do so, but because otherwise he will continue to defeat his own best ends. Moreover, he must learn to act intelligently not merely because other people will like him if he does so (because he actually can like himself *whether* or not they do) but because there are real advantages from good behavior. Although the therapist is verbose and repetitious, he is deliberately so: because he wants to make several points that the patient obviously is not aware of, and he wants to make them vigorously and repetitively, so that they'll have a better chance of sinking in.]

P-46   [*Inaudible*]

T-47   [*Inaudible*]

P-47   But when I'm in that stage————.

T-48   No, but I mean that *even* at that time you can do something to stop yourself. Because at that time you're telling yourself something else to *make* yourself go through with the urge. If you were just calmly telling yourself, whenever you got the urge to handle a man's genitals or something like that, if you were saying to yourself calmly, "I've got the urge; the urge is a perfectly good thing; but my goddamn society doesn't allow it, therefore I can't do it," you would not go through with that urge. When you go into a bank and see those bank notes piled up behind the teller's window, you often get the urge to reach your hand out and take ten thousand dollars. But why *don't* you do it? Because you know you can't get away with it.

P-48   But I don't have the urge.

T-49   Everybody has that urge. If you really see that money there, piled up, lying around, you would like to get it. The reason you don't have the urge any more is that so many times you've told yourself, "I can't get away with it."

P-49   I think you're right. I think you're right there.

[This is fairly typical of rational-emotive method. The patient directly contradicts what the therapist is saying about his urge to steal money from a bank, and his ability to curb this urge; but instead of easily giving up on his point, the therapist carries it through, and soon the patient honestly seems to be admitting that it is valid. The therapist, in this kind of treatment, does not hesitate, often, to contradict the patient's defensive thoughts and feelings, and to insist that he look at the real feelings that lie behind his facade. He believes that the patient is disturbed largely *because* he easily gives up, becomes defensive, and then accepts his defenses as truths. But the therapist has no intention of similarly giving up in this manner if he comes up against patient opposition. Instead of withdrawing, when he meets up against resistance, he frequently attacks the resistance even harder, until the patient tends to give it up. Sometimes, he interprets resistances (as a psychoanalytic therapist would do); but frequently, as in this instance, he logically attacks it, and does his best to make the patient see that it is foolish holding on to it.]

T-50   That's right: because you know it's silly to reach your hand in. After three seconds, you'd be caught and you'd go to jail; and that isn't worth it. And that's the question in the homosexuality: not whether it's the right or wrong, or the sissified thing; but is it *worth* it?

P-50   Oh, God—it isn't!

T-51   That's right; it isn't. Now, if we can just get you calmly to see that it isn't worth it—instead of beating yourself and calling yourself an idiot and a louse and everything else for doing it—then we focus on the problem. Now, as I say to people all the time, "Suppose you're driving straight toward a cliff, and you don't want to go over. It's a simple problem: all you have to do is to ask yourself, 'How do I *not* go over this cliff?' and immediately you'd say, 'Well, I'll take my foot off the gas, or put on the brakes, or something else.' There's no difficulty finding a solution. But suppose you're driving toward that same cliff and you're saying to yourself, 'Oh, my God! What an idiot I am! How could I do this stupid thing?' The chances are, you'd then go over the goddamn cliff."

P-51   That's terrible—to lose your power!

T-52   That's right. Now, your hysteria is caused by the thoughts that you're telling yourself. All emotion, as I said, is really caused by thinking. Just immediately prior to the emotion, you're telling yourself something. If it's a pleasant emotion, like love or joy, you're saying, "That's fine! That's great; that's good!" And if it's a bad emotion, like anxiety or grief or fear or hatred, you're saying, "It's horrible! It's awful!" Now you're saying, just prior to your doing one of these homosexual things, some silly sentence. And if you show me some of the things you do, I can tell you the sentences pretty clearly, because I know what they are; they're all repetitious. There's only a certain limited number of them.

P-52   I'm sure of that.

[The therapist begins, here, to teach the patient the essence of the method of rational-emotive therapy: that his negative emotions and his self-defeating actions are caused by the sentences he tells himself, just before he experiences these emotions or performs these actions; and that if he will look at these sentences, logically parse them, and then vigorously challenge and contradict them and replace them with saner sentences, his feelings and acts will change and will give way to more constructive emotions and behavior.]

T-53   Now, we have to make you aware concretely of exactly the bullshit, the sentences, that you're telling yourself prior to doing these idiotic things. Because *you're* not an idiot. *You're* an intelligent, educated man. You don't *have* to think in this silly way. But you have got in the habit of thinking this way, and you're not contradicting it. As soon as you tell yourself one of these silly sentences—"Oh, my God! What a louse I am!" Or: "I must do this homosexual act or something like that." Or: "How can they stop me from getting what I want?"—instead of looking at the thing and saying, "Now, let's see how *true* this is," you say, "Yes, it's true; it's absolutely right!" and you go ahead to act on it.

P-53   You mean all this is in my subconscious?

T-54   Yes.

P-54   I don't want it to be this way.

T-55   I know; but that's what I'm going to get you to do—change it.

[Although the therapist is very directly telling the patient that he has been wrong in his behavior, and that he has caused himself all his trouble, and in this sense the therapist is confronting the patient with his full responsibility for his actions, he is at the same time clearly showing the patient that he *is* capable of changing, and that he *can* change. In this sense, although rational-emotive psychotherapy is extremely confrontational and might seem to be critical of the patient, it is also highly permissive and supportive. The therapist is not *condemning* the patient for his behavior; and he is specifically telling him that he can behave *differently* in the future.]

P-55   All I do is say, "I want to do it, and I'll get it over with, get it out of my system. I'll feel that I'll have it gone, and————."

T-56 But look at that! That's a silly sentence—because it's bullshit! You *don't* get it out of your system by doing it. You're saying to yourself: "(*a*) I have this horrible urge. (*b*) If I give into it, I'll get it over with. And (*c*) It will never bother me again." Now these are all nonsensical sentences. Because you do have a desire to do it—that's the first part of the chain. You have the desire to touch men's genitals. The reason you have the desire, actually, is because you're overexaggerating the importance of their genitals, for other reasons. You're assuming that genitals show masculinity; and if you identify with this masculinity, you'll be stronger; and so on and so forth. Which is another line of nonsense————.

P-56 I'm very small; I have a very small penis.

T-57 Yes, and you think it's terrible. *That's* the point: not that you've been built small. The sentence that always screws a human being is the little extra sentence: "And that is terrible!" Right now, you're in a bad situation, but that's not what's disturbing you. The thing that's disturbing you right now is, "It's *terrible* that I'm in this situation!" And, you know, it *isn't*. It's too goddamn bad you're in this situation; but it isn't terrible.

P-57 Oh, I deserve it!

T-58 By saying you deserve it, you're just repeating again: "It's terrible!"

P-58 Well, I don't say it's terrible; I want to say to myself that it's too goddamn bad.

T-59 It's true. It *is* too goddamn bad————.

P-59 I say, "God, I deserve it! But don't punish me any more!"

T-60 But you *believe* in punishment; and there's no such thing as self-punishment, unless you believe it. And that's your problem: that you *believe* in this crap.

P-60 I don't want to be punished any more!

T-61 But the only one who can punish you is *you*.

P-61 How?

T-62   By telling yourself this nonsense: "What a louse I am!" The worst that other people can do, the very worst they can do to you, is to put you in jail for six months or so—which is the most they'd give you for an offense like this, normally. So they'd put you in jail for six months; and you still wouldn't have to be terribly unhappy in jail. It would be a pain in the ass to be put in jail; but it wouldn't be that terrible.

P-62   I was there two days and I don't know how I lived through it!

T-63   Because you were telling yourself how *horrible* it was. Now, *what* was so horrible about it? It's a pain in the ass to be put in jail. *I* wouldn't like it. But if they put me in jail for two days or six months, I'd say, "Well, what the hell; they put me in jail; and it will be over in two days or six months. So what? So it's a pain in the ass." And you never say that. You *create* these horrors—by telling yourself, completely falsely, how *horrible* the situation is. Right now you're in a difficult situation; there's no question about it. It's not good; it would be silly to say it's good. But it's not half as bad as you're *making* it up to be. And your unhappiness is caused, *not* by the situation, but by this crap that you're telling yourself: "I can't *stand* this! This is horrible! How did I get into it? I deserve to be punished!" But this is all nonsense. You made a mistake and the point now is, *not* to punish yourself for making the mistake, but to figure out how *not* to make it next time. *That* is the issue.

P-63   I'll make it again when I come out———.

T-64   All right. Now the way we get you not to———.

P-64   My wife said she'd leave me if I didn't come out of it.

T-65   All right; fine. But the point is to stop *blaming* yourself, to stop *catastrophizing*.

P-65   How do I do that?

T-66   By seeing that it's nonsense, that all catastrophizing is nonsense. There *are* no catastrophes in the world; there are just pains in the ass. If the worst comes to the worst, you die; and even that's not a catastrophe.

p-66   No, that's easy!

t-67   All right. And if you live and people don't like you, or some-
       thing like that, so they don't like you! You can still live. Now
       we got to stop your catastrophizing. You're catastrophizing and
       blaming yourself all over the place. And if we can get you to
       stop that, then almost immediately you'll start feeling a hun-
       dred per cent better. If we can really get you to see that all
       your unhappiness is not caused by the event that you falsely
       ascribe it to, but by your attitude toward the event—your tell-
       ing yourself how horrible it is; what a louse you are; how
       could you do that; and so on. Now, *that's* what we have to
       show you.
           The same thing goes about homosexuality. Again, it's not
       the *event* which is so awful, but the telling yourself, "I'm no
       good! I'm a louse! How could I do this?" And then you'll
       drive yourself to go do it again. Now, if we can get you to
       calmly see what's going on, what occurs, and not to say
       "Goody, goody! Look what's going on!"—for that's nonsense,
       too—but "It's too goddamn bad. I'm headed for this cliff; now
       let's see how I stop heading for this cliff." That's the only
       issue—not, "I should be punished for stupidly going toward
       the cliff," or anything like that.
           Now, we have to change your thinking. We haven't got any
       more time this session, but what I want you to do is, by the
       time you see me next, to note—and write down, if necessary,
       because you're going to forget easily—anything that disturbs
       you. By disturbance, I mean, any anxiety, fear, grief, guilt,
       depression, and so on. They're all illegitimate! No human
       being need have any of these goddamn things for any length
       of time in an intense way. And you've been having them for
       years.

p-67   The feeling I have now is just the horror about what's going
       to happen to me.

t-68   All right. But what *could* happen to you? At the worst, you'll
       go to jail.

p-68   I don't want to go to jail!

t-69   You don't want to—but what's *horrible* about it? And if you calm down and start facing things, there's a chance you won't go to jail. The more excited and hysterical you get, the better is the chance you'll go. All right. Now, as I said: I want you to write down, if necessary and you can't remember, all the things that now disturb you. We'll go through them in detail; and I'll show you what you're telling yourself to create the disturbances.

It's not the thing, it's not the situation, not what's happening—it's *your* attitude toward what's happening, your silly beliefs about the events. And if you bring me these disturbances, these griefs and anxieties and upsets, whatever they are—about this situation or anything else, anything that should go through your mind—then I'll show you exactly what you're telling yourself and what *not* to tell yourself—how to do anticatastrophizing instead of catastrophizing. And very quickly, if you get to work on this—because you've got to do homework; you can't just come and listen to me, just like your students can't come and listen to you and learn to read———.

P-69   You don't have to tell me that, Doctor. In fact, all these years I couldn't go to a psychoanalyst; I couldn't really afford one.

T-70   O.K. So let's make another appointment; and you bring me some of the things which currently disturb you and we'll go through them; and I'll show you what you're doing to catastrophize, to make them fifty times as bad as they are. Now, when do you want to make it?

P-70   Well, when do you think I should come back?

T-71   Well, this is Tuesday. I think you should come again probably the end of this week, since we have a problem here which we have to get at right away. Later on, we'll cut you down on appointments. At the beginning, I'll see you about twice a week. Now, what's the convenient time for you?

P-71   Around two in the afternoon.

T-72   Then I'll see you two o'clock on Friday. You just note down anything that bothers you; we'll go through it; we'll get you over this nonsense.

P-72   I'll do everything in my power, because I want to get over it.

T-73   O.K. If you do the work, I can help you get over it.

P-73   I'll write it down. Did you say, anything that bothers me?

T-74   Anything that disturbs you. Any grief, anxiety, fear, guilt, or anything. That's what I want to know. Because if we go through these, then you'll see the pattern. It's all the same nonsense; you'll be able to see it and get over it.

[Usually, the patient is seen about once a week for rational-emotive psychotherapy; and after several weeks, that is cut down to once every two weeks; and then till later, once every three weeks or less. But in this patient's case, since he has to come up for trial soon and is exceptionally upset, he is started off at twice a week. In the remainder of this session, the patient indicates that he is in financial trouble and therefore doesn't want to come too often; but he agrees to come twice a week at the beginning, since he needs help desperately. Actually, he comes irregularly, every two weeks or so.]

Second Session

T-1   How are things?

P-1   Well, a lot of things are happening now. The first thing: I had a change in the charge of felonious assault. That's been reduced to a smaller charge; and this next thing comes up in a week.

T-2   Disorderly conduct, or something like that?

P-2   Yes.

T-3   All right: so it's just a misdemeanor.

P-3   Yes. So I'm not too worried about that now.

T-4   Worried about the case, you mean?

P-4   Yes.

T-5   All right. What good will worrying do?

P-5   Nothing at all. I keep telling myself that. I remember what you told me about nothing is the end.

T-6   That's right—nothing is the end. Even if you went to jail, the world would not open up and swallow you.

[Typically, although this is only the second session of rational-emotive psychotherapy, the patient has apparently already begun to take to heart some of the things that the therapist has gone over with him during the first session; and he has begun to feel better about some of them. In conventional psychotherapies, it frequently takes a great many sessions for the patient to begin to use the material he has been learning in therapy; but in rational therapy, it sometimes takes only a session or two for him to begin to put the therapeutic material to use.]

P-6   In that case, I'm not thinking of the world, really.

T-7   What are you thinking of?

P-7   I have claustrophobia or something. I was so uncomfortable in that jail, I thought I'd die there.

T-8   Well, you wouldn't.

P-8   I couldn't breathe.

T-9   What's so horrible about being in a small, confined space? It isn't pleasant; but what's so horrible about it?

P-9   I just couldn't breathe.

T-10   You told yourself that you couldn't breathe—that was what was horrible.

P-10   I *told* myself that?

T-11   That's right. You said, "I can't stand this! It's too close; I can't breathe!" And that's what created the lack of breathing.

P-11   They let me go out. I even scrubbed the floors, just so I wouldn't be confined in that little space.

T-12   Yes. But what's so horrible about the space?

P-12   I guess the horrible thing was that you have nothing else to do but sit and think about this thing.

T-13   All right; but you could think pleasant thoughts. You could think constructively, "Now, what am I going to do when I get out? How am I going to stop this crap?" and so on. You don't *have* to think, "What a louse I am!"—which is what you were thinking. *That's* what was horrible. That's what does the

damage; and that's what we've got to get you to see and to
stop. You're *not* a louse; you're a human being who makes
mistakes, like all human beings. And if you accept yourself as
a fallible person who makes mistakes, you will soon very
quickly see how not to make the same mistakes. You have
never accepted yourself with your failings. You've always
beaten yourself mercilessly; and you cannot learn thereby.

[Although the session is just under way, and the patient has brought
up something from the immediate past rather than from the present,
the therapist uses what he has brought up as a *raison d'être* for getting back to his main deindoctrinating theme: that *nothing* is really
terrible, aside from intractable physical pain, and that what the
patient *thinks* is terrible becomes so, by his very act of thinking it so.
He also keeps repeating that as long as the patient condemns himself
for his failings, he won't have the time and energy to work against
failings, but will thereby only help make things worse.]

P-13   I always tried not to accept that. What I did was————. Well,
        I'm a little confused now how I went about it; maybe after the
        whole thing is over I————. My mind is so taken up with this
        experience now that I can't think back and think how I actu-
        ally felt about the whole situation. But what I feel is I tried
        not to accept it, in the fact that I definitely want to live a
        normal life. I got married; and my wife sometimes argued
        with me and said that I got married to cover it up—make my-
        self feel like I was a man. I felt that wasn't the kind of life I
        wanted.

T-14   No, I don't doubt you got married to lead a normal life. But
        what made you *not* lead it?

P-14   That quirk in me.

T-15   But what *is* the quirk. The quirk is not that you desire young
        boys or anything like that—not that you desire a man. That's
        not the quirk.

P-15   No?

T-16   No. Because what's wrong with *that*?

P-16   To desire a man?

T-17   Yes.

P-17   Isn't that abnormal?

T-18   No. That's your problem—that you believe it is.

P-18   My wife argues with me all the time, saying it's *so* abnormal.

T-19   No.

P-19   It sort of goes against nature.

T-20   She's wrong. Let me explain to you what nature is. Suppose you were born on a desert island and there were nobody to teach you; you were raised by a wolf, and you were on the desert island; and then, after a while, other people came to the island, males and females. You had no teaching in regard to what was right and what was wrong about sex.

   Do you know what you would do on that island, sexually? You would do everything. First of all, you would masturbate. Second, you would have nocturnal emissions, through dreams and fantasies. Third, you would be screwing females. Fourth, you would be screwing males. Fifth, you would be screwing animals. And sixth, you would be screwing knotholes in trees or some other objects. You'd have at least six major sexual outlets, under those circumstances. Because man, biologically, is a plurisexual animal.

P-20   Or woman?

T-21   Yes, man or woman.

P-21   What does pluri mean?

T-22   Pluri means many. Man's not monosexual. He doesn't go for one sex outlet; and he's not bisexual—he doesn't just go for men and women sexually. He's plurisexual.

P-22   *Every* man?

T-23   Every human being who is normal. If he were not raised with prejudices, he would do all these six things. Now, he would do these differentially; he wouldn't do them all equally. If you were on a desert island and there were six sex outlets, you wouldn't be spending sixteen and two-thirds per cent of your time masturbating, and sixteen and two-thirds per cent with women, and sixteen and two-thirds per cent with men, and so on.

Though there would be individual differences among you and other men, the chances are you would end up by screwing women about eighty per cent of the time, screwing men about ten per cent, and doing the other four sex things combined another ten per cent. For the simple reason that heterosexuality is more convenient—that you would find, after trying the other things, that it's just more convenient: that women have a vagina and men do not. Animals do, in a sense—female animals—but it's certainly not very convenient to screw a porcupine or some animal like that! But women have a vagina; and it's somewhat more pleasant having sex relations with women when you're not biased, than it is with any other kind of person or object. So about eighty per cent of the time, probably, you'd be having intercourse with women and the other twenty per cent of the time you'd be having men or trees or anything else you could find—for variety, if for nothing else. Man is a very definite varietist. But you wouldn't be *guilty* about any of these things, because you wouldn't have learned that one is right and one is wrong.

Now—unfortunately, we might say—you were *not* raised on a desert island by a wolf; you were raised by other human beings. And these human beings are very prejudiced human beings: they have all kinds of rules about sex, most of which are absolute nonsense; and the main rules come from the Bible. The Bible was written about a period which occurred some twenty-five hundred years ago—an agrarian-pastoral society. They raised sheep and grain then; they didn't have factories; they didn't even have remedial reading teachers! Practically everybody had a farm and raised sheep and grain; that's the way they lived. And in order to do this successfully, you had to have labor. And you couldn't hire it, because everybody else had his farm and, come harvest time, he was very busy. So you couldn't go out and hire him to help you, because he had the same problem that you had. There was only one place you could get labor—and that was through your own sons. That was the only main, safe, secure place you could get labor. If you had six or eight sons around, they would plough your land and do your work for you. So all they were interested in, in the Old Testament, was exactly this: getting sons. Women, they didn't give a shit for, because they weren't that much good at labor. And today, in Orthodox Jewish synagogues, the women still are up in the balcony and the men sit on the floor of the temple, because women are looked down on.

But in order to get sons, you had to be the father of the sons. You couldn't go and adopt them in the old days; they had to be yours by blood; that was the ancient Hebrew custom. And there's only one way to get sons by blood, and that's to have a wife and to have intercourse with her, and to make sure that nobody else does. And consequently, they made all the girls be virgins until marriage. Because if a girl wasn't a virgin, some other guy might screw her first and then you'd have to fight him. And they made all women be chaste after marriage—they were against adultery for women. Not for men, incidentally, but for women, in the Bible. Because again, if the guy next door came and said, "I screwed your wife six months ago, and if she has a son it's mine," you'd have to go fight him. Because if he had slept with her, the son would be his, by blood.

And they also banned masturbation, and they banned homosexuality, and they banned any sex relations with your wife where you didn't literally screw her. If you went down on your wife, or anything like that, that was illegal—because you couldn't have children that way. And everything was defined as abnormal which does not lead to having children. There's only one thing that will lead to children, and that's a man and a woman screwing each other. There's nothing else. And therefore we have been calling these other things abnormal, for twenty-five hundred years. Even though our society has changed enormously, so that we do not go after sons particularly today. For if you had six sons, you'd have to send them to college and support them—you'd be bankrupt; you wouldn't want them. But we keep the same nonsense which they promulgated twenty-five hundred years ago.

So there's nothing abnormal about homosexuality, in itself. The only thing which is *really* abnormal—and this is almost funny!—is if you take *one* sexual act and you stick to that exclusively, against all other acts. Suppose, for example, you could only have sex relations with, let us say, a pig—nobody else, no man, nor woman, nor anything. That would be abnormal—not because you were screwing a pig, but because you were afraid, obviously, of screwing people. Otherwise, why would you stick to a pig? It's obvious that there's nothing that good about a pig, compared to having sex with other people.

Now, the same thing goes for heterosexuality. Suppose you were raised, like most of us were raised, with prejudices, biases —that's all they are—to have sex relations just with women. And suppose you have them, and are successful enough. But suppose you only dare screw your wife in one position—let us say, when she's on her back and you're above her—and in no other way; everything else you consider horrible. This is perverse. Because what's *wrong* with the other positions? If you try the other positions and you just don't like them, that's perfectly legitimate. But suppose you never even *tried* any other positions—you refused to do so. *That's* abnormal.

[The therapist, as is not uncommon in the course of rational-emotive therapy, does not hesitate to give the patient a lengthy lecture on what sex abnormality truly is. He assumes, from the patient's previous answers, that he does not really know *why* he is sexually perverse, and has an unscientific attitude in this regard. He therefore tries to set him straight, by making perfectly clear what sex deviation actually is, so that he can then get the patient accurately to attack his deviance. Many therapists, of course, give lectures of this sort to their patients; but most of them have no theory on which to give it, and indeed are contradicting their assumed theory of psychotherapy. In RT, the theory states very precisely that therapy is a form of deindoctrination and reindoctrination: that the patient is disturbed because he subscribes to, and consciously or unconsciously acts upon, various irrational premises; and that the therapist, to help him get better, must show him why these premises are mistaken, and induce him to contradict and challenge them. The lectures given to the patient by the therapist are for this specific depropagandization purpose, and are therefore quite deliberately done, in conformity with the theory of rational-emotive methodology.]

P-23   Well, I don't know. I never tried anything different with my wife.

T-24   All right; that's because you're afraid. That's your problem— fear.

P-24   No, I don't think it's fear. I felt I love her; and I wanted to have a very pure————.

T-25   What's *pure?*

P-25   Well, I thought she was the wife; and that's the way the wife should be.

T-26   But *why?*

P-26   When she first found out about it, my homosexuality, she said, "Is it because you perform differently there? Well, try it with me a different way." I was horrified.

T-27   That's your problem. And this is what we're going to get into in a minute—the reason for your homosexuality, too. But I want to get over to you that the only thing that's wrong about any act of sex is its exclusivity. If you *exclusively* do anything, then you're abnormal in a psychological sense—not in the sense of being wicked. Because it means you're *afraid* of other things. If you only do one or two things————.

P-27   Why can't it be just because you *like* that?

T-28   No, as I was saying, it could be, in a few cases————.

P-28   People just like one thing; they just *want* that. I had a brother who just liked one thing like that.

T-29   But I say that if he had unprejudicially *tried* everything else, and ended up this way, that would be *taste*. But it's very unlikely that he did. He was afraid, I'm sure. He would not *try* anything else. He was off his rocker, in all probability.

P-29   Well, he had a very limited diet. He didn't like this————.

T-30   Well, again: we have to ask *why*. If he really tried fifty thousand things, and he ended up with two or three that he liked, there's nothing abnormal; he just has peculiar taste buds. That's not abnormal psychologically. We could say he was physically peculiar, but not psychologically abnormal. But almost everybody I've ever talked to, who was in this class, just *doesn't* try the other things. They're afraid. Or they try certain things once or twice, and they say, "Oh, no! I don't like this!" They don't really give it a *chance*. But abnormality, or perversion, *means* not giving a thing a chance, and condemning it without that chance. And you've done it abnormally in one way at least—and that is, you only have screwed your wife in this one position. Because, obviously, you haven't tried the others, so you don't even know if they're any good. And you assume that that one position is pure and good; and this is nonsense. What's *pure* about it? What's *good* about it?

P-30 Well, that's your Bible again.

T-31 That's right! But that's peculiar, abnormal. Anybody who would actually follow the Bible is a pervert. It's very amusing! —most of the perverts in our society are married individuals who only do what you do with your wife. They're all perverted! Because they're *afraid* to try anything else. *Why* are they afraid? Because someone, twenty-five hundred years ago, said—for completely different reasons than now exist—that it's wrong. And they're afraid to go against———.

P-31 They're not afraid. They just haven't any *desire* for it.

T-32 Well, but you normally *would* have some desire to try it at some time. You can't tell me that a guy could screw his wife for thousands of times and never get the idea that, "Maybe if she got on top of me, or if we did it from the rear or something, it would be delightful." You *have* to get that idea. Just like some guy who believes in eating potatoes all the time, at some time or other—seeing other people eat other things— would get the idea, "Well, maybe I ought to try it." But the reason he wouldn't try it is because he's afraid. "God will strike me dead if I try it!" Or: "Maybe it'll poison me!" Or some other crap he believes in. That's his sickness—the fear.

Now, homosexuality is sick—not because all people who engage in homosexual behavior are sick. Kinsey found that forty per cent of men have homosexual relations at one time or other in their life; and the other sixty per cent are probably afraid to try. They got the idea of doing it, sometimes; but they just didn't dare. And if they had the guts, the whole hundred per cent would try. But they'd soon put it in its place, and only occasionally they would do it. Because, if they're unprejudiced, as I said before, they'd enjoy women *more,* in most cases.

The other reason why they would put it in its place in our culture is that it's banned. Now, it shouldn't be banned. It's a very stupid law that we have, to make homosexuality a crime. Like a lot of other ridiculous laws we have. It's a very stupid law to not let people go out naked when it's a hundred degrees in the shade. We should let people walk naked if they want to, if we had any sense. But we don't; we ban it arbitrarily. And therefore anybody who lives in our society is crazy if he walks out naked. Not because he's crazy to *want* to walk out naked; but because he's going to get arrested for doing so.

Now, homosexuals, most of them are disturbed for two reasons. One is that they're *exclusively* homosexual. They don't even do what you've done—they don't have wives. Most of them can't have sex relations with a woman. They have no desire to. In other words, they're so afraid of women that they lose all desire for them; they just go with men—and that's abnormal, because it's exclusive. And the second reason they're abnormal is they're doing an illegal act, when they could do an enjoyable legal one.

As I often say: suppose that arbitrarily, in our society, they banned redheads, and they said, "Any man who has intercourse with a redhead goes to jail for five years." Well, under those circumstances, any man who has intercourse with a redhead would be disturbed, he'd be very sick. Because there are plenty of blondes and brunettes; and he can give up redheads. Moreover, there are pretty few redheads around. So he'd be an idiot; he'd be disturbed if he insisted on having sex with redheads.

By the same token, homosexuals are disturbed—not because they like men (that's not a disturbance at all) but because they *give in* to their likes and take all kinds of dangerous chances in this stupid society. Just as they would be disturbed if they went out naked on a regular afternoon. It wouldn't be the nudity that would be their disturbance, or the desire for it; but the fact that they're pigheadedly going against their culture—and therefore they're screwing themselves. Anybody who defeats his own ends is obviously crazy.

Your sickness has been two sicknesses, oddly enough. One is with your wife—where you've been afraid of anything but one position. And two is the homosexuality: not the desire, but the fact that you took all these risks to satisfy it. Now, let's ask *why* you've been obsessed with the homosexuality? *Why* you've wanted males all your life?

[This is a good example of the therapist's persisting in his arguments, in spite of the fact that he is obviously getting little acceptance for them from the patient. He has been trying to show the patient exactly why his homosexual pattern is abnormal: because he is fixatedly, compulsively drawn to it, instead of merely having a moderate *preference* for homosexual behavior. The patient indicates—as is often true when the therapist gives him a good deal of material to work with—that he also is fixatedly and compulsively restricted with a single kind of "normal" position in intercourse with his wife. Whereupon the therapist, instead of retreating and figuring that he may well not get anywhere with this one-track-minded patient, vigorously attacks *that* perversion, too, and tries to show the patient that it is part and parcel of his entire sickness. All along, the therapist is not merely *revealing* to the patient how disturbed he is; he is, even more importantly, forcefully *assailing* the philosophic premises that he reveals the patient to have.]

P-32   That's what I want to know.

T-33   This is a simple business—of what we call channelization. If you're a normal human being with no prejudices, you'll like *x, y, z, a, b, c;* you'll like a lot of things. And sexually, you'll like a hell of a lot. You'll like men and women and children and animals, and everything else under the sun: because your desires are such that they're plurisexual. They're absolutely promiscuous, on a biological basis. A man without prejudice would screw a hole in the wall, literally, and think nothing of it. But arbitrarily, in our society, we channelize these desires. We throw out the animal as a sex object, for example. We say, "Oh, how horrible to screw an animal! This is wicked.

We can't do that!" We throw that out. And most of us throw
out homosexuality.

We throw out incest—which is quite arbitrary, because
there's nothing biologically wrong with screwing your sister.
She's a woman, like any other woman. We arbitrarily ban it:
because, again, it goes back to the Bible; and also for various
other reasons, since family fights would occur, and things like
that. If you screwed your sister, then your father might say,
"Well, why shouldn't *I* screw her?" And there might be
murder. So men decided years ago, "Let's have no incest."
But, really, it's arbitrary: since you could well screw your sister, and it wouldn't be abnormal to desire screwing her instead
of some other girl. What's the difference?

But we throw certain sex acts out, and we start channelizing
our desires into a limited area. And the area normally becomes,
in our society, women—doing certain things, such as having
intercourse, going down on them, and so on. Not having sex
with men; and not with animals. And usually masturbation,
too, declines, because it's more pleasant having sex relations
with another person than masturbating. So we don't go around
screwing knotholes, and so on. We channelize.

Now you've done this channelization—only you've done a
double channelizing. One is toward purity in women, which
you've learned to desire. And, oddly enough, that very thing
is going to turn you toward men. Because, for one thing, if
you just go for purity in women, you're going to be awfully
limited in your sex life. First of all, you'd have to be married
to the woman with whom you had relations. Secondly—as
you've done—you'd have to do only certain things with her.
Everything else is wicked and abnormal, according to you. But
your penis and your sex desires are not going to want to do
just that one thing you say is "good." They want to do other
things. And consequently, you're going to have desires for
men.

The more you restrain yourself with women, the more
you're going to desire men—peculiarly enough! Because if you
had no restraints with women—suppose you just included
women of all kinds, all categories, that you were married to,

you weren't married to; you'd screw this way, that way, the other way—you'd probably have very little desire for men. But from an early age, you were taught, "Oh, no! Don't screw females. You'll ruin them. That's wrong! Wait until you're married, and then do very limited things." Well, this kind of teaching is just going to encourage you to have sex desires at a very young age. And if you've got to throw out women at that age, well, naturally you'll go toward men. That's not unusual.

P-33   I don't remember having a desire for women.

T-33   Well, but it would be unusual if you wouldn't. You would. What happens is————.

P-34   I've just been attracted to men and to men's penises.

T-35   Well, but now let's get into more detail. I guarantee that when you were very young, you were also attracted to women, and you threw them out. Now, why men's penises? The reason you were attracted to men's penises is, peculiarly enough, not sexual. It's this crap about masculinity, in our society. Because you have a little penis, comparatively, and you were raised to believe (wrongly!) that having a small penis is unmasculine— that it's sissified; that a real man is a big brute with muscles, who has a great big penis and can screw a woman's ass off for two hours or so, and then repeat it again in three minutes later, and so on. When you found out, very early in life, that this wasn't you—you must have been, as a boy, a reasonably small boy compared to some of the others; you weren't a big brute; you obviously didn't have a very big penis————.

P-35   One of my great desires was always to be tall. I always wanted to be tall.

T-36   All right. And the other kids, because kids are cruel in this society, probably made comments on your size. They called you peewee. Or if if you went into a shower with them, they'd say, "Oh, you got nothing there!"—things like that, didn't they?

P-36   I can't remember that either. I was ashamed of it, though.

T-37   How can you get ashamed of it, unless these kinds of comments were passed? You couldn't get this from nowhere—you weren't born this way. You read books which talked about big guys; and you'd go to the movies and see the big guys; and you saw the other kids—you must have seen them in showers, and swimming, and something like that. And you got the idea—and it's completely the *idea*—that there was something good, something better about being strong and tall and having a big penis than about being a peewee with a small penis.

Now this *idea*—which again is completely arbitrary, completely so; but you got it in this culture. In some other culture, you mightn't have got it, incidentally. Because in some cultures it's the little guys who are looked up to, peculiarly enough, and the big guys are thought of as galoots, who are ugly and so on. And the big guys are trying to be little guys in that kind of culture. But that's not *our* culture. Our culture definitely goes for the strong, dark, handsome man—the big prick! This is our stereotype. And you were propagandized to believe in this; and because you believed in it and didn't have it yourself, you used what we call identification. You tried to identify, to get close to the guy who did have it—to be in good with him.

Well, how can you get close to a big guy with a big penis better than by being homosexual and doing something sexually for him? This is the most logical way, isn't it? That's the way you have picked. You've tried to identify with, to get close to, to be acceptable to, to please the big guy. And you believed that by that way—by osmosis, sort of—you would get his strength. But this is crap. It's like the guy who goes around and wants to be a big producer or something, in the movies, and he can't be; he hasn't got it; or he hasn't got the money. So he goes and becomes a yes-man to a big producer; he licks his ass.

Now this is what you've done—you've been a yes-man, sexually, all your life. Because you wanted to be big and strong, with a big penis; and you've *defined* that as being good. Now, actually, it's not good; it's no better than anything else. But as long as you believe that this is the greatest thing on earth, as you have all your life———.

P-37   I didn't believe it was the greatest thing on earth.

T-38   Well, *practically*.

P-38   This was a certain *part* of my life.

T-39   All right. Let us say, *one* of the greatest things in your life. You also believed that being a great teacher, or something like that, is a good thing.

P-39   That's the greatest thing.

T-40   Fine. And there you've done well, mind you. You've been a good teacher, and you've helped your pupils, and so on. You picked a socially useful profession—which is fine. It gives you enjoyment. But unfortunately, at a very young age, you picked this socially dangerous thing, and you defined *it* as being good.

   Now, this is what a lot of these delinquent kids we read about do. They define as being good killing somebody else. And they really think they're great guys when they're doing it. They're *not* great guys, but they think they are. And to them it's perfectly normal. When they're arrested and put in jail for this, they think they're being persecuted. Because that's they're *definition* of being good: "If I can knock off more guys than anybody else, then I'm a big shot!" And they never think of the other guy or his family or anything like that. That doesn't occur to them.

   By the same token, you figured, "If I can get close to, get the penis of, as many big men as possible, this is the greatest good in life." And you've been obsessed with that crap. And it *is* crap. You've defined your worthwhileness in terms of that kind of crap. And you've never questioned that at all. You've just accepted it without thinking. And then the worst thing that came in after doing this—after accepting this crap—you then blamed yourself for being this way—which will only get you more and more upset. Because whenever you blame yourself for anything, instead of saying, "I'm doing this thing. I'd better not do it; it's getting me into difficulty—that's why. Not because it's wicked; it's getting me into difficulties; that's why I'd better stop this." Instead, you start up with: "I'm a louse; I'm no good. I'm terrible for doing this." And then you'll do it more and more. You become obsessed completely with it.

You first start with a small obsession—that is, "The good thing in life—to show how great I am, or what a *man* I am— is to get near this other guy's big penis." That's your first obsession. Then your second obsession is: "Jesus Christ! I'm terrible for doing this! How can I do this?" Over and over you say this; and then you become more obsessed. Because as soon as you think, "How horrible I am for doing *x!*" the only thing that's going to remain in your mind is doing *x,* not doing *y.* And that's what's happened in your case.

It's not in the least unusual. I have a dozen patients all the time who keep doing exactly the same thing. And there are literally millions who do exactly the same thing—all because they become obsessed with (*a*) "I must be a great guy, have a big penis, and so on," and (*b*) "I'm a louse for having this thought!" And *both* these ideas are silly. Because there's no reason *why* they must become a great guy and have a big penis, in the first place; and there's no reason why they are a louse for thinking this, in the second place. And you believe both these things. And if we get you rid of both these childish beliefs—and they're typical childish beliefs in our society—that you'll be a big shot if you get a big penis and that if you're homosexual you're a louse and no goddamn good—if we get rid of both these childish beliefs, then you'll still desire men to some degree. Because why shouldn't you? That's not the abnormality, desiring men—looking at other handsome men and saying, "It would be nice to have sex relations with them," just as I said the other day to myself, "Desiring 16-year-old girls is not abnormal."

But being *obsessed* with the desire, and giving in to it all the time because of the obsession—that's the abnormality. That comes from the idea that it would be so marvelous to have a big penis; and that idea that "I'm such a louse for being homosexual." And those are both idiotic, asinine beliefs that you have. And that's what we have to get you rid of—those beliefs. If we get rid of these beliefs, and make you feel (which is true) that you're a good enough guy just being a teacher and a husband, and that having homosexual notions is not abnormal (quite common, quite statistically normal), then you won't find any violent urge to carry these notions out. You'll get the impulse, the desire—who doesn't? Just as you get a desire to get in somebody else's Cadillac, when you see it on the street. But you don't go up to it, when he's not there, and get into it and drive it away, do you? Because you know you'd get into trouble.

Now, when we get rid of these two childish notions that you have—(a) you must be a perfect man and have a big penis, and (b) you are a louse, you're no goddamn good when you're homosexual—then all your compulsion will go. And from time to time you'll look at a man and say, "Wouldn't it be nice if I could go off and have sex relations with him?" Just as from time to time you'll look at an attractive woman and say, "Wouldn't it be nice if I could go off and have relations with her?" But you won't *do* it—there'll be no necessity, no compulsion. That's the problem: to tackle those two silly beliefs.

P-40   It all seems so simple. I wish I had come here a long time ago.

T-41   That's right. We would have got you over it a long time ago.

P-41   Because, you see, I was under the impression that I couldn't be helped. I thought I was effeminate. More than————.

[The therapist has longwindedly, and with deliberate repetition, given the patient the core of the rational therapeutic theory of compulsive behavior in general, and of compulsive homosexuality in particular: namely, that human beings falsely believe that they've *got to* do something, usually in order to prove how worthwhile they are; that this belief leads them into poor behavior; and that then they condemn themselves all the more for this kind of behavior and believe that they've absolutely *got to* compensate for it and prove their worth (or else prove, as they increasingly come to believe with these philosophies, that they *are* worthless and hopeless).

[Where, according to conventional therapeutic theory, the patient should resist this kind of direct teaching, since it does not really respond to his *feelings,* and in fact contradicts many of the points he believes and keeps trying to make in these sessions, it is found, in actual practice, that he does not resist, and that he is very happy to learn that there *is* a specific reason for his homosexual compulsiveness, and that there *is* something he can do about changing this reason and thereby helping himself.

[In other words, the therapist's explanations of how humans behave, how they get disturbed, and what they can specifically do to overcome their disturbances, are quite reassuring to many patients who feel that they are hopelessly muddled and that there is no way out of their dilemmas. The therapist is by no means telling the patient that he personally likes him or wants to help him. He is, rather, telling the patient that he has knowledge and methodology which he can present to the patient which will then help the patient to *help himself*. Although, therefore, the *relationship* between the therapist and patient is minimized in this rational approach, and becomes much more of a teacher-pupil contact than a personal intimacy, the patient is shown that he does not need personal love and sympathy, that he can live very well without *this* kind of support or succorance, and that if he *learns* the principles of human personality he can use them for his own benefit. Supportive, then, rational-emotive therapy definitely is; but not in the same personal way that other therapies tend to be.]

T-42 ———and that it was awful to be effeminate.

P-42 You see, when I was a kid they called me sissy. I liked to play with girls. I had feminine instincts.

T-43 Not instincts; we learn things like that. We all have some of these effeminate traits; but you learned things because you were afraid———.

P-43 Well, why were my other brothers the other way?

T-44 Lots of times one brother is different just *because* the other brothers are different. We often find that. One brother is good at math, so the other takes up music. He's not going to compete at math; so he takes up music.

[The therapist is trying to make the point that the patient was not necessarily born with effeminate traits. Today, however, he might admit to the patient that he *may* have been born with a tendency toward female gestures and mannerisms (since some human beings *are* born much more "effeminate" than others, and since schizophrenics and borderline psychotics, in particular, often seem to be physically fragile, uncoordinated, and "feminine" in some of their behavior and may well have innate tendencies to be this way). But he would have shown the patient that it is not *horrible* to be born with what, in our society, would be considered such a handicap, and that it is possible for the human being to accept his limitations and not condemn himself for having them.]

P-44   My brothers used to call me "sissy."

T-45   Were your brothers older? Were they bigger?

P-45   Not particularly. No.

T-46   But they were fairly rough and tough?

P-46   Rough and tough—yes.

T-47   All right. So you would not want to compete with them.

P-47   See. I was the sensitive one. I always stood in the back.

T-48   Because you were smaller, weaker, younger, and so on. You felt that if you'd compete with them you wouldn't get anywhere; so you went into the area where you felt more comfortable—because they were in that other area. It happens all the time. Did you have sisters?

P-48   Yes.

T-49   Were they younger or older?

P-49   One is younger; one is older. I was very friendly with my sister, my younger sister.

T-50   That's the point, you see: you were friendly with your younger sister because your brothers were bruisers who looked down on you and whom you couldn't get along with. But your sister would accept you. So, naturally, you felt more comfortable to be with her. And the more you went with her, unfortunately, the more your brothers wouldn't accept you and the more "sissified" people looked upon you. And then you said, "Oh, my God! I'm a sissy! What will I do?"

P-50   It's so simple.

T-51   It's tragically simple. We could get all the people out of it if they would come early enough and learn the facts of life. You've just been ignorant. That's been your crime.

[The therapist could get a great deal of background information at this point, but he feels that it is unnecessary to do so. He uses the family material to illustrate what happens to individuals, such as the patient, who think that they have to be great and strong, and who have brothers who look down on them. He guesses, without really knowing, that the patient went toward his younger sister because he felt more comfortable with her (actually, of course, there may have been several other reasons why he did so); and, as the patient's acceptance of this interpretation shows, it looks like he may well be right in his guess.

[Mainly, he is using the past events of the patient's life to illustrate therapeutic theory, just as a physics teacher uses experiments to illustrate scientific theory. If he turns out to be wrong about certain things, he will gracefully withdraw his interpretations, or even revise his theory. But, with a patient whom he knows will only stay for a short series of sessions, he feels that he doesn't have the time to get all the relevant facts, and that therefore he'd better stick to the more essential ones that come up, and use them for the purpose of getting the patient to understand what has gone on in himself philosophically, and what he may do to change his philosophic premises.

[The patient, by remarking, "It's so simple," confirms the fact that the therapist is doing a good educative job in explaining to the patient, in terms he can understand, what the backgrounds of his compulsive homosexuality are. If the therapist allowed himself to get sidetracked into all kinds of background and family details, he would not be able to do this clearcut kind of teaching. So he risks oversimplification, in order to get across to the patient a few major points.]

P-51 It wasn't entirely ignorance. See—at the same time while I had, maybe, no character. After all, what I did was supposed to be like a tramp, or a bum, or what.

T-52 Right.

P-52 I could have had tremendous character. I was fighting it all the time. I just didn't————.

T-53 Fighting it while *blaming* yourself!

P-53 Yes. Well I thought I wanted it, but I wasn't going to let myself have it because it isn't the right thing to do.

T-54   But it isn't a matter of rightness. It isn't a sane thing to do
only because our society punishes it. In other societies—if you
had lived in ancient Greece, for example you would have
had no trouble. You would have been screwing the boys,
having a great time; and then marrying, having a wife, and
also screwing the girls. This is what you would have done, if
you lived in Greece. But you weren't raised in ancient Greece;
you were raised in this society; and you have the attitudes of
this society, and they're very *punishing* attitudes. That's your
problem: that you're punishing yourself all the time; you're
blaming yourself because society is so screwed up. Now, if we
can get you to stop the blame—then, as we said, you'll still
have desires————.

P-54   I think I can stop the blame very easily. Because, from what
you say————. I mean, it makes such a common sense. You say
I'm in a society where they won't accept my type. I'm living in
a town now where I can't have friends, because they don't
speak my language. I can make friends with artistic people,
literary people, and all that.

T-55   Right.

P-55   While coming here, I was wondering if I should leave America. Not that I want to feel cowardly and run away from anything. But the fact that they call————. After my first visit
here, I came to that conclusion: the fact that they call criminal
what I naturally have a tendency to want.

T-56   But you have the tendency to *want* it, partly because you, too,
have the American notion that you should be a man, and so
on. If you didn't have that great *masculinity* notion, you
wouldn't be *as* homosexual as you are. You'd be normally-
sexed.

[The therapist has been trying to get the patient to see that he is not
wicked or intrinsically abnormal for having homosexual desires, and
that he should not blame himself for having them. Somewhat typically, however, the patient temporarily tends to go to the other extreme, and to blame his society for having rules against homosexuality; and he therefore thinks of running away to another country. The

therapist correctively shows him that he *still* accepts the views of his society, by thinking that he has to be super-masculine; and that *this* is the basic cause of his homosexual compulsion—which *is* abnormal, not because it is homosexual but because it is compulsive.

[In therapy, it is frequently found that patients, in giving up one self-defeating idea, immediately go to the other extreme and dream up another one; and that they then have to be patiently corrected by the therapist and brought back to middle ground. They particularly tend to go from one form of blaming—condemning themselves—to another form—condemning others. But the therapist has to keep showing them that *no* form of condemning human beings is legitimate. It is often pointed out, by critics of rational-emotive therapy, that it is dangerous to give patients new ideas, since they may interpret them wrongly and take them to irrational extremes. This is of course true. But *all* therapies essentially have to give patients new ideas, else the patients would not change. And in rational therapy, because of the nature of the continuing, articulated dialogue between the therapist and the patient, the patient's misinterpretations of the ideas the therapist is propounding soon come to light, and can fairly easily be pointed out to him. In less philosophical forms of therapy, this is often not true.

[Thus, if the patient enters Freudian or Rogerian therapy with the idea that he is an unlovable louse, and he begins to feel that his therapist personally accepts him, he may significantly improve (acquire a "transference cure"). But he may still basically believe that he *has* to be loved by others to be acceptable to himself. Because of the nature of the therapeutic relationship, he may well never make clear that he has given up one silly idea—that he's worthless because no one loves him—for another silly idea—that he is worthwhile because the therapist now loves him.

[In rational-emotive psychotherapy, if the same thing occurred (which would be less likely, but still could happen), the philosophic discussions that take place would almost certainly reveal those mistaken notions that the patient *still* believes, and there would be a much better chance that the therapist would be able to correct his false interpretation of himself that he has gained through the therapeutic procedure.]

P-56 I'm not really entirely homosexual?

T-57   No. By no means; but you have been obsessed with male penises.

P-57   Yes. In fact, in my last trouble that was the definite cause. Now I've had many men who weren't right. But this man was just the right one, and I did something I never would have done.

T-58   What do you mean, he was the right one?

P-58   He was just the right type.

T-59   You mean, he was big and strong and you wanted to be like him———?

P-59   And his penis really attracted me. I mean, I've seen other things that didn't attract me at all.

T-60   It attracted you because you believed that you ought to have a penis like his. Now why the fuck should you?

P-60   Why does a child want anything? If a child wants something he cries for it.

T-61   He cries for it because he believes it's good. And what is good about a big penis?

[The therapist may well have missed a cue here. The patient may be saying that, like a child, he has to cry if he doesn't get what he wants; and the therapist could have pointed out that he's *not* a child; he *doesn't* have to get what he wants; and therefore he *doesn't* have to whine and run frantically after what he wants—*even* if the thing he wants is intrinsically good. But the therapist is out to make another point, which may be equally valid—namely, that what we think we want we often want because we *define* it as highly desirable, when it really may not *be* that desirable in itself.]

P-61   I don't know.

T-62   Nothing. That's the tragedy.

P-62   I know.

T-63   It doesn't satisfy women particularly.

P-63   Well, why do I want it?

T-64   Because you were raised to *believe* it's a good thing. It's definitional.

P-64   Because I don't have it.

T-65   Right. The irony of it is that if you were a big guy, six foot
         six—and I had one in here yesterday: a big guy, about six
         foot eight; a real giant, with a big penis and so on. And he's
         disturbed because he's so big! He would like to be much
         smaller. But because you were relatively puny, and were
         raised in America where we got this goddamn wrestler-prize-
         fighter ideal—that every guy should be a big, bruiser ball-
         player type—and you have believed this crap; the irony of it
         is that you're artistic and esthetic and so on, and you're
         ashamed, to some degree, of it. You don't accept yourself
         fully, as an artist, because you haven't got the bruiser build.

P-65   Well, I don't think it goes into my work at all.

T-66   Not into your work; but into the psychic part of it. You want
         to be both the artist, on the one hand, and the big bruiser,
         on the other.

P-66   That's what I want mostly. The other was just a side line. It's
         just that sex meant an awful lot to me.

T-67   What a big side line! Yes, that's the point—and it's pure
         propaganda.

P-67   Now I've had a really small life in homesexuality, believe me.
         It was never all I wanted. I could have it; and I went after it
         and it disgusted me. Not because I thought it wasn't the
         right thing to do; because it just wasn't what I wanted. Now
         this last man, I would have enjoyed. There are very few men
         I would have enjoyed.

T-68   All right; but you would have enjoyed it *because* he had a big
         penis, and you think you ought to have a big penis. You can
         get along perfectly satisfactorily in life with a little penis.
         Your wife hasn't complained.

P-68   You can get along satisfactorily without any penis.

T-69   That's right. You would, without any penis. And your wife
         hasn't complained.

P-69   No, not at all.

T-70   And you get perfectly good sex satisfaction with her. But you believe you *should* have a large penis, just like you believed, as a boy, you should have big muscles and be tall and so on.

P-70   Oh, I stretched myself every night, so I could be tall!

T-71   All right. Now isn't that tragic?

P-71   But before I thought of the penis. I didn't get sex until a long time later.

T-72   That's right. At first, it was the length of the body.

P-72   I wanted to be tall. I wanted to be good-looking, like a movie star.

T-73   Right.

P-73   And my first experience—. I don't know if I ought to go into it yet; but as I think of these things, maybe it will help. My first experience of a sexual thing—I had about three. I went to the movies with my brother, and there was some man sitting next to me. I was only a kid. I don't think I was any more than about eight; seven or eight. There was a sudden movement. Then he put a dime in my hand. And when I went out I said to my brother, I said, "That man gave me a dime." I didn't even know what he was doing.

T-74   But he gave you an idea?

P-74   No, I never thought of it—until I grew up, later on—maybe that's what he was after. And then I remember in school. There was a fellow, a Greek fellow. He wanted me to sit on his lap all the time. I said, "Uh?" I didn't even know what he was talking about. And I sat on his lap. And he said, "I've got a book." He knew I liked literature. I was a very young kid. So I sat on his lap; I felt nothing. I was too young.

T-75   You were too young. Yes.

P-75   I just wasn't awakened.

T-76   But you later remembered these things. So when you got sex desires, you put two and two together.

P-76   I remember one time he saw me and I got scared. And I ran, and he ran after me. Then I didn't have any more experiences like that. The next thing I remember is I was looking at these magazines, at these strong men—.

T-77   Yes, the strong men, and the big crotches in the magazines. Because they had those jock straps on, and they had big crotches. Yeah, that's right.

P-77   Yes?

T-78   You said, "Why can't I be like that?"

P-78   No, that excited me, it gave sexual pleasure. Maybe I did feel it.

T-79   But you probably felt, "Why can't I be like that? And since I can't be like that, then at least I can get close to it?" Isn't that what happens in the movies: the ugly girl, who can't be a movie star, wishes she could be a movie star; and she starts a fan club so that she can be a friend of this great, beautiful movie star. Isn't that what goes on all the time? And you seem to have done the same thing, except that you did it sexually. You wanted to be close to the guy with the big crotch—the big man. One of the things that the penis is called is "little man" or "Long John," big man. You tried to get one by substitution, since you never could get it directly: you couldn't get a bigger penis than the one you had. What's the next best way to get it: to identify with the one who has it. This is how your obsession probably began. And if we get you rid of the idea that you must be a big man, and get you to believe that all you really have to be in life is what you *are,* then you're not going to need this kind of crap. This is what we have to get you to see. If you start to think about it, you'll see. You've been chasing a rainbow. All because you believed as a boy that it's great to be a bruiser, and you weren't. And your older brothers were bigger than you—even though they weren't big guys, they were bigger and stronger than you—and they looked down upon you. And they probably didn't want to play with you, and you played with your sister.

P-79   Well, I used to force myself. I used to make myself play with the boys. But it bored me. I never could be interested at the time.

T-80   You hated yourself because you couldn't be interested probably. You thought you were a sissy. That is the crap we've got to get rid of.

[The therapist determinedly keeps harping on the same thing, hoping that the patient will be able to see it and put it to use. He employs material from the patient's past—such as his relations with his brothers and sister; but he does not state or imply that these past *conditions* caused the patient to be the way he is. Rather, he keeps insisting that the patient, early in life, devised a *philosophy of life* concerning masculinity and a large penis; and that it is this philosophy which has maimed him and caused him to become compulsively homosexual. Moreover, the therapist keeps insisting, only by seeing and *eradicating* this philosophy is the patient going to get better. Merely understanding his past, as he seems to want to do, will not be enough. He must, instead, see his past and current *values* and must challenge and contradict them.]

P-80   I wanted to tell you, there were a few things that bothered me when I was away.

T-81   Yes. Well, we haven't got much time now. You hold them and bring them up next time. When would you like to make it next time?

P-81   Well, I'll tell you what. My case is coming up next week. Can I call you on that?

T-82   Sure.

P-82   I'm supposed to receive a postcard.

T-83   As soon as you know, you call me and we'll make the arrangements.

P-83   There's just one thing. I've been very unhappy about this student leaving me. I've done wonders with him; I've done everything a teacher could possibly do. He now has a good job; he previously couldn't read at all.

T-84   All right. What's the problem?

P-84   Well, he suddenly left and I hadn't heard from him in a long time. No why, no reason. I called him and he said that he had

had a cold and all that. He said he'd call me as soon as his cold was better, but I never heard from him until he came up to visit me with his son; and again, he still didn't call to take any lessons. He really was my pupil. I had taught him for some time. Now he called me today and said he wants to come and see me. I don't know just how to deal with him. He said. "I think it's about time I came and talked to you." I said, "Yes." I said, "I think it is time."

T-85   All right; so what's the problem? Just treat him very nicely and find out why he hasn't been around. If he has some reason, the thing to do is to find out about it, not to take it personally—in case he's gone off and taken lessons elsewhere, or something like that. But by all means just find out the information. O.K.?

P-85   You've helped me so much. It seems so simple. I'm sure I can think about these things.

T-86   I'm sure you can.

chapter 8

Verbatim Transcript of
Recorded Psychotherapy
Sessions with a Married Male
Compulsively Addicted to
Homosexuality—Part II

~~~~~~~~~~~~~~~~~~~~~~~~~~~~~~~~~~~~

Third Session

[The first part of this session, which was not recorded, is concerned with the patient's expressing, again, his terrible fears of the possibility of his going to jail for his recent homosexual offense. The therapist insists that even if he does go to jail, that will merely be an annoyance and inconvenience, and that it will not be terrible unless he makes it so. He shows how other people have been in solitary confinement for years and have not been too disturbed; and he finally calms the patient down in this respect. The patient then brings up his homosexual compulsion again.]

P-1   What I'd like to review again—because what we've been saying has been very good and it's helped me a lot—is this compulsion. I want to make sure what it is. I also want to explain it to my wife. When I get home, it's so hard for me to repeat exactly the way you say things.

T-1   Yes, it takes time to really get it. All right, now. Compulsion is a very simple thing. Take an illustration. Suppose you do anything that you know is wrong. Let us take something like overeating. This is a typical thing. If you really looked at it objectively and said, "Now, look: I overate today; this is getting me fat; it may eventually get me high blood pressure, arteriosclerosis, and so on; this is screwing me. Now how do I *not* overeat?—which is the only real problem here."

If you talked to yourself this way, it's really not a very difficult problem. Because if you overeat, you've got to go through all kinds of motions to overeat: to buy the food, to cook it, to put it in your mouth, and so on. It's really not very hard *not* to overeat, if you just thought of it *as* a problem. Instead of putting the food in your mouth, you just *don't* put it in your mouth. And every time you're about to put it in, you say, "No; I know it would taste good; but it's going to screw me. Ten minutes later, it's eaten; it no longer tastes good; and I've got this extra fat. And *that* I'm going to have for a long time. It isn't worth it!"

And if you kept reminding yourself, just objectively, every single time you started to put the food in your mouth—or even once it was going down, because sometimes you'll unconsciously start eating, but you'll know after a short while what you're doing; you can't eat a whole meal without knowing you're eating—if you said, "Uh-uh! None of that crap!" and you immediately pushed the rest of the food away, and got up and said, "I'd like to eat it, but it's screwing me," it would only be a short while before you got into the habit of *not* overeating.

This, incidentally, is what we do everyday. Because when you have an appointment at six o'clock, a very important appointment—say, you have to catch a train or a boat to Europe or something—several times during the day you remind yourself, "Now, let's see what time is it getting to be? Now two; now 4:30; now 5:30. I have to get going!" And you keep practicing this and you very rarely miss the appointment.

Now, if you took other problems exactly as that kind of thing, "I don't want to miss the boat to Europe," or "I don't want to miss the train; I'll screw myself," you'd keep watching your internal sentences—and thereby pushing the food away from you. Or, in your case, whenever you see a male who attracted you, you'd say, "Uh-uh! Hands off! No use." But there's one thing that comes in to screw this. There are really two or three things—they are all in the same line. The first thing is the catastrophizing. You say to yourself, instead of, "Well, how do I push the food away from the table?"

you say, "Suppose I *don't;* suppose I *do* overeat. This is terrible! This is awful! I'll be a louse; I'll be no good; I'll get fat; I'll kill myself!" And so on.

That's the first thing. Now, mind you, that all this catastrophizing is on the supposition that you're eating the food. You're saying, "Suppose I keep eating. Look what will happen!" And so on and so forth. Well, then by doing this you're still focusing on that goddamn food business. You're concentrating on it: food, food, food, *food.* Like one of my patients who was dieting. She would write cook books and everything else; but it was all about *food.* And finally she just stopped dieting, *without* this kind of overfocusing.

The first thing you do, then, is catastrophize. Then the second thing you do, which is in a sense a form of catastrophizing, though slightly different, is blame. You say, "I just ate that meat!" Not, "How will I not eat it again?" but, "What a louse I am! How could I do this? I'm a bastard; I'm an idiot; I'm no good!" Appended onto every one of your sentences about eating is, "I'm no good for eating that food! I'm a bastard for eating that food! How *could* I have eaten that food?" Again, all you're doing is focusing on the event— on eating the food, and every single thing connected with it.

P-2   You weaken yourself.

T-2   Right! A third thing you say to yourself, finally, is: "Look," you say (very falsely!), "I've tried to stop eating the food,"— which you really haven't. You just tried focusing on how terrible things are; on "What a louse I am! It hasn't worked! It's impossible: I'll *never* be able to give up eating, I'll *never* be able to give up eating, I'll *never* be able to give up eating. . . ." Well, here again, all you're focusing on is *eating.*

Now, that's what a compulsion is. It's saying a million times to yourself: "It would be horrible if I do this thing. I'm no fucking good for doing it. I'll never be able to give it up!" And finally, you particularly convince yourself of this last thing: that "I *can't* stop eating!" Or, in your case: "I *can't* stop going after males; I *must* go after them." Well, this is what the compulsion is: it's those sentences. "I can't stop because I have no control over it. There's nothing I can do about it. I *must* have them!"

All because you keep blaming yourself and catastrophizing. If you didn't blame and didn't catastrophize, then you'd get back to the real problem—which is, "How do I stop this crap?"—which is not a very difficult problem to solve. Just like: "How do I catch the train or the boat?" It's not that difficult. But if you start saying, "How do I catch the boat? And, let's see, if I don't catch it, I'll miss this, that, and the other thing; and if I miss it, I'll be a louse and I won't get to Europe; and I'll lose all the money I set aside for the trip," and so on and so forth, the chances are that you'll miss your boat.

P-3   You'll get all rattled.

T-3   Right. Because you're not any longer focusing on the problem.

P-4   How *do* you focus on the problem? What is the right way?

T-4   Well, the best illustration I can give is what I tell my pupils—that is, my patients. They're other people's pupils, but they're my patients. Particularly those in acting and singing. I've got a slew of actors and actresses for patients. They're as mixed up as anybody! And they come and they say, "I acted for a director today and I screwed up. Why did I do so badly?" And I say, "It's very simple. You didn't focus on the problem. Now what *is* the problem? The problem is not what the director thought of you and how well you can perform for *him*. That wasn't what Sarah Bernhardt was thinking of—because an actress who thinks like that is a ham: somebody who plays to the gallery and somebody who worries what the *audience* is thinking of her.

"The problem, as I am sure Sarah Bernhardt saw it, is: How *you* can take on that goddamn role and make it *yours, be* that role, *do* that singing, focus on the expression of that part or song, or whatever it is. That's the problem; not how well you're doing at it—which seems to be the same problem, but really is a completely different problem."

P-5   Doing *the job*.

T-5   That's right. That's always the answer. The problem is,
        "Here I am with this situation. How will I solve it?" Not:
        "Would I be a *good guy* if I solved it?" Or: "What would
        people think of me if I *didn't* solve it?" Or something like
        that. Now, your problem is that, in this silly society, you're
        not allowed to do a thing you'd like to do—which is to have
        homosexual relations.

        All right; that's not the worst problem in the world. How
        do you *not* have those relations is the problem. Not: what a
        louse you would be if you *had* them; or what a bastard *they*
        would be if they prevented you from having them. And
        those are the things you've been focusing on. "What a louse I
        would be!" or "What a bastard they would be!" And the
        problem simply is, in the reality situation, how can you *not*
        have these homosexual relations. And it's not very difficult.
        Exactly like having to push the food away from the table, or
        how do you catch the train on time, or things like that. Or
        how you read—by focusing on *your* reading and not what
        the other guy is thinking about you.

P-6   It all boils down to a way of thinking—thinking correctly.

T-6   Right!

P-7   You can think and do it rightly.

T-7   And you have to ask yourself the simple question—the
        question is always the same: "I'm over *here;* how do I get
        over *there?* And the over there is anything you pick—whether
        you want to give up homosexuality, or catch a boat, or so on.

P-8   So just what is the first thing I think about? For instance, if
        I see somebody and get that quirk, what do I think? Do I
        think of the ultimate thing that's going to happen?

T-8   Or———

P-9   Or do I think that I don't want it?

T-9   No, the thing you have to think about when you get the urge
        is, not that you don't want it—because that's untrue. Don't
        try to kid yourself—that will get you nowhere. You have to
        think: "(*a*) I would like this, but (*b*) I don't *need* it. And
        since they won't let me have my liking, unfortunately, I'm

going to have to give it up. It won't kill me; I don't need it. But I like it—so do me something! For the rest of my life, I may like it."

P-10 But I never had the courage to say that.

T-10 But that's what you've got to say. Not, "I'm a louse for liking it"—which you've been really saying. "How *could* I like that!" And then you'll like it more. Now, actually, once you admit you like it—but, unfortunately, you can't have it because society doesn't————.

P-11 It's a case of forbidden fruit.

T-11 Yes. Then the like itself will probably diminish a great deal. It won't go to zero—why should it? For the rest of your life, you'll probably look at males and desire them.

P-12 I've been forcing myself not to look.

T-12 No, that won't do any good, because then you'll find————.

P-13 I feel I've formed a habit. I know it doesn't do anything for me. I don't know why I do it.

T-13 Well, one of the reasons you do it is because you're saying, "It's wicked! It's wrong to look!" That's your compulsion. "I'm a louse for looking! That'll make me   ."

P-14 I should just look and say, "So what?"

T-14 Yes—so what? Just like you can look at Cadillacs that you want and say, "So what?"

P-15 It's killing me that it's so simple! It's very simple—that's what I tell my students, too—reading is so simple.

T-15 That's right.

P-16 Yes, it's very simple.

T-16 Yes.

P-17 It's a basic thing, which you have to keep thinking of until you don't have to think any more; it comes your way.

T-17 The reading doesn't come from their eyes, so much as from their heads. You've got to think the right things, focus on the right things, and the eyes will probably take care of themselves. O.K.: the same thing here; it's really so simple.

P-18   Would you mind letting me call you again—because I hate to call you and change the time.

T-18   No, that's perfectly all right. You just call me when you know what the program is.

P-19   Because I definitely———. I have to come in once a week because I feel that you've helped me tremendously.

T-19   Yes. If we can get you to do exactly what you teach your students—you'll see it's the same process. It's just a little different topic! That's all it is.

P-20   Well, I just want to finish my life happy. I've been pretty unhappy, though not entirely unhappy. There have been so many other things I've been interested in life. That wasn't my only ambition.

T-20   That's right. Now, if we can take out this compulsion, then you've got that much more time to———.

P-21   My wife'll be glad to hear that! Do you think it will be advisable for her to come and visit you?

T-21   By all means, if she wants to come once and ask any questions, I'll explain the answers directly to her and she'll probably feel better about it.

P-22   Maybe it's not right for her to come to the same one I go to. To me, it seems sensible———.

T-22   No; there would be no harm if I talked to her, especially about you. If she wants to come once or twice just to understand what's going on, it would be helpful.

P-23   I think I'll have her come in.

T-23   O.K.

P-24   She's really a wonderful person. Of course, my lawyer said that she was all wrong, that she was too easy with me. She should have said that she was going to leave me—that she would get another man and all that. Which I thought was good for him to see [laughs]. And he studied to be a psychologist!

T-24   Well, I'm afraid he's not the best psychologist in the world.

P-25   No, I don't think that was good advice. Like he said, "If she had another man that would make you jealous?" I said, "No, I think that would make me go a little bit more."

T-25   That's right. Two wrongs don't make a right!

P-26   That's right!

T-26   O.K.

Fifth Session

[This fifth session takes place a month after the third session. In the meantime, the patient has been fined for his homosexual offense, after being convicted for it; but he has been given no jail term. He was feeling much better, even before the case was closed. He spent the fourth session largely talking about his wife, who was very upset about his past homosexuality, and wanted to be assured that he is better and will not even think of homosexual acts again. The therapist pointed out to him some of his wife's problems in this respect, and how he might cope with them. He particularly warned him not to become panicked by his wife's perfectionism, and not to berate himself if he did think of homosexual things again. The main thing was for him to face his desires and not give in to them, rather than trying to repress or squelch the fact that he was still having such desires.

[At the beginning of the present session, which was not recorded, the patient talks mainly about some of his reading students, several of whom still owe him for their lessons and have not been paying up. The therapist tries to show him that he must accept their lack of payment more philosophically, and not personalize their behavior by blaming himself or getting angry at them for being the way they unfortunately are. The patient is at first reluctant to accept this view, but then sees that it is essentially correct and seems to come fully around to it. The session continues as follows.]

T-1   There are some things in life which you can't have; and that's too bad again.

P-1   Another thing. I'm a little confused. I'd like to review some of the things we've talked about, about my real thing. I remember the second time I came you told me it's not what we do, it's just what we think about it—how we think about it————.

T-2   Right.

P-2   There are six things?————

T-3   We are all plurisexual, and there are about six major sex things.

P-3   Now, in other words, I've got a way of thinking. I want to get away from it, if I can, because I don't think it's fair to my wife.

T-4   It's not fair to you either.

P-4   Why isn't it fair to me?

T-5   Because then you could get into trouble.

P-5   By disobeying the law, yes.

T-6   Yes. Just in terms of trouble, it's not fair to you.

P-6   Yes. All right, it could get me into trouble. All right. But what I think mostly of is if I should forget myself again and if I should get into trouble————.

T-7   Yeah; but why should you? It's very funny, you see. Now you're dreaming up something that really has little possibility of happening, and you're saying, "What would happen if it happened?"

P-7   I'm not completely cured.

T-8   No. But you can get completely cured, in the sense of *not* doing it. You may not be completely cured in the sense of not *wanting* to do it. But anybody can get cured of not doing it. All you have to do is force yourself not to do it, just as you force yourself————.

P-8   You think I have control of my mind when I get like that?

T-9   Oh, there's no question you have control of your actions. Don't try to control your thinking—that you won't do. That takes much more time.

P-9   I don't understand how to control my actions.

T-10   A simple illustration is stealing. Now, no matter how much you want to steal—suppose you have a real urge to steal— you're not going to control it by telling yourself, "Oh, no: it's wrong to steal. I shouldn't have the urge," and so on. Because for the time being, you're *going* to have the urge. We can find out *why* you've got the urge, and work on it; but that's going to be a while before we find out and it goes away. But no matter how much you have the urge to steal, you don't *have* to steal. You can definitely control the action of stealing. What could *stop* you from controlling it? The *urge* won't make you steal. You get lots of urges which you control every single day in the week. Now, why don't you give in to *them?*

P-10   Well, I think this is a stronger thing. I don't have as much control over it as————.

T-11   Oh, bullshit! Suppose you were on the street and you really got a violent urge to urinate—a real physical urge—and there was no place where you could go. What would you do—do it right in the street?

P-11   Well, I once did. Not right in the street. There was a park, and I went under a tree, so nobody could see me.

T-12   Oh, all right. But suppose there's no park and no tree—just open street. What do you do under *those* circumstances?

P-12   You just don't do it.

T-13   That's right. You look around. You finally, after 10 or 20 minutes or so, find a place where you can go. Now this is a real physical urge to go—to urinate. You couldn't *get* a stronger urge.

P-13   I know. I get them often.

T-14   And if you can control that, of course you can control the action of the homosexuality. You can't control the urge. You're going to get the urge to urinate. There's no use starting to argue with yourself, and say, "No, I don't want to urinate." That's ridiculous: of course you do.

P-14   But would you compare those two items?

T-15   Oh, I'd say the urinating urge is much greater than the urge to have homosexual relations. Because this is a real painful thing, when you're not urinating. While when you don't have homosexual relations or anything, that's not so painful. Nobody is treading on your toes. That's a desire; but the physiological urge to urinate is really quite an *urge*. And you can go to a concert, for example, and get really enthused about the playing of the soloist; but if it's the first movement of the concerto, you won't clap after it's over. It may be the best goddamn first movement you ever heard anybody do—but what do you do, clap? You wait until the end of the concerto, don't you?

P-15   Uh-huh.

T-16   Now, how is it you're able to wait? You're really enthused. The soloist has done a truly beautiful first or second movement————.

P-16   It's training. It's growing up and learning control.

T-17   That's right. It's telling yourself, "I would love to clap right now, but it's not cricket. Therefore I won't do it. I don't *have* to. I'd love to, but I don't have to." Now, on the homosexual business, you're saying, "I would love to, and I *do* have to." Now it's that additional sentence, "I have to," which makes it uncontrollable.

P-17   In other words, I could say, "I would like to, but I don't have to."

T-18   Right. You can say, "I would like to very much. I would adore to. But I don't have to." We do this all the time. Every day we get urges to do all kinds of things. If it gets very hot, you certainly get the urge to take your shirt off on the street. But do you ever do it? You're really uncomfortable; you're sweating away; the temperature is 100. And, as a matter of fact, in certain places you could have a coat, a tie, and everything on— with very hot temperature—and you would never take off the coat and tie.

P-18   But—I asked this before—it's hard for me to realize that a physical urge is as strong as the other thing.

T-19   It's stronger, in most instances. Because a physical urge has both the mental *and* the physical behind it. You see, if you're slightly uncomfortable on a warm day, and you say, "I think it would be a good idea to take my coat off," this we'd call a mental urge. But if you're really very uncomfortable and you're sweating there, and it's a formal affair, and there's no air conditioning, and so on, and you're very uncomfortable—then we have the original mental urge tenfold over what it was originally: and in addition, your body is practically demanding that you take off your clothes. So it's much stronger. You can't have a physical urge without also having a mental.

P-19   The reason we're able to do that is because we've grown up, trained ourselves to do that.

T-20   Exactly. We've always told ourselves, in those situations, "I don't like to keep my coat on, but I can and I will." And in the other situations we tell ourselves, "I don't like to do it. Fuck it! I won't. I'll go and not hold back." And it's completely a matter of training—completely. And it's really so funny: because I have so many patients who don't do lots of things—usually they find these things onerous so they don't do them.

For example, I have some patients who get up every goddamn morning late for work. Every morning! And their bosses are screaming and yelling and docking their pay; they get fired, and so on and so forth; and very often, it's only five minutes that they're late. It isn't that they're a half hour late and that they really need that sleep. It's five minutes; and despite the screaming and so on, they come in late. They say to me, "I can't stop this; I just can't get there earlier." This is bullshit—because the same patients, mind you, may clean their teeth four times a day; and they don't like cleaning their teeth; it's a hell of a nuisance. And lots of times, in the morning they spend five minutes cleaning their teeth. If necessary, they could go to work without their teeth cleaned. It would be safer and saner that way.

P-20   I know what you mean now.

T-21   So it's just that in one area, they learn. They say, "Fuck it! I've got to clean my teeth; and let's have no nonsense about it, or I'll lose them." In the other area, they *don't* learn to say, "Fuck it! I've got to get to that job, and no nonsense about it or I'll lose it." Now that's very childish in one way—telling themselves childish sentences—and in another way they're very grown up—telling themselves adult sentences.

P-21   Well, that's me. I can control anything. I went on a diet. I never had any trouble. I'm quite methodical in everything. But it's just this————.

T-22   Crap! You mean you *think* it's just this. Now I had one case which was very funny. This very brilliant guy came in here. A real brilliant boy; and he was complaining all over the place: "My goddamn boss! I can't stand him. He opens his big mouth and he says things, and I could kill him! One of these days, I'll sock him in the jaw."

So I tried to show him that that was abnormal to feel that way. He said, "But it's normal. Anybody would get angry under the same circumstances." And I said, *"You* don't." And he said, "What do you mean?" I said, "First of all, let's take the government. You live in New York City. You're a bright boy. You know goddamn well that every year you're spending at least a thousand bucks **extra** in rent and taxes and other things because of the graft in this city. Isn't that so?" He said, "Yes, I know that." I said, "Well, are you angry every time you pay the rent?" He said, "No." I said, "Why not?" He said, "Well, years ago I was. But then I started saying to myself, 'Go fight City Hall! You can't do it.' So I gave up the anger." So I said, "Exactly!"

And I said, "What's more, you told me that when you were 17 or 18 years of age your father, who was a real lulu, would annoy you continually. He would send you out to get butter or something and then send you out one minute later to get bread, and then send you out one minute later to get marmalade or something to go with it. You told me that you got over being disturbed by him." He said, "Yeah." He said, "I don't give a shit. I know he's crazy; it doesn't bother me at all. I don't get angry at him." I said, "Now this is the same crap. You got over the City Hall deal; and you got over your father —and God knows your father is closer to you than your boss is. And if you can accept your father with the shit he gave, you can certainly accept the boss—who you only have to go in and see, you tell me, once a week or so." That's all he ever————.

P-22   It was the same thing as his father.

T-23   Only it was less. Because, as I said, he only had to confer with his boss once or twice a week. It wasn't a boss who was over him every day: it was an upper boss; and he himself ran the department and once or twice a week he'd have to confer and the boss would say stupid things to him. No stupider, of course, than, "Go out and get the butter," after you just got the bread.

[The therapist is doing several things that are common to the rational-emotive approach. First of all, he is doing most of the talking and is actively depropagandizing the patient. Second, he is not being dissuaded by the patient's counter-arguments, but is vigorously showing their invalidity. Third, he is giving the patient a new idea, which may seem to be somewhat contradictory to the previous ideas of changing his homosexual behavior presented by the therapist, but is actually a supplementary attack on it.

[The prior idea was that the patient was *creating* his homosexual desires, mainly by demanding that he be very masculine and have a big penis, and trying for a magical identification with strong men with large penises; and the therapist was trying to show him that he could redefine his desires—or, rather, needs—in this respect, and become less homosexually oriented. But now, realizing that it will very probably take quite a while for the patient to work on his basic philosophic outlook, and therefore to undermine his homosexuality, the therapist brings up a new idea; namely, that even while the patient is still in the throes of strong homosexual urges, he doesn't *have* to give in to them in the form of overt behavior, but may frankly acknowledge their existence and then consciously suppress or squelch them.

[The therapist is *not*, in this respect, advocating repression—or looking away from his homosexual desires—but is advocating, at least temporarily, conscious suppression—or facing the desires and then refusing to carry them out in practice. He knows that this method will only prove to be palliative, and that the patient's underlying problem is still to rid himself of the overpowering compulsion to *be* homosexual; but he feels that the patient may well get into serious trouble, in the form of another arrest, if for the present he does not suppress some of his overt sex activity; so he offers an additional method of doing so, partly designed to keep the patient out of jail again.

[Even this new method, however, the therapist shows the patient, is largely based on changing his thinking, and the internalized sentences of which this thinking largely consists. Because the patient now believes, "I *can't* suppress my homosexual urges, when they are imperious," and the therapist is trying to get him to believe, "It would be a hell of a hassle suppressing my homosexual urges, and would leave me uncomfortable; but I *can* remain uncomfortable with the unfulfilled urges, just as I can remain uncomfortable, but still get along in life, with the unfulfilled urges to urinate in public or take my jacket off at a formal affair when the temperature is very high."

[Even in advocating conscious suppression, therefore, the therapist is teaching the patient to suppress in a logical, *thinking* manner, and not merely to do so blindly, against the grain of his own internalized beliefs.

[Finally, the therapist is using different kinds of stories, fables, and illustrations from work with his other patients. He is thereby doing what teachers and debaters do: being as persuasive as he can be, by making use of a whole armamentarium of logically propagandizing methods.]

P-23   Well, that isn't my problem. Actually mine is different.

T-24   Why is it?

P-24   Well, I feel it's different, in that one thing is so completely common sense.

T-25   Everything is common sense. That's exactly what this other patient thought at first. But one thing is so obvious: well, if your father is a crackpot, you accept it and let it go at that. And you say to yourself, "So what?" And also: "So what—so your boss is a crackpot."

P-25   Sure.

T-26   And the same thing goes with you. If you can give up all kinds of things which you desire—because it would be rash for you to get them. For instance, you have some money in the bank. I'm sure you normally have a few hundred dollars in the bank. You could go out tomorrow and buy yourself a down payment on a beautiful car, or something like that, which you'd enjoy. Or you could go out and buy your wife a fur coat. What stops you from doing that—things you'd really like to do? You could go and spend every penny in the bank in one day, if you wanted to do so, very easily. Now, why don't you go and do it?

P-26　Well, I have to realize that I just *can't*.

T-27　In other words, you would screw yourself, if you did that. Well, the same thing goes for this homosexual crap. If you can forego taking money which you have, and which you earned, and which you're legitimately entitled to, to buy a new car or something that you want, if you can forego that because *you* might need that money—and you're not sure you will, but you *might* need it tomorrow for something else—then certainly you can forego a sexual pleasure, if it is still a pleasure, when you know goddamn well that you may get in trouble with the police—you already have—and you're certainly going to spend time and energy at it, and there's a very good chance you'll get in trouble with your wife. Now, what's the difference there?

P-27　Well, one thing I can reason with; the other thing, it's hard for me to reason with.

T-28　Because you haven't tried.

P-28　I haven't trained myself.

T-29　That's exactly right! That's exactly it. You even see it in your own students all the time. They'll do one thing, and they'll really apply themselves to it. But there's something right next door that they just won't do any work at. And they screw themselves in that area, and then they come and say, "But I can't do it———."

P-29　Now, does that go back to the fact that I had a guilt complex and that I was drawn to this thing, because every time I wanted to punish myself I allowed myself to do this? Was it a guilt complex? That is what I'm confused about.

T-30　No. No, that doesn't mean this.

P-30　Now this is a different approach that you're telling me today. The other approach made me feel, "Well what the hell am I guilty about? I'm not doing wrong and all that. Then why punish myself every time, and go and do that thing————."

T-31 Let's get one thing straight. There are *several* reasons why a human being does anything. If you even go into a restaurant and eat a meal————. Let's take a certain restaurant. There are several reasons. One is, for example, you may like the food; it may be a special kind of food. You may like the decorations; you may like the waiter; or you may go there mainly to be seen, because it's a place where you should be seen. Now, why did you go in? We can't say you were in *just* because you liked the food. There are several reasons.

Now the same thing goes for this homosexual business. There are several reasons—some of them, oddly enough, completely conflicting; which is peculiar. Because let's take this guilt one; and what we would call—let's see if we could give it a good name—the childish gratification one. Two reasons. These are two of your main reasons. They may not be the only reasons, but they are two of the main ones. One of the reasons why you did the homosexual business is you *did* blame yourself, and you still have been blaming yourself all along. And if you do a thing that may get you into danger and difficulty, and that you make yourself feel guilty about—which means you think you should atone for your sins—then you do atone, you punish yourself, and you actually may do the thing *more*.

Now that's *one* of the reasons you engage in compulsive homosexuality. That's not necessarily the only reason or the main reason. Another reason is this childish gratification—which is almost an opposite kind of reason. And it's very humorous, almost: because the reason people go in for childish gratification—people like you—is just *because* in other areas they *don't*. They're very sane and respectable; and they don't do things amiss; and they don't spend the money they have in the bank; and they don't run around with women; and so forth. Just because they're virtuous in those areas, they often leave themselves a little loophole and say, "It's quite all right for me to be childish in this *other* area. I'm a nice guy and a scholar and so on. Why *can't* I have my little fun? Look at all

I give up!" Now that's an opposite reason from that of the guilt; and yet you can be doing the homosexual thing for *both* reasons. That's the peculiar part. You see?

P-31   Uh-huh.

T-32   And then there may be two or three other reasons as well. But these are two of the major reasons. And I frankly feel, in your case, that the childish gratification—the lack of training yourself to give up this homosexual stuff—is probably the main reason. Not the guilt—the guilt is a subsidiary one; an important one; and, incidentally, it only comes into play after a while. Because you don't get guilty right at the start. It takes a while; and then that adds to the other reasons. And that's one reason why you can't logically look at the whole mess and say, "Look: it *is* childish gratification! Let's stop the crap!" Because you're getting so guilty and so tense and so on that you're never calmly looking at the situation. So the guilt adds to the enormous harm which is there; but it doesn't necessarily create it from the start, you see.

P-32   You feel that the fundamental thing with me is the childish gratification?

T-33   Yes, that you *like* this homosexual thing. You happen to like it for the wrong reasons, but that's irrelevant. Because, as we said before, the reason you like this thing is so you can identify with a strong guy, and so on. But that doesn't matter. If you like a thing, you're entitled to like it for the wrong reason—just as you can like going into restaurants to show off. It's really a very silly reason, to go and spend a lot of money on a meal to show off, because other people will see you there. But lots of people do it; and they're entitled to act like children in that respect. So they do the thing originally for the wrong reason. They get the desire.

But suppose, for example, there are two guys—you and some other guy—and suppose the other guy is affluent; he's wealthy and so on; and he has the prestige reason. He wants to eat every day in Sardi's, the Waldorf Astoria, and places like that, which are overpriced. Well, he can afford this childish gratification. You can't. Therefore, it's more logical for him to do it—for this *poor* reason of prestige—than for you. If you have plenty of money, then go ahead: go have the childish gratification———.

P-33 In other words, I can't afford to be homosexual.

T-34 That's right. In this society. If you want to go to North Africa, or some other place, where they don't prosecute you, well I can't think of any reason why you couldn't afford to do it there. Everybody—or at least a lot of people—do it in these places; there are no laws against it. Among the Arabians, you wouldn't be prosecuted at all; and in some Scandinavian countries there is no problem. But in the United States, in your profession and so on———! Because there are even some people in the United States who can afford it, because it doesn't matter greatly in their case if they get caught.

P-34 If a person is unmarried and he wants to live his life as he wants———.

T-35 That's right. Everybody knows a certain wellknown playwright is a homosexual. As long as he doesn't do anything too outlandish, he's going to be all right. Even if he gets caught, he may be able to pay off the cops, or something like that. So there's not much likelihood of much happening to him. Though a famous English actor got picked up in England for a homosexual offense, and they won't let him into this country now. He can't get into this country, on grounds of moral turpitude. So some of the big guys, too, get caught. But there are certain guys who can get away with it. A Bowery bum, for example—what the fuck does he care? So they put him in jail for thirty days—does it make any difference?

But in *your* position, with *your* wife, with *your* pupils, you could get absolutely ruined. Like one of my patients just did. He ruined his whole professional life. This guy went up to the very top of his profession. He studied for years and years. He had about every academic degree imaginable. And now he can't carry on his work for the rest of his life. Because he got arrested for a homosexual charge, convicted of it, and nobody in his field would hire him now. At the moment, he's in a completely unrelated field, which is mainly manual labor. And for the rest of his life he's never going to get back, probably, to his original field.

P-35 Isn't that sad?

T-36 Yes. And, incidentally, this was a very well-disciplined guy in most areas. But in that area he just persisted in saying, "I'll screw them and get away with it! Why should I train myself?" And so on, and so forth. He just didn't want to work at it.

P-36 If I had just come to you sooner! I say—well, it's never too late. It isn't. I'm liable to enjoy the rest of my life.

T-37 That's right. You've got thirty more years————.

P-37 Yes. Because I'm a very great disciplinarian of myself. I even like it that way.

T-38 Right. But that's the way you have to be.

P-38 I even love it that way. And that was what was disturbing my wife. I think she'll be much happier now—if I tell her the approach is a little different now.

T-39 Yes: it's getting rid of the guilt on the one hand—which just obfuscates the issue. But it's getting down to the real necessary self-discipline under these circumstances. Under other circumstances————.

P-39 At least, now I know why I'm that way. It's childish gratification. I always wanted to be big, tall—I understand that thing very well now. All I want to do is keep studying every day now, keep telling myself————. Does your book go into this? Maybe I ought to get hold of your book.

T-40 My book, *Sex Without Guilt,* has some material in it. It has a chapter and a half on homosexuality, and it goes into sex guilt in general. So it will certainly do you no harm to read it.

P-40 I think I'll keep reading and studying it. Because things are so clear when I'm here with you. Then, when I go out, I get a little jumbled on it.

T-41 It takes a little time.

P-41 Yes, like everything else.

[This indicates another aspect of rational-emotive psychotherapy:

since it is frequently found that patients gain by reading the proper books, in between sessions. The present session was recorded some years ago, when only a few books on RT were available. Today, in addition to *Sex Without Guilt* (Ellis, 1958), the therapist would have recommended the chapters on homosexuality in *The Art and Science of Love* (Ellis, 1960), *Reason and Emotion in Psychotherapy* (Ellis, 1962a), *If This Be Sexual Heresy* ... (Ellis, 1963a), and *Sex and the Single Man* (Ellis, 1963b). As more general adjuncts to psychotherapy, these books are often found to be of great value in helping the patient to understand his basic problems and in shortening the length of therapy: *How to Live with a Neurotic* (Ellis, 1957); *Creative Marriage* (Ellis and Harper, 1961b), *A Guide to Rational Living* (Ellis and Harper, 1961a), and *Reason and Emotion in Psychotherapy* (Ellis, 1962a).]

T-42 That's right; like everything else. Like your students do. You tell them a thing or two; you outline it; and they do the wrong thing and they have to come back and get it corrected.

P-42 I have to get a solid thing. That's what I give my pupils: a definite thing to think about. I say, "If you think of anything else, don't come here. That's my idea and it's going to help you. If you're going to listen to this son of a gun or that one, you're going to get all haywire and get mixed up again."

T-43 My patients come in and say, "I heard a lecture by so and so. He said this." I say, "Fuck that! If you want to go to him, go to him."

P-43 Yes. You just mustn't go off in too many ways. I think it's more tightened up now. I think I have a little better approach. Well, I was just frightened. Right now, I couldn't care if I never saw a man! [*Laughs.*]

T-44 Like this guy, too, I just told you about. He got caught a couple of years ago and managed to get out by sheer luck. And after a couple of years, he just slid back.

P-44 Well, I'm going to get stronger and better all the time—because I've got something definite to think about. And it's so different from what I've ever thought. But, as my wife said, I've never thought————.

[It is apparent here that the therapist's authoritative lecturing is beginning to pay off. This patient, like so many patients, wants definitely to know what is what: exactly what causes him to do what he has done, and precisely what he can do to stop being compulsively homosexual. Instead of antagonizing him—as it should have done if Freudian and Rogerian and Sullivanian and much other therapeutic theory were true—and instead of bolstering his resistances, the therapist's didactic and vigorously counter-attacking approach has helped him see things that he never saw before, and led him to believe that he can now help himself by putting these new ideas to use. The pupil is beginning to learn and take the teacher's lessons to heart—even though he obviously has virtually no personal relationship with the therapist, and though the transference aspects of this therapy have been minimal.]

T-45   Right! In this area you never thought. In other areas, you think fine. But in this area you've never bothered. You emoted instead.

P-45   I just let myself go. I thought if I did it, I could forget about it. I didn't particularly want it. I may get a certain urge—my childish gratification again.

T-46   That's right: it's just childish gratification.

P-46   Now there's one more very important thing that is bothering me now. It's my sexual association with my wife. It never— we've had some very good sex and all that. Lately, I'm not feeling so good, and I got scared of it. I feel I'm not going to do so good, and I'm afraid to approach it.

T-47   All right; but that's just fear of failure. And that's silly—because you can't very well fail with your wife. As I say in the book, *Sex Without Guilt*, if you define sex accurately, it's almost impossible to fail with her: because all you could do is fail to have intercourse, and sex doesn't just consist of intercourse. Sex consists of intercourse—and fifteen other things. And as long as you're out there to satisfy your wife one way or another, you can't fail; it's impossible. As long as you've got a good right arm and a tongue and all, you can't possibly fail at sex. You can fail at intercourse. And the only reason you would fail at that is because you'd worry about it. But you can't fail at sex.

P-47   I wake up with erections. I have sexual urges and all that. But when I get with her I get sort of————.

T-48   Because you're afraid it'll go down; and if you're afraid, you're interfering with your own sex thoughts—and it *will* go down. Because you've got to be thinking of something sexual to sustain an erection. And you're thinking of something antisexual. It's the same thing as reading. If your pupils are worrying about how they're reading, or if they're thinking of the kitchen sink while reading, are they going to read very well? They can't do it. But the main thing, as I said, is to focus on satisfying your wife, one way or another—then it doesn't matter whether one time you don't get an erection. Sometimes you don't. Nobody's always potent, to the end of his life sexually, all the time. It would be almost impossible—especially for a male. Females are more fortunately situated anatomically. Because even when they don't want sex relations, they can have them; they don't have to do anything particularly. But a male has to get an erection, and he can't always get and sustain it. So what? What difference does it make? It's not a great failure. It's not horrible.

P-48   See: the whole thing is—she feels I'm not centering on her; I'm thinking of my homosexuality and all that; and it makes her very unhappy. And I try to tell her it's not that————.

T-49   No, you're not worrying about that; you're worrying about failure with *her*. And, by her attitude, she's helping you increase your negative attitude.

P-49   Well, she sort of makes me feel a little—not annoyed that she doesn't trust me, because I can't blame her; because, in a way, I betrayed her.

T-50   But so what? The past, you can't go over again.

P-50   But I mean, it's hard for her. She'd like to believe me; but it's hard for her. I think she's coming in to see you; but not this week. She has to get some of her pupils through a special test they're taking.

T-51   When she can get around, you see that she makes it. I'll calm her down. I'll answer her questions directly.

P-51   Well, I think we've touched on something that will help her a lot, today now. I was making too much of it, and I shouldn't feel too guilty about it. "What if it happens again and you get arrested again," I said. Well I just don't want it; I just think that it's something I mustn't have, I don't have to have.

[The therapist, in a manner very typical of a rational practitioner, not only shows the patient that he's telling himself anxiety-creating sentences to make himself fearful of sex relations with his wife; but he also teaches him some useful information about sex: namely, that he doesn't have to satisfy his wife with his penis, but may easily do so in various other ways. Then, if he sees that it is not absolutely necessary to maintain long-lasting erections with his wife, his anxiety will probably drop, and he will be much better at actually maintaining them.

[In this regard, the rational-emotive therapist does not hesitate to teach the patient side information which may be helpful to him in the course of his life. Largely, he teaches psychological information, so that the patient can understand himself and others, and therefore be less emotionally upset. But if there are any good sexual or nonsexual techniques that the patient may use for his enjoyment, and that may incidentally serve to decrease his anxiety, the therapist is quite willing to impart this information, just as any good teacher would.

[The rational therapist, in a sense, is a teacher of methods of happy living: most of which involve self-understanding, but some of which involve practical matters that the patient just may not happen to know about. Sex information is frequently given by the therapist, especially in the case of heterosexual patients who are impotent or frigid. It is also quite useful, at times, with homosexual patients who have sex difficulties.]

T-52   That's right. You don't *have* to have. So you like certain things—so what?

P-52   Well, she doesn't even want me to *like* it.

T-53   There she's unrealistic; and that's why I should talk to her; she's completely unrealistic. If you like a thing, whatever the reasons are, you like it. So what? We like all sorts of crazy things. But we normally don't do them. Because we know we'd get into trouble. Millions of guys have loved, loved enormously, 17-year-old girls. But they don't screw them. There's a law against it. It's a crazy law. You'd have a hard time defending the law; but it exists.

P-53 You mean 17? Or do you mean 15?

T-54 No. In New York State, girls have to be 18 or over.

P-54 Really? Oh, because we just had a friend, a school teacher, who had a terrible experience. He was having an affair with a little girl who was not quite 16. In Maryland, where he lives.

T-55 Well, it may be, in Maryland, a little different.

P-55 And everybody defended him. They all said that this little girl was a tramp and everything. But he was a school teacher, and had to set an example.

T-56 Statutory rape.

P-56 He got six months in jail—the nicest, loveliest person———.

T-57 All right. In New York State, he wouldn't have gotten away with it, if she's a day under 18. Really, is there any difference between a girl 17 and a few months and one who has reached her 18th birthday? There's none. And yet that's the law. And these girls are luscious, and many of them would jump into bed with you. But you just have to say, "No dear; we'll have to wait until you grow up." And that's all there is to it. Not because it would be wicked; but because it would be foolish. Lots of people can't eat lots of foods, to which they're allergic, or where they'd gain weight, or something like that. They love the food; but they just can't eat it. Now, that's too bad; we have to accept these limitations of being human.

P-57 It could be so simple; and I've made it so difficult.

T-58 Right.

P-58 The same thing with reading technique. It's so simple, and people make it so difficult.

T-59 Exactly.

[Where the therapist has previously been trying to show the patient the similarity between how to read well or how to teach reading well and how to function in life, the patient now seems to have truly internalized this analogy and to be giving it back fairly consistently to the therapist. This frequently seems to happen in rational-emotive psychotherapy: the therapist keeps propagandizing along a certain line, and then the patient takes up this line as if it were his own, and as if he thought it out for himself. Sometimes he realizes that he got it originally from the therapist; but often he seems to forget this and think that he originated it himself. As long as he finally *gets* this new way of thinking, it does not matter if he realizes where he got it; and it is not necessary for the therapist to point this out to him (though he may sometimes do so, as a teaching technique, or in an attempt to get maximum, conscious understanding on the part of the patient into his own thinking and rethinking processes).]

P-59 Because you don't get off on the right track.

T-60 And because the guilt comes in there—and they blame themselves. They say, "Oh, I'm a louse for not doing it the right way." And they don't just say, "Now let's see now; what is the right way? Let's see how I can do it?" They forget that completely. Now, if you simplify it down to its elements, then there's no question whatsoever that you can do it; none at all. Well, do you want to call me or make an appointment?

P-60 Perhaps I'd better call you, Doctor, because my schedule's so irregular. I have to see people when they come, right now.

T-61 It's perfectly O.K. with me.

P-61 But I'll try to get here at least once a week, because I feel————.

T-62 Yes, we want to get this over with, once and for all. It shouldn't take long, to really get it out of the way.

P-62 I definitely want to get rid of it. It's so simple it frightens me.

T-63 Yes, people tell me that all the time. They say, "How can it be so simple?" I say it is.

P-63 I know it should be simple. I just want something I know I shouldn't have.

т-64   Right. O.K., you call me. We'll finish it up.

[Here again, the therapist goes on in a most unorthodox way, compared to what he would do if he were practicing most other forms of psychotherapy. First of all, he definitely indicates that it should only take the patient a short time longer for him to overcome his homosexual compulsion—even though he has had it for many years, and even though symptoms such as these are only removed, if at all, by several years of intensive psychoanalytic therapy. But the therapist sees no reason why the patient cannot get better quickly, now that he seems to be getting the main therapeutic message, and to be understanding that he has to tackle his guilt feelings and has to learn to define his homosexual urges, as long as they still remain, as *desires* or *preferences* rather than dire *needs*.

[Second, the therapist keeps emphasizing the *simplicity* rather than the *complexity* of the patient's understanding himself and doing something constructive about his self-understanding. Many therapists, particularly psychoanalysts, stress the supposedly "deep unconscious" roots of the patient's disturbance, and indicate that his symptoms are caused by such complex underlying causes that it will take him several years of therapy to comprehend and work through these complex fellings and relations.

[Rational-emotive psychotherapy, on the contrary, gets away from this kind of mysticism, vagueness, and deliberate over-complicating, and insists that there are almost always quite simple, and easily understandable, philosophic tenets that underlie and cause the patient's symptoms. It insists, moreover, that he can fairly easily be helped to understand his basic value system, to parse it into the sentences of which it essentially consists, and then to vehemently challenge, question, and contradict these sentences, until he disbelieves them, and believes instead a much saner set of philosophies of life.

[Rather than try to get the patient to "understand" every minor aspect of his history (most of which is fairly irrelevant to his present disturbed behavior), the rational therapist tries to get him to understand a few "simple" things about the basic *causes* of his past and his present dysfunctioning. Once he comprehends these, and *uses* his understanding to *change* his ways of believing (and, especially, of evaluating himself and others), he can then much more comfortably live with the complexities of being human and residing in a difficult world.

[Where the patient himself, then, has a natural and an acquired tendency to *over*-complicate his thoughts and feelings, and where psychoanalytic and several other methods of therapy help him to become sicker by encouraging this tendency, rational-emotive psychotherapy shows him how to cut through many of the unnecessary complications, to see some of the bare bones of his self-indoctrinated nonsense, and to remold these bones. In consequence, RT not only usually takes much fewer therapy sessions than conventional forms of therapy, but also gives the patient more help in the course of these sessions than he is likely to get with other kinds of methods.]

Seventh Session

[This is a recording of the seventh—and, as it proves to be, the final—session with this compulsively homosexual patient. Only the first part of this session was recorded, since the recording machine was overheating: it looked like the session would merely be repetitious, and the therapist turned off the machine. As ironically happens, in many cases like this, the patient took a new track soon after the machine was turned off, and began to show that he really was getting the therapist's message, and was beginning to act on it. He went into detail as to how he had met four different men in the last few weeks— since the seventh session took place almost six weeks after the previous, sixth session (when he had also reported some progress)—all of whom would have been quite attractive to him when he first came to therapy, and with at least some of whom he would have started up a homosexual episode. But he was able, in each of these cases, to admit his attraction without believing that he *had* to have sex relations with the man in question.

[In addition to the technique of challenging himself mentioned in the recorded part of this session—namely, the technique of convincing himself that he had his own good points and that he was not "smaller" than the other man—he also started to see that he did not really have to measure himself at all against others, and that he was a valuable individual, in his own right, *whether or not* he was superior to others. The therapist particularly stressed this point, too: showing him that if he only accepted him*self* as good because he had good *character-istics* or because others had poorer *traits* than he, he was leading himself up the garden path—for the obvious reason that his own good characteristics might wither or fade, or others might improve their traits and therefore surpass him. In any event, he would be left in the uncomfortable position of always paranoically *spying* on himself and others, to see if he *still* equalled or surpassed them; and consequently he would always be underlyingly anxious and self-deprecating.

[The patient clearly saw this in the course of the interview, but wondered whether he would be able to hold to this view and carry it out in practice. The therapist showed him that his very wondering, in this regard, was another manifestation of his lack of confidence in himself, and his doubt about whether he was *as good as others* in retaining the valuable things about himself that he learned. The patient admitted this, and said that he would try hard to work on accepting himself unconditionally, whether or not he compared well to other people.

[At the end of the session, the patient said that he thought he understood what the therapist was telling him, and that he thought he now could carry on pretty much by himself—especially since he had great financial problems and could not too well afford much more therapy. The therapist agreed that he was doing much better, and thought that it might be well for him to try it by himself for another couple of months, and then come back to check on what was happening and how he was handling—or not handling—his homosexual and other problems. He said he would call for an appointment in a couple of months; and the therapist fully expected that he would do so.

[At that time, however, he did call, and said that he was getting along so well that he would like to try it on his own for the present, and only make an appointment when he was running into some real difficulty. Details of this call are described at the end of the typescript of the first part of the seventh session.

T-I　　Well, how are things going?

P-I　　Well, pretty good. I've got a lot of little things worrying me; but I'm not going to be concerned about those. I'm just concerned about one big thing. Isn't that sensible—just to think about the big thing?

T-2   Yes.

P-2   The main thing I'm concerned about in my life right now is this compulsion. I find I'm still attracted and all that by seeing a big guy. I'm attracted and I get a little thought in my mind; but what you've given me to think about, it helps me. I just feel, "Well, he's bigger than I am. I'm big in other ways." I think of good things about myself not to let it get me. But I'm just worried, "What if it should happen to me again, an act of compulsion, where I have no control over it, and I get into trouble again?"

T-3   But it can't happen to you again if you don't believe that nonsense—that you have no control over it. We *always* have control over our impulses—with very rare exceptions. It's the *belief* that you can't control it which makes for the lack of control. Because what would happen? You'd get very attracted to some male and you'd want to make some kind of an overture toward him—right?

P-3   Yes.

T-4   All right. Now, how is it possible for a human being *not* to control that kind of desire, unless he's telling himself that he *can't* control it? If he tells himself that he can't control it, then he won't.

P-4   But what is this compulsion idea? That's what————.

T-5   Compulsion is the notion that "I can't *stop* doing this! That "I *must* do it." That's what the compulsion is—it's an idea.

P-5   But I don't have that. My wife thinks I have it, but I don't.

T-6   Then what are you worried about, if you don't have it?

P-6   Well, I want it; but I don't have the idea that I must have it.

T-7   That's right. Then there's no————.

P-7   I used to feel that I must have it, because that's what was going to get it out of my system. I'd get it over with. I'd forget about it.

T-8   Right. You were screwing yourself. So————.

P-8   But the main thing I'm worried about is this. I thought compulsion is something that you can't control. For instance, when this thing originally happened to me this summer, I thought I wanted it. It was something very unusual: I don't just go for anything. And what I was doing—I didn't truthfully know it was against the law; that's why I got into trouble. And then when I did get into trouble, and I saw those plainsclothesmen, I thought they were just holding me up. I didn't think they were cops, so I added insult to injury. I became hysterical.

T-9   Right. All right: but you believed at that time—to some degree, perhaps a mild degree, then—that you must have this thing. Not that it was just a desire.

P-9   It's not that I had to have it—no. I felt that I had a very strong desire.

T-10   All right. Like somebody who wants to have a million dollars.
P-10   Right.

T-11   Or somebody who wants to have a beautiful car: "I don't have that. I'll look at it and say, 'I like it; but I could enjoy a Ford just as much as that.'"
P-11   Yes.

T-12   But how is it you were able, at that time, to *not* know the law? That's rather unusual—that you didn't know you could get into trouble for that. How did you *avoid* knowing about the law all those years? You're a bright guy. You read the papers. You read about homosexuals getting into trouble, and so on. Now, how is it that you could convince yourself that there was no danger, when there obviously was? We have to be a little suspicious of that—and believe that you convinced yourself, because you very much *wanted* to convince yourself.

P-12   Well, truthfully you see—I've been in trouble once before. And when these people picked me up, these plainsclothesmen, they said, "Why are you so foolish? Why did you try to do everything out in the open? Why don't you go to your home?"

T-13   Right.
P-13   Well, all I did—I asked this man if he'd come to my place. I didn't do anything in the subway or anything like that?

T-14   Well, now—wait a minute! *How* did you ask him? Were you touching him, or anything?

P-14   I said, "Would you like to come up to my place?"

T-15   Were you touching him?

P-15   Yes.

T-16   All right, now: that's the point! Just *asking* somebody to come up to your place is not going to get you in trouble. But you were touching him, also. Now, is it that you didn't realize that it's against the law to do it in that manner?

P-16   That was just ignorance.

T-17   Is it ignorance—or are you pushing it out of mind, because you just don't *want* to realize it?

P-17   Well, I realize it now.

T-18   Yes. But *then* I think you had such a strong desire to get away with it, that you were kidding yourself. And telling yourself, "Oh, there's no harm in this. It's not against the law." When it obviously *was* against the law. And then you got a rude shock and got confused and hysterical, and those other things happened.

P-18   Yes.

T-19   All right. That's too bad. But the point that I want to get out is, that you not *only* had a strong desire—the wish was father to the thought and the strong desire was leading you to kid yourself. Now that isn't true any more. Now you're very well aware that you will get into trouble if you do this. You're not kidding yourself on that count. You still have a definite desire to do it; but what could *compel* you to do it now? Where could the compulsion come from if you weren't making it up? A compulsion is a *definition*. It's the individual telling himself, "I must do this; I must do this; I must do this." Now, if you're not going to tell yourself that, you're not going to have any compulsion. And I agree with you, that I don't think you ever had anything but a weak compulsion. You had a strong desire, but a relatively weak compulsion. You never had the real terrible compulsion of some of the people I see.

P-19   I didn't want that sort of life. I always wanted to live a nice married life. I was married twice. My wife, now, she doesn't believe me. She said I got married because she loved me and all that; but it's changed her so that I think she's become sick from that.

T-20   I don't doubt it.

P-20   And she thinks I just married her for a cover-up and all that. I said, "I didn't do that. If I wanted that sort of life," I said, "there are plenty of respectable men who are living that type of life."

T-21   That's right.

P-21   I said, "Our next door neighbor. You respect him. He's a great artist and everything. He lives with another man. They mind their own business." She said, "Maybe it would be better if you lived that way." I said, "Well, that's not what I want." I said, "I'm in love with you and I want you. I don't want anything like that. Because to me it doesn't seem natural. It isn't natural; it's just some peculiar quirk or desire that I have————."

T-22   That's right. A quirk that you grew up with—a desire to get close to men with big penises, because they were "greater" than you because they *had* big penises. All right: a lot of people, for example, want to get close to beautiful women. I have patients who only go for beautiful women, even if they're dumb as hell, because they think that *does* something for them; it makes them bigger. This is the same kind of quirk, actually.

[The therapist, as usual, keeps trying to show the patient that it's not his homosexual behavior, in itself, that is important, but the ideologies that lie behind it and cause it; and that these ideologies, actually, are not very different from some of the ideas that drive heterosexual men to do foolish things, too. The patient thinks that he has to be big, he has to be great; and it just so happens that he has picked on a homosexual way of "becoming" great and big; but if he had picked on a heterosexual way of achieving this, he could be just as emotionally disturbed.]

P-22   Why wouldn't I have been drawn to big women?

T-23   Well, for the simple reason that you probably were so afraid of getting rejected by them. And besides, your problem originally was not a *sex* problem—don't forget that, as we've said before. Originally, your problem was one of strength: of being a man. When you first got the problem, you were a kid. You didn't get it in your teens; you got it before your teens. You wanted to be a man; you didn't want to screw.

P-23   Do you think it might have been something a little physical also—a lack of hormones or something?

T-24   Male hormones?

P-24   Yes.

T-25   It's most unlikely. Because then, if you were lacking in hormones, you would be lacking in desire. Actually, when we feed the male hormone, testosterone, to homosexuals who have deficiencies, they get *more* homosexual. They don't become heterosexual.

P-25   Really?

T 26   Yes, because they just get greater desire. The *direction* of the sex desires is psychologically centered, although the power of the desires may be physiologically influenced; so when the power of the sex urge is increased by hormonal increase, the individual becomes more of what he was in the first place—that is, more heterosexual if he was heterosexual, and more homosexual if he was homosexual. It's a mistake to think that homosexuality has anything directly to do with the sex hormones; for it doesn't. Most homosexuals have plenty of male hormones; in fact, many of them are out screwing far more than heterosexuals are, and they couldn't do so without being plentifully supplied with male hormones. So it isn't the hormones.

Occasionally, some homosexuals are asexual—that is, without sufficient hormones and therefore without erectile capacity—and they therefore may become "fairies." They can't screw very well; so they prefer to be screwed, and to take a wholly passive role in sex relations. But that's very rare. The great majority of homosexuals, I would say, tend to be higher rather than lower-sexed; and they are masculine in the sense that their secondary sexual characteristics—beard growth, hair distribution, body build, and so on—are quite normal. But the object of their sex desire, *psychologically,* is another male, instead of a female.

P-26   They become homosexual just for the strength—to have strength?

T-27   Well, they don't all become so for the same reason. A lot of them become homosexual because of another kind of weakness. They're afraid that they're not going to be able to compete well for and to capture a good female. And they're afraid that they won't be able to support her adequately, to be responsible as a husband, and so on. You see, you don't have that. You're willing to be a responsible husband. So you're not in that class. But a great many of them *are* in that weak class. They just say to themselves, "I'm no fucking good! I couldn't be a good man—and therefore I'll go with other men rather than with women." Some of them hate their mothers, their sisters, or other females—and therefore they stay away from the entire sex. In your case, it seems to be fairly clear that you wanted to identify with strong, big-penised men.

P-27   Why the penis? Why not just a big man?

T-28   Because that's the symbol. In our society, a large penis is a symbol of masculinity. It's a stupid symbol—since men with the largest penises may actually be among the weakest individuals—but that's the way we view it. And you have accepted this view, and insisted to yourself that you would be a "big man" if you were able to get close enough to, and identify with, a man with a huge penis.

[The recorded part of the session ends at this point. As noted above, it was arranged that the patient, at the end of this session, would call the therapist for another appointment in about two months' time. He did call at that time, but to report that he was doing excellently, and wondered whether he had to come in at all. He had first had several occasions when he strongly desired to have sex relations with big men who looked as if they might have big penises (since he had stopped going to public toilets and did not actually spy on men's penises as he previously had done); but he had easily been able, in each case, to show himself that he still believed that he was small, in character as well as stature, and needed acceptance of a "big" man to compensate for his weakness; and he was then able forcefully to contradict this idea and to rid himself of it. After several such incidents, he found that he was not even looking at big men any more and was not being particularly impressed by them when he did happen to encounter them.

[For the past several weeks before he called, he had been spontaneously becoming less and less attracted to males of any sort; and he was also enjoying sex relations much more with his wife. In these circumstances, the patient felt that he could probably do without more therapy at the present time, especially since he still was in great debt and was having a rough time getting by financially. The therapist agreed that he could stop his appointments—as long as he made sure that just as soon as he began becoming upset, or began to become compulsively attached to men again, he would immediately come in for treatment. He said that he certainly would do so if this happened. He did not call again; but some track was kept of him, since he kept referring other patients for psychotherapy, and some of them were his close friends and relatives. They voluntarily reported that he was doing remarkably well; that he now was a great advocate of therapy, and frequently helped others with their problems; and that he had even confessed to some of them that he used to be compulsively homosexual, though he no longer was.

[From these reports, it would seem that this patient, up to six years after he stopped treatment, was free from his presenting symptoms and that he was getting along in life considerably better than he had ever done before. The therapist doubts that he is by any means completely cured, and suspects that he still has a great need to prove his own worth to himself by pleasing others and by doing well in his work. But it would appear that he by no means depreciates himself as much as he used to do and that he has lost much, if not all, of his dire need to be accepted by others, and especially by strong, masculine-appearing males.

[Here is a case, then, where only seven sessions of rational-emotive psychotherapy were apparently instrumental in getting a patient to understand his lifetime pattern of compulsive homosexuality, to change some of his basic attitudes toward himself, and consequently to rid himself of this compulsion. This seems almost too magically good to be true. How come?

[For one thing, it should be admitted, at the start, that this patient was not exactly a typical homosexual, in that he was able to have satisfactory heterosexual relations, too, and was only at times overwhelmed with his homosexual compulsion. More important, he was not a general evader or goofer, as so many homosexuals are. He was able to make a good adjustment at his work; he was generally a responsible human being; and he had a fairly satisfactory relationship with his wife. In other words: in many aspects of his life he concertedly *worked* at making his way in the world and accepting the grim realities around him.

[A great many homosexuals, on the other hand, do nothing of the sort: but are general (as well as specifically sexual) goofers; avoid responsibility in many areas; and are not able to maintain almost any kind of a good sex-love relationship, even in the homosexual world. This patient, then, was distinctly emotionally disturbed, but not quite so badly as most fixed homosexuals are. Whereas they are (as noted previously in this book) usually psychotic or borderline psychotic, he could possibly be described as a severe anxiety neurotic, with a major compulsion.

[This patient, again, only had the problem of getting over his homosexual compulsivity; and he did *not* have the additional problems of going out to find a girlfriend and to achieve a satisfactory sex-love relationship with her. I find that these difficulties constitute a great additional hazard for many homosexuals whom I treat: since even heterosexuals in our society do not have the easiest time in the world meeting suitable members of the other sex, inducing them to have sex relations, and relating to them in a loving (or at least non-hostile) as well as erotic manner. Whenever, therefore, I induce a fixed homosexual to try heterosexual relations, and whenever he *also* fortunately knows or meets an attractive, intelligent girl who is more than willing to cooperate with him in this regard, I usually have little trouble in getting this individual to enjoy heterosexual activities, and thereby to eliminate his homoerotic fixation. But when my homosexual patients try reasonably hard to succeed with girls, and they unfortunately keep meeting with one rejection after another, I then find that many of them become discouraged, give up the battle, and sink back to exclusive homosexuality. So in this particular case, with this compulsively homosexual patient, he at least did have a willing female sex partner, his wife, easily available; and there is no telling what might have happened if this had not been true.

[Nonetheless, in many ways this patient was typical of individuals with a clearcut homosexual neurosis. He decidedly depreciated his own strength or "masculinity," and felt that he needed to impress others in this respect. He was most concerned about his physical appearance, especially his small build and penis. He magically tried to gain "masculinity" by winning the sexual approval of, and thereby being able to identify himself with, strong-looking, big-penised males. And he was not merely homosexual by choice or preference—indeed, his conscious choice was to be heterosexual—but was literally driven, most compulsively, to engage in homosexual acts which were generally unsatisfying, dangerous, and exceptionally self-defeating.

[What is more, he was in the usual vicious circle: where his self-depreciation led to compulsive behavior, which he then in turn blamed himself for severely, and thereby even more compulsively drove himself to male sex partners. Typically, too, before he entered therapy this patient was afraid of a wide range of heterosexual activities with females, and only allowed himself, because of guilt, to experience various extravaginal sex contacts with males. In many ways, then, he was even more typically homosexual than many other homophiles who have no heterosexual experience whatever, and who would hardly even think of marrying a female.

[This case seems to show, then, that with a highly disturbed, compulsively driven, exceptionally noninsightful, and relatively resistant patient, the rational-emotive therapeutic technique still worked unusually well, and worked in seven sessions which were interspersed over a period of four months. Similar results have also been obtained with many other fixed homosexuals, the majority of whom have had little or no heterosexual experience before they came to psychotherapy (Ellis, 1959b). I find that the more active-directive and rational-emotive my techniques of therapy have become (in contradistinction to the psychoanalytic psychotherapy that I was trained to practice and that I did practice for several years when I first became a therapist), the better my results with homosexuals have been. Although they are still very difficult to treat—for reasons given previously in this book— if they will come for a dozen or more sessions of therapy, they will usually make considerable improvement in desiring and having actual heterosexual relations.]

chapter 9

How Homosexuals Can Help
Themselves Through Rational
Methods of Psychotherapy

Although I have on several occasions incensed many homosexuals by insisting that just about all fixed or exclusive homophiles are distinctly emotionally disturbed, this does not mean that I think they cannot benefit considerably from making use of the methods of rational-emotive psychotherapy which I have expounded during the last decade. They most definitely can. In fact, whereas the usual Freudian psychoanalytic methods are next to useless, and often harmful, in the treatment of homosexuals (and, for that matter, of virtually all other kinds of disturbed individuals), active-directive therapeutic techniques, and rational therapy in particular, are often quite valuable in this respect.

Fixed homosexuality is definitely curable, in the sense that every homophile who truly *wants* to learn how to enjoy (and not merely tolerate) heterosexual relations can, with the help of a good therapist, do so. Most confirmed homosexuals, however, obviously do not desire to change their basic pattern of sexual behavior, but merely want to live more successfully *as* deviants. If so, is there anything that the methods of rational-emotive therapy can offer them? Yes, quite a lot.

Let us first consider anxiety. Most homosexuals, however "well-adjusted" they may be to their condition, suffer from various forms of worry or over-concern. They are terribly afraid that they will be exposed, ridiculed, and made to look foolish. Or they are guilty about their nonconformist behavior. Or they are frequently depressed about the hopelessness of their ever finding the kind of sex-love companion whom they really want (and who is so pitifully rare in the gay world).

In terms of rational-emotive therapy, these homosexuals are saying to themselves (a) a fairly sane sentence and (b) an utterly insane one; and if they will clearly see and logically parse and attack their insane sentences, they will not only immediately tend to become less anxious, guilty, or depressed, but will eventually much less often bring on these calamitous feelings again. Thus, the homosexual is usually sanely telling himself, (a) "I would not in the least like being exposed as a homosexual and ridiculed by others in my community for being one," or "It may not be the best thing in the world for me to be a sex deviant when most of the other people I know are sexually straight," or "I wish that I could find the kind of a sex-love companion whom I keep looking for, but it looks as if the chances are not very great of my doing so in the near or even distant future." If he quite rigorously stuck with *these* observations, the homophile would tend to be sad, regretful, frustrated, or displeased—but he would *not* be anxious, guilty, or depressed.

What causes his anxiety, guilt, or depression are various utterly irrational interpretations (b) that he gratuitously *adds* to his sane observations (a). For anxiety-creation: "Because I would not like being exposed as a homosexual and ridiculed by others for being one, *it is a terrible thing* to be thusly exposed, and *I could not possibly stand* others not liking me if they knew I were gay." For guilt-inculcation: "Because being a sex deviant in this heterosexual society is not very desirable, *I am no damned good,* am indeed *a worthless slob* for being a homosexual, and I deserve to be *everlastingly punished* for engaging in these sinful kind of acts." For depression-producing: "Because it is so difficult for me to find the kind of a sex-love companion whom

I keep looking for, *I'll never find one;* and if I never do, then *I can't possibly ever be happy* in the course of my entire life."

Why are these evaluations at point (*b*) insane? Because if one looks at them closely, it will be seen that they are all *non sequiturs,* and that none of them are factually related to the observations (*a*). Even if one *is* exposed as a homosexual and ridiculed by others for being one, it is *not* a terrible thing—but only a great nuisance or annoyance; and one *can* stand it (though one may very well never *like* it).

Even if sex deviation in a heterosexual society is not very desirable, one is *not* a no-goodnik or a worthless slob for being in this undesirable condition; and certainly no one, including a fixed homosexual, ever deserves to be condemned and punished for being the unconforming way that he is.

Finally, even if it is most difficult for a homophile to find the kind of sex-love relationship he prefers, there is no evidence that he'll *never* find it; and, assuming that he never did, there is still no evidence that he could never possibly find *other* kinds of happiness in his life.

Anxiety, guilt, and despair, then, are not caused by the situation a man is in, no matter how frustrating or dislikable this may happen to be, but (as the philosopher, Epictetus, remarked some two thousand years ago) by his *view* of this situation. Or, as we say in rational therapy, it is not the individual's *condition* which bothers him when he is emotionally afflicted; it is his irrational, needless catastrophizing or self-condemnation *about* this condition. Certainly homosexuals are severely excoriated and penalized by the antisexual culture in which we live; but there is no law which states that they have to depreciate and punish *themselves* just because their fellow citizens often try to do so.

If, on the contrary, they will strongly *question and challenge* the negative philosophies that they imbibe about homosexuality in this society, and if they will firmly keep contradicting their *own* internalized sentences which usually mirror this negativism, they can fairly quickly (though with a large amount of work and practice) rid themselves of almost all the anxiety, guilt, and depression that tend to accompany their homosexual behavior.

Similarly with their hostility and rage. Homosexuals often believe that they are angry against the world because it unfairly and gratuitously persecutes them for being different. Hogwash! The statement that they make to themselves at point *a,* that their community treats them unjustly and meanly, is indeed true and sane. But their view that this *unfairness* makes them angry is nonsense. What really upsets and enrages them is their own irrational *b* sentence: "Because the world is unfair and nasty to me, *I can't stand it;* and it *shouldn't* be that way!"

Who said so? What's the empirical evidence for this *b* statement? *Why* can't homosexuals stand the world's unfairness? They'll never *like* it, of course. But why can't a human being *stand* what he doesn't like? A little thinking about this will show that he damned well can.

And *why* shouldn't social conditions be the unfair way they are? It would be nice, naturally, if they weren't that way. But how does that prove that they *shouldn't* be? The only manner that we could sensibly say that something bad *shouldn't* or *oughtn't* or *mustn't* be bad is to assume that some magical God or Fate says that it shouldn't; and that assumption, obviously, is unfounded. The world *is* often bad; and homosexuals *are* frequently unjustly persecuted by it. So it is perfectly silly to say that it *shouldn't* be this way, when you really (if you are to make sense) mean that you wish to hell it weren't. But it *is.* And while it is the unfair way it is, you'd better calmly accept it the way it is, unragingly work to change it, and stop giving yourself a needless pain in the belly by idiotically demanding that right now, at this very moment, it simply *cannot, must not* be the way it palpably is.

Homosexuals, then, if they start facing the fact that their

gut-ripping hostility is fully their *own* creation, and stems not from the world's inequities (which are clearly enough true) but from their own childish grandiosity which prevents them from accepting (while actively disliking) the grim realities around them, can soon rid themselves of virtually all rage and psycho-pathic rebellion. At the same time, they can sanely retain their annoyance and displeasure over antihomosexual mores and laws in our society, and can calmly work to change these regulations (as, for example, by working in the Janus, Mattachine, Daughters of Bilitis, and other homophile organizations).

As has been consistently pointed out throughout this book, if homosexuals really want to help themselves in regard to their fixed deviations, there is little doubt that practically all of them can retrain themselves so that, at the very least, they begin to enjoy heterosexual activity, even though they may not lose their homoerotic leanings. If they are truly interested in attacking their own deepseated anxieties and hostilities, they can, by using the rational-emotive approach to understanding and eradicating their disturbances, almost invariably acquire a good measure of heterosexual adjustment and thereby overcome the fixations and obsessive-compulsive tendencies which are keeping them ex-clusively in the homosexual area of behavior.

Realistically, however, it must be acknowledged that many homosexuals—exactly like many other nonsexual neurotics and psychotics—will not thoroughly and persistently attack the philosophic sources of their disturbances, but will be content with more superficial change. This is a "normal" human tendency, in that the emotionally sick individual is frequently both born and raised to be an idler or a goofer; and although he theoretically *could* combat his underlying tendencies and *could* almost com-pletely reassess and reorder his self-defeating values, he most frequently does so, if at all, only in a partial and intermittent manner.

Many fixed homosexuals, therefore, will want to rid themselves of the worst disadvantages of their ways of living, but at the same time they will not want to work hard or long enough to become heterosexually or ambisexually oriented. For these individuals who want to have limited, but still definite, emotional gains, the principles of rational-emotive psychotherapy can still be employed to good effect. If they take these principles to their logical conclusions, they will give up virtually all their anxieties and hostilities, and therefore will not remain fixed homophiles. But if they partly employ rational-scientific ideologies, they may well be able to remain homosexually fixated and still not defeat themselves *too* badly in their life pursuits.

Terminal Essay:

Homosexuality and the
Mystique of the Gigantic Penis

by Donald Webster Cory

It would seem that every aspect of homosexual behavior has by now been examined: the gay world has been looked at from within and from without, by journalists and jurists, by therapists and apologists, by those seeking to make a buck and others seeking to make a trick.

The homosexual has been put on a couch and taken off, his orgasms counted and his shoulders measured, his drinking patterns analyzed and his sexual partners scrutinized.

At first, he was studied alone; later in dyadic relations; and finally in groups—both informal and amorphous as well as structured and organized groups, including the reformist and social protest homophile movement.

Little seemed to remain that was still untouched in this area of human behavior, and if there was considerable controversy, on the one hand, or ignorance, on the other, it could no longer be said that a wall of silence surrounded the homosexual.

But now Albert Ellis, never one to fear a promenade on hitherto untrodden grounds, has focused attention—for the first time in writing, I believe—on the mystique surrounding the love for the big penis among homosexuals. If one may mix some metaphors, Dr. Ellis may have opened up Pandora's box and found therein a gigantic phallus; and if to this one may add the sin of a pun, he has come up with an hypothesis to explain the phenomenon, but the hypothesis, if generally applied, may contain a small phallus and a big fallacy.

First, let us get one thing straight—if I may be excused the word. The observation that Dr. Ellis has made in his private practice as a therapist—namely, that male homosexuals are attracted by and aroused by other males who have big penises—is true not only of those disturbed gay men who come for treatment, but is almost universally true of males attracted to other males. Dr. Ellis, then, deserves commendation on three grounds: first, for making a cogent observation from his clinical practice; second, for attempting a generalization to explain the phenomenon; and third, for bringing to light, for the purpose of investigation and discussion, a previously uninvestigated area of homosexual behavior.

Unfortunately, generalization from a single case has many dangers, as the neo-Freudians discovered in connection with Freud's basing some of his most sweeping theoretical formulations on a single insightful study—for example, of Dora. If a scientist looks at only one case, no matter how careful the observation nor how astute the analysis, it is impossible to know what is idiosyncratic about that case and what is representative of the entire class of instances of which it is one member.

Thus, the investigation of one homosexual who happens to be excited by large penises may prove atypical in many respects. It may be that other homosexuals are not similarly aroused by an oversized phallus, but that only a few are. Or it may be that most homosexuals do go for a penis nine inches in length and equally fantastic in diameter, but for a variety of different reasons, that may have to do with their own body-build, or what they like to do in bed, or whether they were narcissistic masturbators, or whether they are searching for father figures, or what not. Unless one examines a number of members of a class or category, generalizations are hypothetical and speculative.

Now, it is entirely possible, and most believable, that Dr. Ellis had a patient who had three characteristics: (*a*) he was compulsively homosexual; (*b*) he had a very small penis, or at least thought he did; and (*c*) he liked to have male lovers, tricks, bedmates, and others, whose genitals bulged like a pornographic picture out of the magazines that have come to be called beefcake.

From this, one is tempted to draw the conclusion—which, I might emphasize, Dr. Ellis never draws, but which can be overgeneralized from the second verbatim case discussion he presents in this volume—that one of the correlates of the big-penis-loving homosexual is the little-teeny-weewee-having guy, who imagines that he is worthless because he is underendowed in a not unimportant area, and who, as a result of this or concomitant therewith, doubts his own masculinity, sees himself as being less than man, envies true manliness, and hence wants to be close to the epitome of those whom he envies. Somehow, as if by osmosis, some true "manliness" will seep through to this effeminate man whose virile member would not look too big under a magnifying glass and would never make much of a mouthful for a partner. Masculinity will be felt, or so the gay guy believes, if only he can get his hands on, or his body next to, something that looks like a caveman's club or an elephant's trunk.

It might be concluded, from a cursory reading and rash jumping to conclusions about Dr. Ellis's case, that male homosexuals (or specifically, those who like big-phallused partners) are themselves small-penised; and that there is a high correlation between those who have little themselves and those who want a great deal in the other male. But this is dubious.

What are the facts? First, it is part of the entire homosexual drive, part of what I consider the homosexual mystique, to go for sizeable sex organs. This is not at all restricted to those poorly endowed in this respect. Gay males, large and small themselves, and the large as much as the small, spurn the lover with a penis that resembles a cocktail frankfurter.

In fact, there is possibly only one other factor among homosexuals that is so universally strong as a drive for the big penis; that is, the interest in youthful lovers. Now and then, the homosexual is found who has interests directed toward older men, father images, and even grandfather images. Frequently, there is interest in mates of one's own age. But sexual arousal generally takes place when the homosexual views a youthful male. He may be tall or short, blond or dark, quiet or garrulous, but he should be youthful—and have an impressive-looking phallus.

Some of the homosexuals who have this strong interest in quantity may themselves be small, but they are indeed in the minority. Certain observers of the homosexual scene, having done little research and having almost no homoerotic experience, have postulated that homosexuals are genitally undersized. But the fact is that there is no sign of any inverse ratio between size of penis and interest in homosexual behavior. I have, in my personal experience, physically examined many homosexuals, perhaps hundreds if not thousands; and I can recall only two or three who were genitally small, a handful (figuratively, not literally) who were unimpressive, while most were normally big and abnormally big—and, incidentally, were extremely proud of this feature of their anatomy. I would guess that homosexuals, in this respect, are indistinguishable from heterosexuals. Information on this matter may be present in the files of the Institute for Sex Research, but if so has not yet been disclosed.

Are big-built gay males interested in other big-built males? Yes. Do they also become aroused by and direct their interests toward the man whose penis resembles a little boy's pinkie? They do not. The drive toward the big penis seems to be a part of being homosexual, and seems to take in those who themselves are small, big, and in the not-too-happy medium. Seeking for a large-phallused partner, then, is a trait characteristic not of the men with small penises, but of men interested in males.

The homosexual who is on the small side may be in a particularly disadvantageous position. First, he is not in demand, and as the word gets around in the gay circles that he is so small, he is spurned and scorned. Second, in his contact with other homosexual males, he is constantly reminded of his deficiency. The two penises next to one another serve to bring home his own shortcoming. If he were with a woman, even if she were aware of this, he would not be so acutely aware of her awareness.

He is likely, under these circumstances, to scorn his own body, to have a feeling of self-worthlessness (as described by Dr. Ellis); and in at least one instance that I am familiar with, a homosexual male with a small penis was also a masochist. He had a horse-whip in his bedroom, would get undressed, beg to be whipped, ask the partner (hardly an appropriate word) to spit at him and to call him by various pejorative epithets and invectives, and then, as he became aroused by the pain, would lie almost prostrate on the bed, and implore the whipper to enter "through the rear door."

Most homosexuals, however, are not at all small in the genital area, are quite proud of being adequate, and yet want a bedmate who is equally big, if not bigger. This is not explicable on the rational grounds that more can be done, in the way of arousal and gratification, if one's partner possesses a larger instrument with which to do it. Oddly enough, many of the males who seek a partner who is big will have an intimate front-to-front body contact (fondling or frottage) with him; will engage in mutual fondling and some degree of mutual masturbation; and then will seek to ignore the other person's penis entirely, and will want to continue and conclude the relationship by being the insertor partner in fellation or anal intercourse. It is true that, while these acts occur, the penis of the bedmate can be, and often is, fondled; but more frequently, if only because of physical convenience, it is ignored. Thus, except for preliminary arousal, the degree to which a person can be satisfied is little affected by size of his partner's organ, although he may be highly excited by its size.

What about the partner who acts as receptor, in anal relations or fellation, or the one who indulges in mutual fellation? Again, it is difficult to see how heightened satisfaction can account for attraction to size of penis. The large size is definitely ill-fitting, painful, uncomfortable—all of which could serve as reasons to account for the mystique surrounding it only if we are to hypothesize (as some authorities have in fact done) that the receptor in such a relationship generally plays a humiliating, self-degrading, self-denigrating, and essentially masochistic role.

One case history, personally known to me, is worth a brief summary.

Hans is a 20-year-old white youth, born and brought up in a large urban center. He was playfully involved in homosexual relations with peers at about the age of nine, more seriously so from 13 onward. He had infrequent heterosexual relations from time to time after the age of 15, but always preferred males, usually his own age, but occasionally somewhat older. Goodlooking, unattached to any family since his early adolescence, free to move in and out with roommates and lovers, Hans found all of the sex he wanted: perhaps an average of two or three different partners a week between the ages of 15 and 20. He has been with men of all ages and all races, and is popular with them. They return to him and beseech him to repeat what started as a one-night stand. He is aware that a major reason for this popularity is that they discover that he is unusually big.

How big? Hans claims that, comparing his erection to another's, he has never seen a male whom he did not outsize by at least one inch, and usually by three. He admits, somewhat reluctantly, that he has met men whose penises were thicker, fatter, heavier, but never longer. Those who approached him in size, although not reaching his length, were invariably Negro, and most of these men would make a remark, somewhat to the effect: "If I ever met anyone bigger than me, I thought it would be another colored guy." Or, as one put it: "I thought the good

Lord didn't make white guys as big as us, but I was wrong, you're bigger than any of us. Maybe the Lord got mixed up, and thought you was going to be colored."

I have personally examined Hans, and can attest that this is not an exaggeration. But, lo and behold, Hans himself is deeply attracted to partners with big organs, is excited by the bigness, by seeing an oversized penis, fondling it, hugging and kissing it. Now, one might be tempted to conclude from this single case history that homosexuals with extraordinarily big penises have a liking for men with big organs, so that the former can out-distance and humiliate their partners and bedmates.

But Hans, like the man with the little penis described by Dr. Ellis, is typical of a large group of homosexual males: a group that consists of men with phalluses big, small, and medium-sized; fat, thin, and medium-diameter; straight or curved, cir-cumsized or uncircumsized, white or black or red or yellow; and having any other physical characteristic within the range of human variety. All these male homosexuals are aroused by and attracted by partners with something to show.

In fact, we must also note that women, too, are interested in big phalluses—partly for the rational reason that a large penis can be more stimulating to a woman during intromission, because it will cause greater penile-vaginal friction and consequent satisfaction.

Considering the preference that women have for the large penis (in spite of the fact that it plays a minor although not miniscule role in their sex arousal); and considering the almost unanimous interest of the male homosexual in this phenomenon, how can this near-universal preference be explained? I should like to hypothesize the following:

1. The attraction of the large penis should be thought of in terms of lovers of males; not in terms of homosexual males, as one category, and heterosexual females, as another. These two categories have something in common, so that on another and

higher level of abstraction, one conceptualization can be made of the two; namely, that both heterosexual females and homosexual males are interested in sexual gratification with males.

2. Nonetheless, for a variety of reasons that are related to the etiology of homosexuality, to the difficulties of playing the role of a homosexual in Western society without becoming disturbed by the social pressures, and to the inherent biological limitations on male-male relationships, the homosexual becomes more exclusively body-oriented and body-aroused vis-à-vis other males than does the heterosexual woman. She, although undoubtedly interested in the male's shape, body, face, etc., is also interested in his personality, mind, occupation, social status. Thus, attention on the body, and on any one part of it, becomes for the woman diluted in the general attraction to the total person, which she calls "love."

3. Further differentiating the male-loving male and the male-loving female in this regard is the biological difference, which may or may not be culturally reinforced, between males (whatever their sexual preference) and females (whatever theirs may be). Men generally are easily aroused by the sight of a body, a face, or a part of the anatomy, so long as the person doing the arousing is of the right sex. Thus, heterosexual men stare at breasts bobbing up and down beneath the sweater, and heterosexual men find it easy to fantasy themselves with, and make arrangements to be with, females whom they had never before seen. Homosexual men are similarly easily aroused by other males, and by their faces, muscles, and penises. The important conceptual category here is no longer the person who is aroused by males, but the person who is himself male; and most males seem to be eye-directed to a potential (heterosexual or homosexual) sex partner, and highly attracted to his (or her) zones which are conceived as being erogenous.

4. Homosexual men are usually seeking males, and very masculine ones, at that. The "fairy" or the "nellie" gets spurned

by most homosexuals, not only because of the social stigma attached to being seen with him, but because the gay guy is looking for a man, not for a woman. Wanting a man, he feels reinforced that he has found one if the symbols of manhood are pronounced, even if they are exaggerated.

5. It may be that the homosexual is more in contact with the genitals of the partners, rather than with the whole body and the whole person, than is the heterosexual. For psychological and cultural reasons, it is possible that many homosexuals are having a genital-to-genital relationship, rather than a person-to-person relationship. Thus, we have the common fly-by-night affairs, one-night stands, the extreme depersonalization of reaching through a gloryhole for someone who has not been seen. We also have a great deal of nonsexual love, or highly affection-laden relationships that homosexuals establish among themselves—loves that are person to person, but devoid of physical contact. If, as would seem true, numerous homosexual relationships are either genital or love contacts, but seldom a combination of both, the homosexual might well be more prone to concentrate on the existence of his partner's genitals, their size and shape and form. If the penis is so good, then more of it should be even better.

Bibliography and Index

The figures in parentheses following a reference indicate the pages in this book on which the reference is cited.

Abrams, A. Homosexuality. *Med. Rev. of Revs.*, 1918, 24, 528. (21)

Adler, A. The homosexual problem. *Alien. & Neurol.*, 1917, 38, 285. (22,57)

Adler, A. *The practice and theory of individual psychology.* New York: Harcourt, Brace, 1939a. (22, 46, 57)

Adler, A. *Social interest.* New York: Putnams, 1939b. (57)

Allen, C. Homosexuality: the psychological factor. *Med. Press,* Sept. 3, 1947, 222-223. (46, 47)

Allen, C. *The sexual perversions and abnormalities.* London: Oxford University Press, 1949. (22, 46, 56, 57, 94)

Allen, C. On the cure of homosexuality. *Int. J. Sexol.*, 1952, 5, 148-150. (46)

Allen, C., Broster, L. R., *et al. The adrenal cortex and intersexuality.* London: Chapman and Hall, 1938. (22, 32)

Allen, L. Just how paranoid are homosexuals? *Mattachine Rev.*, 1960, 10-17. (41)

Barahal, H. S. Constitutional factors in psychotic male homosexuals. *Psychiat. Quart.*, 1939, 13, 398. (33, 36, 37)

Barahal, H. S. Testosterone in psychotic male homosexuality. *Psychiat. Quart.*, 1940, 14, 391. (22, 31, 57)

Barr and Hobbs, 1954. Cited in British Medical Association, *Homosexuality and prostitution.* London: British Medical Association, 1955. (29)

Bauer, J. Homosexuality as an endocriminological, psychological and genetic problem. *J. Crim. Psychopath.*, 1940, 2, 188. (21, 41)

Benjamin, H. In time we must accept. *Mattachine Rev.*, April, 1958, 4-7. (30)

Benjamin, H. Seven kinds of sex. *Sexology*, 1961, 27, 1-8. (30)

Benjamin, H., and Ellis, A. An objective examination of prostitution. *Int. J. Sexol.*, 1954, 8, 99-105. (56, 88)

Bergler, E. *Homosexuality.* New York: Hill and Wang, 1956. (57)

Berne, E. *The mind in action.* New York: Simon and Schuster, 1947. (46)

Berrios, C. H. Sex life of the Incas. *Sexology,* 1961, 27, 698-700. (48)

Bieber, I., *et al. Homosexuality.* New York: Basic Books, 1962. (22, 35, 46, 57, 94)

Bien, E. Why do homosexuals undergo treatment? *Med. Rev. of Revs.*, 1934, 40, 10. (43, 46)

Bloch, I. *The sexual life of our time.* New York: Rebman, 1908. (21, 36)

Bloch, I. *Anthropological studies in the strange sexual practices of all races.* New York: Anthropology Press, 1933. (37)

Branson, H. K. Why should deviates seek voluntary treatment. *One Inst. Quart. Homophile Studies,* 1959, 2, 91-92. (46)

Bredtschneider, W. E. About the prejudice against homosexuality. *Realife Guide,* 1959, 2, No. 1, 19-25. (41)

Brill, A. A. Conception of homosexuality. *J. Amer. Med. Assn.,* 1913, 60, 336. (22)

British Medical Association. Special Committee of the Council. *Homosexuality and prostitution.* London: British Medical Association, 1955. (41)

British Medical Journal. Editorial: the treatment of homosexuality. *Brit. Med. J.,* June 7, 1958. (41)

Brown, D. Transvestism and sex-role inversion. In Ellis, A., and Abarbanel, A., *Encyclopedia of sexual behavior.* New York: Hawthorn, 1961. (44, 51, 56)

Brown, R. M. *Preliminary report of the Subcommittee on Sex Crimes of the Assembly Interim Committee on Judicial System.* Sacramento, Calif.: State Assembly, 1950. (31)

Brunori, N. *Bestiality in pedagogy and in criminology.* (in Italian) Florence: Macri, 1958. (30)

Buckle, D. The treatment of sex offenders. *Int. J. Sexol.,* 1949, 3, 1-8. (46, 92, 94)

Caprio, F. S. *The sexually adequate male.* New York: Citadel, 1952. (22, 46, 57)

Carpenter, E. *Love's coming of age.* New York: Kennerly, 1911. (21, 41)

Carpenter, E. *Intermediate types.* New York: Kennerly, 1914. (21)

Cleckley, H. *The mask of sanity.* St. Louis: Mosby, 1950. (93)

Cory, D. W. *The homosexual in America.* New York: Paperback Library, 1963. (22, 57, 84)

Cory, D. W. *The lesbian in America.* New York: Citadel, 1964. (51, 57)

Cory, D. W. Homosexuality. In Ellis, A., and Abarbanel, A., *Encyclopedia of sexual behavior.* New York: Hawthorn Books, 1961. (22)

Cory, D. W. and LeRoy, John P. *The homosexual and his society.* New York: Citadel, 1963. (51)

Cowles, E. S. *Conquest of fatigue and fear.* New York: Holt, 1954 (46)

Creadick, R. N. Management of homosexuals. *South. Med. J.,* 1953, 46, 455-460. (94)

Curran, D. Homosexuality. *Practitioner,* 1938, 141, 282. (21, 41)

Darke, R. Heredity as an etiological factor in homosexuality. *J. Nerv. Ment. Dis.,* 1948, 107, 251-268; 1948, 108, 217-240. (24)

Davis, K. B. *Factors in the sex life of 2200 women.* New York: Harper, 1929. (22)

Dean, D. F. Significant characteristics of the homosexual personality. Ph. D. thesis, New York University, 1936. (22)

de River, P. *The sexual criminal.* Springfield, Ill.: Charles C Thomas, 1949. (92)

Deutsch, D. A case of transvestism. *Amer. J. Psychother.,* 1954, 8, 239-242. (94)

Devereux, G. Institutionalized homosexuality of the Mohave Indians. *Human Biol.,* 1937, 9, 498-527. (22, 53, 57)

Dickinson, R. L. Gynecology of homosexuality. In Henry, G. *Sex variants.* New York: Hoeber, 1941. (33)

Dingwall, E. Homosexuality through the ages. *Sexology,* 1959, 25, 284-89. (48)

Eglinton, J. Z. *Greek love.* New York: Oliver Layton, 1964. (53)

Ellis, A. The sexual psychology of human hermaphrodites. *Psychosom. Med.,* 1945, 7, 108-125. (22, 29)

Ellis, A. *How to live with a neurotic.* New York: Crown Publishers, 1957. (98, 246)

Ellis, A. *Sex without guilt.* New York: Lyle Stuart, 1958. (22, 246)

Ellis, A. Treatment of a homosexual with rational psychotherapy. *J. Clin. Psychol.,* 1959a, 15, 338-343. (22, 42, 46)

Ellis, A. Homosexuality and creativity. *J. Clin. Psychol.,* 1959b, 15, 376-79. (22, 46)

Ellis, A. *The art and science of love.* New York: Lyle Stuart, 1960. (42, 78, 92, 94, 98, 246)

Ellis, A. The psychology of sex offenders. In Ellis, A., and Abarbanel, A., *Encyclopedia of sexual behavior.* New York: Hawthorn Books, 1961a. (92)

Ellis, A. The sex offender and his treatment. In Toch, H., *Legal and criminal psychology.* New York: Holt, Rinehart, and Winston, 1961b. (92)

Ellis, A. *Reason and emotion in psychotherapy.* New York: Lyle Stuart, 1962a. (22, 70, 85, 93, 98, 110, 246)

Ellis, A. Psychotherapy and atomic warfare. *Realist,* Oct. 1962b, No. 38, 1-4. (22, 42, 46, 82, 98, 124)

Ellis, A. The case against religion: a psychotherapist's view. *Independent,* Oct. 1962c, No. 126, 4-5. (98)

Ellis, A. Rational-emotive psychotherapy. Paper read at the American Psychological Association Convention, Aug. 31, 1962d. (98)

Ellis, A. *The American sexual tragedy.* New York: Lyle Stuart, 1962e. (78, 98)

Ellis, A. The power of the printed, written, and recorded word in psychotherapy and counseling. Paper delivered at the American Psychological Association Convention, St. Louis, Sept. 3, 1962f. (93)

Ellis, A. *If this be sexual heresy . . .* New York: Lyle Stuart, 1963a. (22, 84, 98, 246)

Ellis, A. *Sex and the single man.* New York: Lyle Stuart, 1963b. (84, 98, 120, 246)

Ellis, A. *The intelligent woman's guide to man-hunting.* New York: Lyle Stuart, 1963c. (98)

Ellis, A. *The origins and development of the incest taboo.* New York: Lyle Stuart, 1963d. (98)

Ellis, A. To thine own therapeutic lust be true??? Paper read at the American Psychological Association Convention. Sept. 1963e. (98)

Ellis, A. Toward a more precise definition of "emotional" and "intellectual" insight. *Psychol. Reports,* 1963f, 13, 125-126. (98)

Ellis, A. Rational-emotive psychotherapy: a critique of three critiques. *Bull. Essex County Soc. Clin. Psychologists,* Spring 1963g, 7-11. (98)

Ellis, A. The psychology of assassination. *Independent,* Nov., 1963h, No. 139, 1, 4, 5. (98)

Ellis, A. The nature of disturbed marital interaction. Paper read at the American Psychological Association Convention, Sept. 7, 1964. (98)

Ellis, A., and Brancale, R. *The psychology of sex offenders.* Springfield, Ill.: Charles C. Thomas, 1956. (22, 42, 46, 77, 99)

Ellis, A., and Harper, R. A. *A guide to rational living.* Englewood Cliffs, N.J.: Prentice Hall, 1961a. (22, 70, 98, 246)

Ellis, A., and Harper, R. A. *Creative marriage.* New York: Lyle Stuart, 1961b. (70, 98, 246)

Ellis, A., and Sagarin, E. *Nymphomania; a study of the oversexed woman.* New York: Gilbert Press, 1964. (98)

Ellis, H. *Studies in the psychology of sex.* New York: Random House, 1936. (21, 33, 56, 78)

English, O. S., and Pearson, G. H. J. *Common neuroses of children and adults.* New York: Norton, 1937. (41)

Fain, M., and Marty, F. Aspects fonctionnels et rôle structurant de l'investissement homosexual. *Rev. franc. psychanal.,* 1959, 23, 608-611. (46)

Ferenczi, S. *Contributions to psychoanalysis: sex in psychoanalysis.* Boston: Badger, 1916. (22, 38, 57)

Ferenczi, S. *Further contributions to the theory and technique of psychoanalysis.* London: Hogarth. 1926. (22, 57)

Fielding, W. *Love and the sex emotions.* New York: Blue Ribbon, 1932. (22, 57)

Fink, H. K. *Long journey.* New York: Julian, 1954. (46, 94)

Fink, H. K. The psychodynamics of the homosexual. *Mattachine Rev.,* July, 1960, 4-11. (46)

Forel, A. *The sexual question.* New York: Medical Arts, 1907, 1929. (21)

Foster, A. W. Treatment of sexual offenders. *Ment. Hyg.,* 1947, 1, 77-80. (46, 92, 94)

Freud, A. Clinical observations on the treatment of manifest male homosexuality. *Psychoanal. Quart.,* 1951, 20, 237-238. (46, 94)

Freud, S. *Collected papers.* London: Imago Publishers, 1924-50. (22, 36, 41, 57, 82)

Freud, S. *Basic writings.* New York: Modern Library, 1938. (22, 57, 78)

Freud, S. *Letters.* New York: Basic Books, 1960. (41)

Freund, K. The problem of the treatment of homosexuality. (In Spanish). *Acta Neuropsiquiat.,* 1959, 4, 233. (41)

Fried, E. *The ego in love and sexuality.* New York: Grune and Stratton, 1960. (41, 46)

Fry, C. F., and Rostow, E. G. *Mental health in college.* New York: Commonwealth Fund, 1942. (46)

Glass, S. J., and Johnson, R. H. Limitations and complications of organotherapy in male homosexuality. *J. Clin. Endocrin.,* 1944, 11, 540-544. (30)

Glass, S. J. and McKennon, B. J. The hormonal aspects of sex reversals. *West. J. Surg.,* 1937, 45, 467-473. (21)

Glueck, B. C. Psychodynamic patterns in the homosexual sex offender. *Amer. J. Psychiat.,* 1956, 112, 584-590. (22)

Goldschmidt, R. *Physiological genetics.* New York: McGraw Hill, 1938. (24)

Gurvitz, M. Sex offenders in private practice: treatment and outcome. Paper read at the American Psychological Association Convention. Sept. 3, 1957. (92, 94)

Hadden, S. B. Treatment of homosexuality by individual and group psychotherapy. *Amer. J. Psychiat.,* 1958, 114, 810-815. (47)

Hadfield, J. A. Some aspects of the psychopathology of sex perversions. *Proc. Royal Soc. Med.,* 1933, 26, 1029-1030. (35)

Hadfield, J. A. The cure of homosexuality. *Brit. Med. J.*, June 7, 1958, 1, 1323-1326. (46, 94)

Haggard, H. W., and Fry, C. C. *Anatomy of personality*. New York: Harper, 1936. (41)

Hamilton, G. V. *An introduction to objective psychopathology*. St. Louis: Mosby, 1925. (57)

Hamilton, G. V. *A research in marriage*. New York: Boni, 1929. (22, 57)

Hamilton, G. V. Defensive homosexuality. In Robinson, V., *Encyclopedia sexualis*. New York: Dingwall-Rock, 1936. (22, 57)

Hammer, E. F. A psychoanalytic hypothesis concerning sex offender. *J. Clin. Exper. Psychopath.*, 1957, 18, 177-184. (22, 57)

Harper, R. A. Can homosexuals be changed? *Sexology*, 1959, 26, 548-553. (46)

Healy, W. *Personality in formation and action*. Boston: Houghton Mifflin, 1938. (41)

Hemphill, R. S., Leitsch, A., and Stuart, J. R. A. A factual study of male homosexuality. *Brit. Med. J.*, June 7, 1958. (41)

Henry, G. W. Constitutional factors in psychosexual development. *Proc. Assn. Res. Nerv. Ment. Dis.*, 1933, 14, 296-297. (34, 36)

Henry, G. W. Psychogenic and constitutional factors in homosexuality. *Psychiat. Quart.*, 1934, 8, 259. (51)

Henry, G. W. *Sex variants*. New York: Hoeber, 1941. (22, 34, 46, 51)

Henry, G. W. *All the sexes*. New York: Rinehart, 1955. (22, 34, 46, 51)

Henry, G. W., and Galbraith, H. Constitutional factors in homosexuality. *Amer. J. Psychiat.*, 1934, 13, 1249-1255. (34)

Henry, G. W., and Gross, A. The homosexual delinquent. *Mental Hyg.* 1941, 25, 420. (51)

Hirscheld, M. *Die homosexualitat des mannes und des weibes*. Berlin: Marcus, 1920. (21)

Hirschfeld, M. *Men and women*. New York: Putnams, 1935. (48)

Hirschfeld, M. Homosexuality. In Robinson, V., *Encyclopedia sexualis*. New York: Dingwall-Rock, 1936. (32, 40)

Hirschfeld, M. *Sexual pathology*. Newark: Julian, 1940. (24)

Hoch, P. and Cattell, J. P. The diagnosis of pseudoneurotic schizophrenia. *Psychiat. Quart.*, 1959, 33, 17-43. (82)

Hoch, P. H., and Zubin, J. *Anxiety*. New York: Grune and Stratton, 1950. (44)

Hoffer, A. Correspondence of Oscar Wilde. *Amer. J. Psychother.* 1957, 14, 176-177. (47)

Hooker, Evelyn. The adjustment of the overt male homosexual. *J. Projective Tech.*, 1957, 21, 18-31. (83)

Hughes, C. H. An emasculated homosexual. *Alien and Neurol.*, 1914, 35, 278. (30)

Hutchinson, G. E. A speculative consideration of certain possible forms of sexual selection in man. *Amer. Nat.*, 1959, 93, 81. (28)

Jensch, K. Zur genealogie der homosexualität. *Arch. Psychiat.*, Berlin, 1941a, 112, 527. (24)

Jensch, K. Weiterer beitrag zur genealogie der homosexualität. *Arch. Psychiat.*, Berlin, 1941b, 112, 679. (24)

Jones, H. W., Jr. and Scott, W. W. *Hermaphroditism, genital anomalies and related endocrine disorders*. Baltimore: Williams and Wilkins, 1958. (29)

Kahn, S. *Mentality and homosexuality.* Boston: Meader, 1937. (22, 57)

Kallmann, F. J. Comparative twin study on the genetic aspects of male homosexuality. *J. Neurv. Ment. Dis.,* 1952a, 115, 283. (24)

Kallmann, F. J. Twin and sibship study of overt male homosexuality. *Am. J. Hum. Genet.,* 1952b, 4, 136. (24)

Kallmann, F. J. Comment on papers by Rainer, *et al. Psychosom. Med.,* 1960, 22, 259. (28)

Karpman, B. *The sexual offender and his offenses.* New York: Julian, 1954. (46, 94)

Kelly, E. L., and Terman, L. M. Chapter on homosexuality in Terman, L. M., and Miles, C. C., *Sex and personality,* New York: McGraw Hill, 1936. (22, 39)

Kinsey, A. C. Criteria for a hormonal explanation of the homosexual. *J. Clin. Endocrinol.,* 1941, 1, 424-428. (22)

Kinsey, A. C., Pomeroy, W. B., and Martin, C. E. *Sexual behavior in the human male.* Philadelphia: Saunders, 1948. (22, 26, 51)

Kinsey, A. C., Pomeroy, W. B., Martin, C. E., and Gebhard, P. *Sexual behavior in the human female.* Philadelphia: Saunders, 1953. (22, 26, 31, 51, 56)

Koller, S. Uber die Anwendbarkeit und Verbesserung der Probandenmethode. *Zschr. Menschl. Vererb.,* 1942, 26, 444-447. (24)

Krafft-Ebing, R. von. *Psychopathia sexualis.* Brooklyn: Physicians and Surgeons Books Co., 1886, 1922. (21, 23)

Kunkel, F. *What it means to grow up.* New York: Greenberg, 1936. (37)

Laidlaw, R. W. A clinical approach to homosexuality. *Marr. Fam. Living,* 1952, 14, 39-46. (46)

Lang, T. Studies in the genetic determination of homosexuality. *J. Nerv. Ment. Dis.,* 1940, 192, 55. (21, 24)

Lenz, H. Zur kriminalbiologischen bedeutung der hormon-therapie. *Weins, Z. Nervenheilk.* 1958, 15, 195-200. *Excerpta Medica.* VII. 1959, 12, 541. (30)

Lewinsky, H. Features from a case of homosexuality. *Psychoanal. Quart.,* 1952, 21, 344-354. (46, 94)

Licht, H. *Sexual life in ancient Greece.* London: Routledge, 1932. (53)

Lichtenstein, P. M. The "fairy" and the lady lover. *Med. Rev. of Revs.,* 1921, 27, 372. (32)

London, L. S. Analysis of a homosexual neurosis. *Urol. and Cutan. Rev.,* 1933, 37, 93. (22, 57)

London, L. S. *Mental therapy.* New York: Liveright, 1937. (46, 57)

London, L. S., and Caprio, F. S., *Sexual deviation.* Washington: Linacre, 1950. (46, 57, 94)

Maclay, D. T. Boys who commit sexual misdemeanors. *Brit. Med. J.,* Jan. 16, 1960, 1, 186-190. (46)

Maslow, A. H., and Mittelmann, B. *Principles of abnormal psychology.* New York: Harper, 1941. (41)

Massion-Verniory, L., *et al.* Le taux des 17-kétosteroïdes dans diverses sexopathies masculines. *Acta Neurol. Psychiat.,* 1957, 57, 890-897. *Excerpta Medica,* VIII, 1959, 12, 364-365. (30)

Mead, Margaret. *Sex and temperament in three primitive societies.* New York: Morrow, 1935. (38, 49)

Meehl, P. Schizotaxia, schizotype, schizophrenia. *Amer. Psychologist,* 1962, 17, 827-837. (83)

Mendelsohn, F., and Ross, M. An analysis of 133 homosexuals seen at a
    university student health service. *Dis. Nerv. Syst.*, 1959, 20, 246-
    250. (46)
Menninger, K. Somatic correlations with the unconscious repudiation of
    femininity in women. *Bull. Menninger Clin.*, 1939, 3, 110. (46)
Mercer, J. D. *They walk in shadow.* New York: Comet Press, 1959. (41)
Money, John. Hermaphroditism. In Ellis, A., and Abarbanel, A., *Encyclo-
    pedia of sexual behavior.* New York: Hawthorn Books, 1961. (29,
    44, 51, 54)
Money-Kyrle, R. E. *Development of the sexual impulses.*   London: Kegan,
    Paul, 1932. (22, 57)
Monroe, R. R., and Enelow, M. L. The therapeutic motivation in male ho-
    mosexuals. *Amer. J. Psychother.*, 1960, 14, 474-490. (46)
Morse, B. *The lesbian.* Derby, Conn.: Monarch Books, 1961. (46)
Nedoma, K. Homosexuality in sexological practice. *Int. J. Sexol.*, 1951, 4,
    219-224. (46, 94)
Nedoma, K., and Freund, K. Somatosexual findings in homosexual men.
    (In Czech.) *Csl. Psychiat.*, 1961, 57, 100-103. *Excerpta Med.* VIII,
    1961, 14, 1335. (33)
Neugebauer, F. L. von. *Hermaphroditismus beim menchen.*   Leipzig: 1908.
    (29)
Neustadt, R., and Myerson, A. Quantitative sex hormone studies in homo-
    sexuality. *Amer. J. Psychiat.*, 1940, 97, 524. (21, 30)
Neustetter, W. L. Homosexuality from the psychiatric viewpoint. *Matta-
    chine Rev.*, May 1962, 4-7. (41)
Newman, H. H. Twins and sex. In Robinson, V., *Encyclopedia sexualis.*
    New York: Dingwall-Rock, 1936. (21)
Overzier, O. Chromosomatic sex in transvestitism. *Dtsch. Med. Wschr.*,
    1958, 83, 181. *Excerpta Medica,* VIII, 1959, 12, 139. (56)
Pare, C. M. B. Homosexuality and chromosomal sex. *J. Psychosom. Res.*,
    1956, 1, 247-251. (29)
Pascoe, H. Deviant sexual behavior and the sex criminal. *Canad. Med.
    Assn. J.*, 1961, 84, 206-211. (46)
Poe, J. S. Successful treatment of a 40 year-old passive homosexual. *Psy-
    choanal. Rev.*, 1952, 29, 23-36. (46, 94)
Polani, Hunter, and Lennox. Cited in British Medical Association. *Homo-
    sexuality and prostitution.* London: British Medical Association,
    1955. (29)
Pollens, B. *The sex criminal.* New York: Macauley, 1938. (22, 57)
Pomeroy, W. B. Paper delivered at the annual meeting of the Mattachine
    Society, Sept. 8, 1958. (22, 51)
Prosin, S. The concept of the lesbian, a minority in reverse. *The Ladder,*
    July 1962, 6, 5-22. (39)
Rainer, J. D., Mesnikoff, A., Kolb, L. C., and Carr, A.   Homosexuality and
    heterosexuality in identical twins. *Psychosom. Med.*, 1960, 22,
    251-259. (28)
Rasmussen, E. W. Experimental homosexual behavior in male albino rats.
    Acta Psychol., 1955, 12, 303-334. (30)
Reckless, W. C. *The etiology of delinquent and criminal behavior.* New
    York: Social Science Research Council, 1943. (38)
Rickles, N. K. *Exhibitionism.* Philadelphia: Lippincott, 1950. (92, 99)

Robertiello, R. *Voyage from Lesbos.* New York: Avon, 1959. (46, 94)
Robertiello, R. *A handbook of emotional illness and treatment.* New York: Argonaut, 1961. (46)
Robinson, W. H. My views on homosexuality. *Amer. J. Urol.,* 1914, 10, 550. (21)
Rosanoff, A. J. *Manual of psychiatry.* New York: Wiley, 1938. (21, 33, 36, 41)
Rosenzweig, S. and Hoskins, R. G. A note on the ineffectiveness of sex-hormone medication in a case of pronounced homosexuality. *Psychosom. Med.,* 1941, 3, 39. (31)
Rubin, Isadore. Homosexuality: conflicting theories. *Sexology,* 1960, 27, 318-322. (24, 31)
Rubinstein, J. Psychotherapeutic aspects of male homosexuality. *Brit. J. Med. Psychol.,* 1958, 31, 74-78. (46, 94)
Ruitenbeek, H. M. (Ed.). *The problem of homosexuality in modern society.* New York: Dodd, Mead, 1963. (61)
Russell, S. Ten years of history. *The Ladder,* 1962, 6, 4-21. (41)
Sanders, J. Homosexual twins. In Robinson, V., *Encyclopedia sexualis.* New York: Dingwall-Rock, 1936. (24)
Sauls, James R. The crime of feeling guilty. *Realife Giude,* Feb, 1960, 6-13. (41)
Schilder, P. *Goals and desires of man.* New York: Columbia, 1942. (22, 57)
Schlegel, W. S. *Körper und seele.* Stuttgart: F. Enke Verlag, 1957. (33)
Scott, C. Talk at World Psychiatric Congress, Montreal, 1961. (24)
Scott, E. M. Psychosexuality of the alcoholic. *Psychol. Rep.,* 1958, 4, 499-502. (39)
Shentoub, S. A. De quelques problèmes dans l'homosexualité masculine active. *Rev. franc. psychanalyse,* 1957, 21, 485-534. *Excerpta Med.,* VIII, 1959, 12, 958. (46, 94)
Sherman, M. *Mental conflicts and personality.* New York: Norton, 1938. (37)
Silverberg, W. V. The personal basis and social significance of passive male homosexuality. *Psychiatry,* 1938, 1, 41. (22)
Smith, A. B., and Bassin, A. Group therapy with homosexuals. *J. Soc. Ther.,* 1959, 5, No. 3. (47)
Socarides. C. W. Theoretical and clinical aspects of overt male homosexuality. *J. Amer. Psychoanal. Assn.,* 1960, 8, 552-566. (46)
Solomon, R., and Wynne, L. C.: Traumatic avoidance learning. *Psychol. Rev.,* 1954, 61, 353. (44)
Sorenson, S. Normal sexuality. In Forbath, A., *Love and marriage.* New York: Liveright, 1938. (21)
Sprague, W. D. The lesbian in our society. New York: Midwood, 1962. (57)
Srnec, K., and Freund, K. Treatment of male homosexuality through conditioning. *Int. J. Sexol.,* 1953, 7, 92-93. (46, 60, 94)
Stearn, J. *The sixth man.* New York: Macfadden, 1963. (46)
Steinach, E. *Sex and life.* New York: Viking, 1940. (21)
Stekel, W. *Bisexual love.* Boston: Badger, 1922. (22, 46, 57, 78)
Stekel, W. *Sexual aberrations.* New York: Liveright. 1930. (94)
Storr, A. The psychopathology of fetishism and transvestitism. *J. Analyt. Psychol.,* 1957, 2, 153-166. (56)

Swyer, G. I. M. Endocrine malfunctioning and homosexuality. *Practitioner,* 1957. (22)

Tarail, M. New treatments for the homosexual. *Sexology,* 1961, 27, 674-677. (46)

Terman, L. M., and Miles, C. C. *Sex and personality.* New York: McGraw Hill, 1936. (51)

Thoma, H. Männlicher transvestismus und das verlangen nach geschlechtsumwandlung. *Psyche,* 1957, 11, 81-124. *Psychol. Abstr.,* 1958, 32, 510. (56)

Thompson, Clara. Changing concepts of homosexuality in psychoanalysis. *Psychiatry,* 1947, 20, 183. (82)

Thompson, G. N. Electroshock and other therapeutic considerations in sexual psychopathy. *J. Nerv. Ment. Dis.,* 1949, 109, 531-539. (47)

Thompson, P. G. Report on forensic clinic group psychotherapy programs. *Int. Ment. Health. Res. Newsl.,* June 1961. (47)

Thouless, R. Introduction to *The Invert* by Anomaly. London, 1929. (46)

Vincent, L. Toward an enlightened society. *Mattachine Rev.,* 1961, 7, 12-14. (41)

Wasserman, S. Casework treatment of a homosexual acting-out adolescent. *Ment. Hyg.,* 1960, 44, 18-29. (46)

Weil, A. Sprechen anatomische grundlagen für das angeborensein der homosexualität? *Arch f. Frauenk.,* 1924, 10, 23. (32)

West, D. J. *The other man.* New York: Morrow, 1955. (22, 51)

Westwood, G. *Society and the homosexual.* New York: Dutton, 1953. (22, 46, 51)

Westwood, G. *A minority.* New York: Longmans, 1960. (43, 83)

Wildeblood, P.: *Against the law.* London: Weidenfeld, 1955. (41)

Witschi, E. Sex deviations, inversions and parabiosis. In Allen, E., *Sex and internal secretions.* Baltimore: Williams and Wilkins, 1932. (21)

Witschi, E., and Mengert, W. F. Endocrine studies on human hermaphrodites. *J. Clin. Endocrinol.,* 1942, 2, 279. (21)

Wittels, F. *Critique of love.* New York: Macaulay, 1929. (22, 57)

Wolfenden, Sir John. *Report of the committee on homosexual offenses and prostitution.* London: Her Majesty's Stationery Office, 1957. (41, 92)

Wood, Robert. Sex life in the ancient civilizations. In Ellis, A., and Abarbanel, A., *Encyclopedia of sexual behavior.* New York: Hawthorn, 1961. (53)

Woodward, M. The diagnosis and treatment of homosexual offenders. *Brit. J. Delinq.,* 1958, 9, 44-59. (46)

Wortis, J. A note on the body-build of the male homosexual. *Amer. J. Psychiat.,* 1937, 93, 1122-1123. (34)

Wright, C. A. Further studies of endocrine aspects of homosexuality. *Med. Rec.,* 1938, 144, 449. (21)

Wright, C. A. Results of endocrine treatment in a controlled group of homosexual men. *Med. Rec.,* 1941, 60, 154. (30)

Yalom, I. D. Group therapy of incarcerated sexual deviants. *J. Nerv. Ment. Dis.,* 1961, 132, 158-170. (47)